The Sex Seminar: Are you ready for the Red Pill?

By Joseph Angel Maldonado, M.A., and Lynn Traub-Maldonado, CHT

IAM Center, LLC

Copyright 2014

We'd like to start by thanking all the participants who without their openness and honesty this book would never have been possible. Additionally, a special thanks needs to go to all our teachers.

* * * * *

The following narrative is based on a 3 day seminar. The names of the 18 participants have been changed to protect their anonymity.

"Every museum in the world is filled with art created from this basic impulse, the greatest literature, the most beautiful music, the study of sex is the study of the beginning of all life, and science holds the key, yet we sit huddled in the dark like prudish old cavemen, filled with shame and guilt, and the truth is nobody understands sex."

Dr. William H. Masters, "Masters of Sex"

DAY ONE

(Joseph and Lynn walk into a room of 18 seminar participants; Joseph immediately begins to speak.)

Joseph: Why do you have sex? . . . Come on, WHY do you have SEX?

(Group slowly begins to speak out answers as Joseph writes their responses on a chalk board.)

Group: Love, attachment, boredom, comfort, assurance . . .

Joseph: Come on . . . you can do it.

Group: Control, fear, competition, acceptance, peer pressure, escape, money . . .

Joseph: Yeah, dollar bill ya'll!

Group: Gratitude . . .

Joseph: Remember that one everybody. I'll be collecting on Sunday!

(Laughter)

Group: Power, lust, feels good, to connect, to release . . . *(Group is now responding at a rapid fire pace)* . . . when I feel empty, to explore, chemistry, freedom, curiosity, growth, procreation, obligation, recreation, revenge, to play, attachment, to relieve loneliness, healing . . .

Joseph: Okay, great . . . Now, what do you have sex for?

Group: Pleasure, value, orgasm, security, commitment, safety, self expression, ego gratification, to feel free, barter, entitlement, satisfaction, intimacy, romance, for a sense of worth, closeness, to get high . . .

Lynn: Actually, sex is the first drug. It was found that the effects of cocaine on the brain are similar to those we experience during sex. Tell us more on what you have sex for.

Group: Confidence, procreation, domination, power, expansion, closeness, because it's awesome . . . *(Laughter)* . . . empowerment . . .

Joseph: Okay. So it seems some of you have it a little confused between why you have sex and what you have it for; they overlap a little. What do you make of your lists?

Angie: *(Angie is a 25 year old single female who works in the fashion industry)* I'm surprised there are so many different reasons.

Day One: *The Sex Seminar*

Nathan: *(Nathan is a 31 year old single male who works for the City's Parks Department)* Yeah, I couldn't tell the difference for myself, after a while.

Mercedes: *(Mercedes is a 31 year old single female, public relations executive who comes from a wealthy family)* They all seem rather shallow. I mean, isn't there more to sex than what we've just said?

Joseph: How about Sex as a form of communication, as something transcendent? Okay, let's stop here and start right . . .
Hello everyone, I'm Joseph.

Lynn: . . . and I'm Lynn. We'd like to welcome you to "The Sex Seminar."

Joseph: So let's start with a different question . . . Where are you?

Reese: *(Reese is a 27 year old male nutrition and fitness trainer)* What do you mean?

Joseph: Where are you at?

Mercedes: In this room.

Joseph: What does that mean? Where's that?

Susan: *(Susan is a 58 year old recently divorced mother of two adult children whose daughter, Lisa, is also attending the seminar She has worked in the banking industry for over 20 years)* At the North Shore Country Club.

Joseph: And what does that mean? Where's that?

Simon: *(Simon is a 29 year old videographer and photographer from London, England)* Vancouver.

Joseph: Yeah. You're still not telling me anything.

Nathan: I don't understand what you want.

Joseph: I don't want anything. Where are you at? If I blindfolded you and knocked you out, and then dropped you off on Main Street and Vine, how would you know where you're at?

Eddie: *(Eddie is a 35 year old male who owns and operates a chain of successful private businesses)* I'd look at a map.

Day One: *The Sex Seminar*

Joseph: A map from where? What if there were no maps?

Alexia: *(Alexia is a 25 year old female artist and the girlfriend of Simon)* I'd use a cell phone or GPS.

Joseph: What if there was neither of these available?

Tami: *(Tami is a 24 year old female who has recently started teaching preschool)* I'd ask at a gas station or I'd ask a stranger on the street.

Joseph: Again, what if these weren't available?

Alex: *(Alex is a 27 year old male plumber)* I'd be fucked!

Joseph: Right. Because the truth of the matter is that I could have dropped you off on Main and Vine on Mars. You all assumed you knew where you are at, when in reality you don't. The way we know where we're at is by finding the context we're in. In other words, you first have to know you're on earth, in North America. None of you asked "where is Main and Vine?" You all assumed you knew. And it's these assumptions that have us not understand where we are in our lives in relation to things that are larger than ourselves. So with that, ladies and gentlemen, we will look at Sex from a historical context. Because, without knowing where we came from, we can never know where we're at or where we're headed.

Lynn: We'll get to the history part, shortly; but before we do, tell me . . . why are you here?" And, since this is a graduate seminar, tell us, why don't we ask you that in the beginning of our introductory seminar?

Jeremy: *(Jeremy is a 45 year old highly successful entrepreneur, husband and father of four)* Because you don't care . . .

Joseph: That's true, in part. If you understand or feel I don't care, then you'll know you're not being "taken care of." With that, vulnerability follows. Why else?

Angie: So people can reveal themselves in their own time.

Joseph: Yes. In *The Communication Seminar* you're given more freedom to expose as much or as little as you choose. This is a graduate course, though, so more is expected of you.

In this seminar you'll be allowed to go down the relationship continuum by yourselves. It will be more challenging to do that because of the subject matter--sex. It will be more personal and intimate. It will demand more courage from you than a basic communication course requires. So, on that note . . . what's brought you here? Why are you taking this seminar? And when you speak, please state your name.

Reese: I'm Reese . . . and I'm always here in one way or another either volunteering or participating because I just like to be here . . . uh, I learn a ton and get a lot.

Joseph: But why this seminar?

Reese: I think I need it. I don't remember a lot from the last Sex Seminar that I did with you guys. I feel like I need a refresher, for sure.

Joseph: Yes, it's been three years, so a refresher helps. But, at the same time, we take what we can handle and you're probably going to show up with a larger cup than last time. Why else?

Parisa: *(Parisa is a 34 year old Middle Eastern female who has worked in the airline industry for over 10 years)* My name is Parisa . . . and why I am here is because I don't know if I suck in sex or if I am good in sex, but I know I have issues. So, if I can learn to improve and be happier, I'm open to it.

Nathan: I'm Nathan, I chose to come here because I've been to a few seminars and they are always fantastic. With this one, I'm a little uncomfortable. I'm not going to lie. You all look very nice.

(Laughter)

Joseph: Dare you say, sexy?

(Laughter)

Simon: Hi, I'm Simon. I came to this one because I think sex has pretty much ruled my life in where I've gone in the world and what I've done. So, I want to understand it so I can understand my life better.

Nisha: *(Nisha is a 34 year female from Pakistan who works for a large marketing company)* Hi, I'm Nisha and I'm here to find an understanding outside what my religion tells me. My family seems to think they have a lot of say over who I will marry, and they use our religion to try to do this.

Joseph: Why is a sex conversation so uncomfortable for us? How does *culture and religion* play into it? I'd like to suggest that maybe they're the two main culprits of sexual suppression in our society. What do you think?

Mercedes: Anything that doesn't fit within the mold is judged as sick, wrong, or unacceptable.

Joseph: Yes, culture and religion makes it really serious . . . Actually, you're all so damn serious about this weekend. "I'm scared, I'm nervous; I don't know what to expect. This seminar troubles me more than the other ones. I'm not feeling a tingle in my dingle so something's wrong here." We come by it honestly. Culture and religion have created Sex into a serious subject matter. This weekend, we'll take a look at how they've affected us and how we can, at least, sidestep them. We'll look to see what it will take to find a natural comfort with it as a subject.

Anyone who knows me and has sat with me during a meal knows that I play with my food. How often? Always. I'm always playing with my food, picking it apart, breaking it down in order to extend my experience with it. By the way, I never pray before I eat. It has always been awkward for me to pray or give thanks because it's in my play that I give thanks. When I play with my food I'm filled. It fills me. I feel nourished and it brings joy. I never got the praying part. I'm not saying "don't pray when you eat and give thanks," but praying was so damn serious, where playing was quite the opposite for me. I was joyful while in gratitude. Playing allowed me to be more conscious as I ate, and the playfulness actually had me chew more, take my time, and eat slower.

The first person to acculturate me was my mother, who constantly complained and told me to stop playing with my food. My mother wanted me to fit in. I get it. And, since culture told her "you don't play with your food," she desperately wanted me to acclimate. She tried really, really hard to stop me. She used all the traditional methods, too, falling just short of capital punishment. But she couldn't beat it out of me. I kept playing with my food. And like with food, it was very difficult for me to take sex seriously. There is a progression from sex to food. What's the connection between sex and food for you? Are there any similarities?

Group: Satisfaction . . . pleasure . . . sticking that sausage in your mouth.

Joseph: If that's your preference . . . or rather *inclination*, which we will use from here on out because preference suggests there's a choice. To say "your sexual preference is . . ." implies you can prefer not to be attracted to what you're attracted to. Religion and culture would love to have you believe that this is the case . . . Back to your point . . . yes, you can find very sexual objects in food, and so many foods look sexual, such as oysters, sausages, bananas . . . anyone else . . . food and sex?

Day One: *The Sex Seminar*

Mercedes: I studied that when we are forming as an embryo our gonad and the digestive system are actually formed together in our genetics. Food, sex, and breathing are all formed together.

Joseph: So, now we are starting to understand how we are actually created, versus how we are acculturated. What's more natural to us? What's the first food you take in?

Angie: Mother's milk.

Joseph: And where does mother's milk come from?

Nathan: Breasts.

Joseph: Which is an aspect of her sexuality isn't it? Women have had orgasms while breastfeeding. It is a very common thing. The physical connection mixed with the intensity of her intimacy with the child.

Food and sex go hand-in-hand in so many ways. Therefore, without realizing it, I started to form my sexual approach by how I approached food. I wouldn't allow it to be changed in me. I was acculturated in many other areas but for some reason, it just didn't seem to sink in with food. So, sex was never as serious, to me, as it is to most of you here. What's missing with sexuality is playfulness, but pain makes it serious. What makes it so serious for you?

Mercedes: The chance that someone's going to judge me for something I say. Because no one ever talks about it, I'm usually clueless about what others are doing in their sex life. And on the occasion when I've shared, even with close friends, I've experienced being laughed at in judgment. It's like, "Ha ha I would never do that." This has left me feeling apprehensive about opening up and talking about sex.

Joseph: Yeah, it's still very difficult to talk about it out in the open. Much has improved over the last few decades, but a lot of it is kind of random. There isn't enough awareness. It's awareness that decreases sensitivity, and it's this combination that decreases judgment. There's still an undercurrent of fear of being judged. So what's being judged?

Kelly: *(Kelly is a 34 year old mother of four who is married to Jeremy)*

What we do . . .

Joseph: What are the judgments you're afraid of? That you're good, bad, too fat, too small . . . what are you afraid of hearing sexually?

Parisa: That I'm not good enough.

Joseph: And when you hear it, do you feel they're saying it about your whole being? That it's not good enough, not just your sex? What else?

Angie: Whether I'm normal or not normal.

Joseph: Yeah, to the point of whether you even fit in or not with the world, whether you're normal or not normal . . . we often measure normalcy by sexuality. Why only sexuality? We don't do it around money so much . . . we don't do it around how we eat and what we eat, or what games we play. But we do with sexuality. We use it as a measurement of whether we're normal or not. That's a lot of pressure on a three letter word. What are the other judgments?

Kelly: What about like being boring?

Joseph: Boring . . . similar to being not good enough. How do you improve on boring? That's a big task. Personally, I celebrate being sexually boring at this point.

(Laughter)

It's a lot of work **not** being boring sexually.

(Laughter)

What else?

Parisa: I would say shame. Shame that's induced from our belief systems and from our childhood experiences.

Joseph: Yeah, induced through words and actions . . . very painful. What's the purpose of this shame? There's natural shame and then there's man-made and woman-made shame. Human-made shame versus real shame. Let's make that distinction.

You're never going to begin to explore your sexuality until you see what's blocking you from exploring it. You want to understand it's, almost 100% of the time, blocked by a pain of some sort. Pain is the big block to sexual exploration of any kind; even if it's just conversational. Therefore, we need to begin pinpointing the little things that create the pain we're in and that make us so damned serious.

Lynn: Pain is one of the pre-requisites you are going to have to allow yourself to feel this weekend.

Joseph: Yes, pain needs to be felt for it to pass. When you've done this, you'll be left with plenty of empty space where you can begin your sexual exploration. Sexual exploration, like space exploration, requires empty space. Empty space which is presently occupied by pain.

What else, what other things are you judged about?

Nathan: Being a freak?

Joseph: A Freak: a person who expresses their sexual deviance to an extreme. All you have to do is look through a list of fetishes and you'll see there are all types of freaks! There are many variations of them. In general, still, freak is a derogatory term.

We relish saying "screw you, I'm a freak," while, at the same time, battling feelings of shame about it. We're not free! We've been blocked up, so to talk about this playfully, is painful for us.

Claudia: *(Claudia is a 26 year old single mother who has been hairdressing for four years)* How about power?

Joseph: What about power?

Claudia: I don't know I've been dating for the past year and there's always different advice from people about not putting out and holding on to whatever power you have because, apparently, for women they let go of their power when they have sex, right? When they are sexual . . .

Joseph: The biggest pain of all is your lack of understanding of what sex is. So one your definitions of what sex is, was power. Are we sure we're right about that?

What is this thing called sex? We need to see it . . . but we have to remove a lot of the aforementioned blocks. We have to remove our pain and just look at this thing called "sex."

Now what is sex? We've looked at how pain is blocking our awareness and that we all share some pain and embarrassment in and over it. But we don't really have an understanding. What is sex to you?

Claudia: Intercourse.

Joseph: There's no right or wrong answer, just say what comes up.

Alexia: An opening, a space where you can be in and potentially lose all sense of time and space.

Joseph: Good, characteristic number one of sex, it's timeless. It's always timeless. You always go beyond time within it. There's something about time that, kind of, begins to disappear as you find yourself somewhere else. The boundaries of time do not have the same affect over sex as it does over other aspects of our lives. So, we can, at least, say that sex is timeless. Tell me, how long has it been going on? And how long will it go on?

Eddie: Forever.

Joseph: Now, by the way, we're the only animals on earth who are consumed with sexuality. It's always about sex, in some form or another, for us. The other animals just do it when they do it and they don't when they don't. But, we tie everything to sex; even when we are repressing it we're being consumed by it. If you're a very repressed religious individual, all you'll think about is sex and how we shouldn't be doing it, so they're sex obsessed as much as the whore . . . by the way, the whore can be male or female . . . so, one of the qualities about sex is that it's timeless. What else? What is sex?

Angie: I think it's hilarious . . . if I were an alien from another planet and I popped in on two people having sex, I'd find it funny.

Joseph: Yes, viewed from what you do in your everyday life, it might be seen as something so different that it's laughable. Now, I guarantee you that aliens will be laughing at everything you do in your life. Everything. From the way you brush your teeth, how you set up your medicine cabinet and never throw away the old medicine, how you run this thing through your hair called a comb . . . you understand? Everything could be considered odd and funny, so an alien isn't a good example. Actually, considering what we do from our own perspective, it can be perceived as funny.

What is sex?

Alexia: Creative and playful.

Parisa: Surrender.

Joseph: What do you surrender to?

Parisa: To the emotions, to the feelings, to the pleasure.

Day One: *The Sex Seminar*

Joseph: But what do you surrender to in life? Do you surrender to this pen?

Parisa: I surrender to the pleasure.

Joseph: You can only surrender to something you believe is greater than you. You can only surrender to something greater than you. That implies sex is greater than all of us. Sex is bigger than you! That's why you're scared. And you know it.

Kelly: But how can it be bigger than us if we're the one's doing it?

Joseph: Just because you're doing it doesn't mean you're bigger than it. We do a lot of things on this earth that we're not bigger than. A good example is the ocean. We can do a lot of things in the ocean. We fish in it, swim in it, boat in it. Yet, it's bigger than us and we still don't know everything about it. We know more about outer space than we do about the oceans on our own planet. We don't know much about the ocean. It's bigger than us, even though we do it. You get it? So, sex is the same. This is a useful way to look at it. That's the problem, in a nutshell. We think just because we can do sex that we're bigger than it. That we have more power than it, or that we have power over it, or that we have power to use it against someone else. Oh, silly kids. It is so much bigger than you! It has created everything you see around you in one form or another. Pollination of plants or how fish cycle. It is huge and much bigger than all of you! You're all little tiny dots compared to sex. It is timeless. It has been here long before you and will continue long after you. None of you are going to master it. You can play in it. You can feed from it, just like you do from the ocean. You can enjoy it and you can expand upon it, but you're never ever going to control it. You're going to TRY and control it for most of your life, until aging forces you to accept its power over you.

When I was about 19 years old an older friend of mine said, upon hearing me brag about my sexual exploits, "You gotta get it; you can't wear out a hole with a pole." And in my youthful arrogance I responded with, "Watch me old man, I can!" and all he said was "Okay." Of course, he was right and he could have called me an ass, or worse, but why should he have bothered?

Sex is bigger than all of us. So we can't go wrong this weekend. No matter where we go and whatever we play in, we're going to leave here with much more. More perspective, understanding, and, hopefully, a lightness and freedom about sex than we've ever had before. If we could let go right now, and admit that we don't know shit about it, that we don't know dick about it, we'll get even more. This weekend's not about how to do sex, it's about why and what! What it is and why we do it. It would behoove us to go forward with the understanding that we are going to explore something bigger than us.

Lynn: So on that note, the other two pre-requisites you're going to need for a successful seminar is the willingness to be in boredom and to take risks. To the degree that you're willing to feel the pain, take a risk, and even be bored, is the same degree that you're going to grow.

Joseph: It's larger than all of us! How cool, you can't go wrong this weekend. There's a lot to learn and experience and the interesting thing about sexuality is you can have hands on, mind on, body on, full-on experience with it. The ultimate experience, that has been documented, is when a human being has surrendered to it. We'll get to that by day three.

So let go of what you think you know. Drop it to the floor! You don't have to be bigger than it anymore. It's okay that you don't know much! Just imagine we're all in the first grade so we can begin to understand this thing rather than trying to prove what we know about it. It's preoccupied your lives forever, so it's a good time to finally take a look at this, wouldn't you say?

Mercedes: I really like the comparison of food and sex. I just realized, for the first time, that cultural expectations of how you're supposed to be in your sexuality . . . well, it's like an eating disorder. Do you think an anorexic person doesn't think about food all day? That's all they think about, even though they may feel they don't warrant it.

Lynn: Their whole life is designed around it.

Mercedes: Even someone who's trying to diet, all they're going to do is think about that cookie they can't have.

Joseph: You couldn't be more on! What she's suggesting, that we agree with, is that we are sex obsessed, like someone with an eating disorder. This is because we are deprived of the proper information about it, overloaded with it in most places in our lives, we aren't allowed to talk fully about it and we can't even use certain words without somebody giggling. What do you think of that?

Angie: We're getting really offended.

Joseph: After the Boston bombings, David Ortiz, a Boston Red Sox baseball player, went out onto the field in front of a packed stadium and proclaimed that "We're fuckin' strong people in Boston!" Now, what you need to understand is he was on a live microphone and, according to the U.S. Federal Communications Commission, the FCC, the stadium is under their jurisdiction and they determine what is or isn't proper communication in a public stadium. He could have been fined, or worse. But what happened was that he got up there, said blah, blah, blah, and then dropped the "F-bomb" and the FCC instantly said it was okay. Normally he could have gone to jail for doing that on a public stage, but they deemed it acceptable under the circumstances. They have the power to determine whether we can say fuck or not in public! I understand the need to protect children from certain things, but their control and repression goes beyond our children. It's about the oppression we've created where we can't even say the word without a strong reaction. We've created a fear of it.

So, there are no children in this room. Can you say the word fuck? Can you all say it? Say it!

Group: Fuck, fuck, fuck . . .

Joseph: Come on, Say it!

FUCK, FUCK,FUCK,FUCK,FUCK,FUCK,FUCK,FUCK,FUCK, FUCK, FUCK, FUCKFUCKFUCKFUCKFUCKFUCKFUCK.

Joseph: Great, now try shit.

Group: SHIT SHIT SHITSHITSHITSHITSHITSHITSHIT

Joseph: Pussy

Group: PUSSYPUSSYPUSSYPUSSYPUSSYPUSSYPUSSYPUSSY

Joseph: DICK

Group: DICKDICK DICK DICKDICK DICK

Joseph: COCK

Group: COCKCOCKCOCK COCKCOCKCOCKCOCK

Joseph: CUNT come on, you know how to say it . . .

Group: CUNTCUNTCUNT CUNTCUNTCUNTCUNT CUNTCUNTCUNTCUNTCUNT.

Joseph: Great, how does that feel?

Angie: Liberating!

Joseph: Yeah, so how suppressed are you!?

Day One: *The Sex Seminar*

Kelly: I say those words all the time.

Joseph: I understand that. Still, there is suppression because you still feel good saying it under certain scenarios--scenarios that are repressive or which you've deemed to be repressive. The fact that you just felt more comfortable is direct proof that there's suppression in you. Feel free, this weekend, to use any word you want to use!

Lynn: You might be comfortable but what if you say it in a room of people you know are uncomfortable; is it not their judgment that has you repress yourself or even stop you. We have to be able to say it comfortably with ourselves, then comfortably in front of others, until we're so comfortable with these words that we find additional uses for them. It's not only these words that some of you have a problem with; it's also the other ones that have clear sexual connotations behind them. Saying vagina is difficult for some of you; you'd rather say pussy. You don't want to say penis or testicles, clit or clitoris. These are uncomfortable for a lot of people.

Joseph: If you watch TV you can see that we're finally getting comfortable with these words. I remember back in the day when Oprah couldn't say vagina; she'd call it vajayjay. What the fuck was that all about. Thank goodness she took Dr. Berman's advice who educated her on the distinction between a vulva and a vagina and the need to call it by what it is. Now, don't get me wrong, I love Oprah because she was willing to expose herself in order to bring these words and subjects to the forefront. Because of people like her we hear words like penis, vagina, and masturbation more readily than we did just 20 years ago.

Why so much repression of your expression?? When you all got to express yourselves, a short time ago, you were left with a feeling of relief. Relief is good, but it's not enough. What comes after relief? If I get to express myself and all I'm left with is relief, then there must be more that I need to say. Relief is from built up pressure so if I've relieved myself, like when I go to the bathroom, then that means I must be ready for more. If not, then life is all about going to the bathroom.

Think about being in a foreign country that doesn't speak English, or any language you know, how does it feel when you finally come across a person who speaks your language?

Group: Relieved.

Joseph: That relief comes from finally being able to express yourself! That's how much we need to express ourselves! But you don't stop at casual conversation once you're relieved, do you? No, you go on speaking. You go on looking for deeper conversation. We have a need for intimacy, but we don't tend to realize it until we are deprived of it. By the way, for you movie buffs, this idea was wonderfully illustrated in the old movie *Cast Away* with Tom Hanks . . . Our truly authentic communication lies on the other side of relief; as it does with Sex.

Unfortunately, for the majority of us, we do sex for relief. Relief from pressure, from feeling weak so we seek power in it, relief from loneliness, relief from feeling inferior by dominating, or even relief from boredom. There seems to be an endless list of reasons we have relief sex.

Our repression around sex has caused us to look to each other for understanding. Repression of this sort limits where we can learn from. We've been doing this for a long time. Therefore, at this point, we are convinced that humans are the final authorities in the subject. It's no wonder, then, that we look to mimic each other and care too much about what others think about sex. And while we're busy referencing sex from each other, this big, giant, endless, timeless thing called Sex, with a capital S, spins around, like the air we breathe, creating, controlling, and causing all that is sexual. The funniest thing is that we don't even realize it exists without us. You think Sex only exists between us or yourself? NO! It exists independently. When we all leave this earth, it will continue to exist.

So what is this thing that we've labelled "Sex?"

Claudia: Energy.

Kelly: Yes. It's definitely energy. It's creation.

Joseph: Yes. Have you ever thought of Sex in that way?

Lynn: Feel what you're saying. If it's energy, then it's, likely, bigger than me. Feel . . . it's bigger than me, it's bigger than you! It's not MY energy because I see she has it and he has it. So it doesn't belong to me!

Joseph: Yes, absolutely, we do several things with this energy. We might battle for it thinking we have the power to give it or take it. That's hysterical because, imagine being in an ocean and taking a cup of water from the ocean and then fighting over that cup of water. That's what it's like when you use Sex as power. And you convince each other to just ignore the water around you. "I'm in charge, I have the power; oh no, now you have it, so you have the power. Give it back . . . you bitch!"

(Laughter)

Day One: *The Sex Seminar*

. . . And all along you're standing in an ocean of this water. How silly does this look to someone who can see they're in the water? That's how silly it would look to you if you could see Sex all around you. It's everywhere, because Sex is creative. It creates and is in everything that has been created! All creative energy is Sexual energy. It's the same thing! And we wind up in little childish power struggle game over it.

Now, of course, we can sit here and look at it as psychologists, anthropologists, scientists, or even physiologists to understand what these power games are and why we play them, but we're not going to waste your time this weekend doing that. This isn't as much about you as it is about IT. We're here to understand what IT is so then we can understand how we fit in all of IT. We have the opportunity to understand IT's greater purpose, IT's calling for us in our lives, and what IT wants from us. Have you ever even wondered what IT wanted from you? Because if IT's bigger than you, if IT's timeless, if IT creates, IT must be pretty fuckin' smart. IT has to have some intelligence. IT's bigger than all of us! Shouldn't IT have something to teach us? IT utilizes IT's energy to procreate and keep things going, even if we don't want to. IT will get to you no matter where you hide. Leave a few people on a deserted island and I'll give them about five years before, even if they're related, they're fucking. IT goes beyond us, beyond procreation. We are really obnoxious thinking we can control IT, or we have power over IT.

When you dance to music do you try to control the music or do you let it control you? Now those who can't dance would say they control it. That means you can't dance. I don't need to watch you.

(Laughter)

Please, don't dance. It's the same with Sex.

Alex: I surrender fully to music.

Joseph: Then if you understand it in reference to music can you begin to expand that understanding to Sex? So, let's take a look at where we got these wild perceptions of what Sex is in the first place!

Who taught you Sex?

Group: Nobody . . . everybody . . . teachers in school.

Joseph: Who and how? Directly or indirectly, who taught you Sex?

Group: Friends, parents . . . teachers in school, through Sex education.

Joseph: Anyone else? Who taught you Sex?

Kelly: Your partners . . .

Joseph: So you had to wait till you had a partner to begin to be taught about Sex. Kind of like somebody teaching you about pregnancy after you've already been knocked up. Who else?

Group: Your siblings . . . media, television, imagination.

Joseph: You can imagine it . . . like the person who wrote the Kama Sutra who had never had Sex; there is power in imagination. Is it possible that, through the imagination, we get to connect with this Sexual energy where it informs us about itself? Maybe the writer surrendered to it which allowed IT to source him. That's a fascinating fact.

Anyone else? . . . Okay, let's try parents.

So, how did your parents teach you about Sex? Did they do it verbally or by action, showing you? Did they do it awkwardly . . . Did they have talks or have "coded" talks? Just try to remember.

Lisa: *(Lisa is a 29 year old female elementary school teacher who lives with her boyfriend and is the daughter of Susan)* My parent's told me I had to be 'in love' before I had sex. Well, that was what I *should* do.

Joseph: Yeah, yeah. You have sex after you're in love . . . but you still don't know what Sex is.

Lisa: No.

Joseph: So you have to figure it out when you're in love. Then you get married, too, or is love enough?

Lisa: Love is enough.

Joseph: Okay, so love, and then you have sex and then all of a sudden you realize "I KNOW SEX," right? No, of course not. Can you begin to see what a small part of Sex we experience when we have it for the first time?

Simon: Its control, isn't it, when parents teach us that way? That we have to be in love?

Joseph: What do parents teach you sex for?

Day One: *The Sex Seminar*

Kelly: So we don't get pregnant.

Reese: So, we don't get any diseases.

Joseph: Right, raise your hand if your parents taught you about sex in order for you to have pleasure.

(No one raised their hands)

Joseph: Parents teach sex for protection, not pleasure. That's not their interest.

Tell me something. If they're teaching you that you have to protect yourself from Sex what do you think they're implying about IT? What are they saying about this energy?

Brennan: *(Brennan is a 26 year old male chef from a well-to-do family)* That it's something to fear.

Joseph: Yes, think about it . . . these are the first feelings you receive about sexuality from your parents, aren't they? That it's a scary thing, you have to be careful and protect yourself. No wonder there was so much fear and uptightness when you walked in. I'm not saying we are looking to turn you into hedonists.

But, we are interested in looking at who taught us, how did they teach us, and what was the motive behind it?

How do we come into this world?

Nathan: Through a vagina?

Jeremy: Through a pussy.

(Laughter)

Joseph: We come out into this world through a vagina, pussy, or C-section, absolutely. But how do we truly begin to be part of this world?

Angie: We're a product of an orgasm . . . one would hope.

Susan: Well, at least one person did.

(Laughter)

Joseph: As far as I'm concerned, the right someone.

(Laughter)

Lynn: You would say that!

(More laughter)

Joseph: We come into this world through Sex. Sex is what brings us here. It's the doorway for us. It's the doorway! And the first thing we do, when we come into this world, is start exploring; including the body. The child starts exploring the world it's in and itself; including everything that's sexual about it . . . all of itself.

So we come into this world through Sex. A child has no distinction between private and public, right? That distinction is taught. "No, no, you don't play with yourself out here in the middle of the playground!" A child has to be taught the distinction between private and public; they don't understand private from public. For a child, Sex is neither public nor private, it's both, and it's all of it. A parent's job is to teach the difference between these two areas, which is a big responsibility, especially if you don't know much about it yourself! . . .

Here's your assignment for tonight:

Homework:

1. Go home and look at all your sexual body parts using mirrors.
    a. What do **they** look like?
    b. What do you think of **them**?
    c. What do you feel when you look at **it or them**?
    d. Touch **them or it**.
    e. How do you feel touching **it or them**?
    f. Does **it or they** look like they're a part of you?
    g. Does **it or they** feel like they're a part of you?

2. Write down your findings

... That's enough for today.

"We cannot expose ourselves properly to the world until we expose ourselves to ourselves, and that is the hardest part of the process."

DAY TWO

Joseph: Welcome back, everyone!

So let's begin with the homework, what was that like for you?

Mercedes: I just looked at myself in the mirror and I was still fully clothed, but I just thought that our whole bodies are our sexual body parts. When I'm attracted to someone it's because I find their face attractive, or the outline of their body is attractive. Even something like smell I can find attractive. So, I don't know if it was avoidance on my part . . . actually, yes, I know it was avoidance that I didn't actually take any of my clothes off. I was fully clothed when I looked at myself.

Joseph: So, why didn't you take your clothes off so you could see all your parts?

Mercedes: Because it said to look at your sexual body parts, and I guess my definition of sexual body parts wasn't necessarily any one part.

Joseph: So your body was clothed throughout?

Mercedes: Yeah . . . not that a naked body isn't sexual . . . of course that's sexual, too, but I guess I just . . .

Joseph: There are different ways of exposing ourselves. The claim Mercedes is making is that she's fully exposed to herself, with or without clothes. Therefore, she looked at herself, and exposed herself to herself, that's if she's being honest with herself.

A lot of people can go naked and still not expose themselves, while many other people can be equally exposed fully dressed. How do you think exposure relates to sexuality?

So did you touch them, your body parts?

Mercedes: Yeah, I ran my hands along myself . . . and it was . . . I mean it wasn't . .

Joseph: How did you touch them? Slowly? Fast? Because, right now, it sounds like you did it really fast?

Mercedes: Yeah, I did it really fast!

Joseph: Okay, why? Why did you do it quickly?

Day Two: *The Sex Seminar*

Mercedes: I did it quickly, probably, to avoid the feelings that it would bring up.

Joseph: So now I have to wonder whether you didn't undress for that reason . . . and you could consider asking that of yourself.

Mercedes: Yeah, I'm not sure about that either.

Joseph: You get it? Because if she had taken her time, unclothed or even clothed, then I would have said okay . . . you actually are exposing yourself to yourself.

Mercedes: Yeah, and I touched my arms and my chest and my legs but that's it.

Joseph: Okay. So try it again tonight. You can be dressed or not, but now touch the rest of it; touch it till you feel you. Your body parts appear to you as if they're a part of you, they're not. Now you can see where you stopped yourself last night. Reflect on that. Why did you stop? Where did you stop? When did you begin to speed through the touching?

It might unlock things you don't really want to feel.

Mercedes: Yeah, (nervous laugh) that's why I didn't want to do it.

Joseph: So, try it again.

We cannot expose ourselves properly to the world until we expose ourselves to ourselves and that is the hardest part of the process. We think that to expose ourselves to others is the hardest act in life. No. The hardest act is to expose ourselves to ourselves; to really stop and see you and BE WITH yourself. This is an opportunity to be genuinely with you, but as you've seen with Mercedes, it will instantly bring stuff up. Of course it does, that is why it was easier for you to keep your clothes on, or to move through the assignment quickly, or to dart your eyes around your body without taking in all parts of yourself. These were just avoidance tactics you were using.

So, Mercedes, this now begs the question: is this an old feeling or a new feeling?

Mercedes: Umm, it's new and I think I've actually come a long way because last time I didn't even do the homework.

Joseph: No, your face is telling me that you're hiding from an old feeling.

Mercedes: Yeah, it's old. (Holding back tears) I know exactly what it is; I don't really want to go there.

Joseph: Okay, then it's best to sit in the feeling without looking for what has caused it; that's key. You're stuck at what's caused it, which allows you to avoid the feelings. Understand, it's not what caused it that harms us, but the effects of the feelings themselves that we carry around; the sensations. For now, I'd like you to be with the sensation, as difficult as that will be. It will require great courage on your part but this is how you'll release it. This action neither forgives nor not forgives the cause or *causer* of these feelings. It has nothing to do with the causer; it's about how you take your power back. After which, you'll find that the event that prompted this pain will take on a different meaning for you. You can find freedom by going to the sensation. Are you following?

Mercedes: Yeah . . .

Joseph: Okay. So good luck tonight.

Lynn: I just want to say that we often think it's the story that's causing us the pain when it's actually the sensations associated with the experience that's hurting us. We need to feel so we can heal.

Joseph: Anyone else? How did the homework go?

Angie: I really liked the homework.

Joseph: I don't care if you liked it or not. What was it like?

Angie: It was fascinating. It's actually something that I kind of do all the time but having it in an assignment form made it a little different. It made me question what I already do. It's like dividing it up into, like, actual questions. Like, what did they look like . . . in one way my experience was kind of similar to Mercedes. For me, my entire body is my sexual parts. Because, like, all of it for me is involved, from, like, my fingertips . . .

Joseph: You really LIKE the word like!

(Laughter)

What do you mean by you "kind of do it all the time?"

Angie: Well, I grew up attending nude beaches all the time and I guess nudity is really kind of natural for me . . . it's neutral.

Day Two: *The Sex Seminar*

Joseph: So did you do the assignment? Did you break yourself down to body parts?

Angie: Not necessarily . . .

Joseph: Okay so you didn't do the homework. Why did you avoid breaking them down?

Angie: I did and I didn't . . . I wanted, like, for me the first thing I did was, kind of like, I thought of it as a whole because . . .

Joseph: Why?

Angie: Because parts kind of felt negative to me.

Joseph: This is why it has to be broken up into parts for you. You get it?

Angie: Yeah.

Joseph: You're comfortable in the wholeness and we can't see in the comfortable; we see in the uncomfortable. You stop yourself from going into the uncomfortable.

We grow more from the discomfort than from comfort. So if any part of this homework was uncomfortable, consider my approach which is, "If it makes me uncomfortable . . . I gotta do it!" But be careful not to fool yourself and disconnect when you're feeling uncomfortable, that's not being in discomfort. When we expose from a disconnected place, then there is no discomfort, hence there is no growth.

Angie: Okay, I'm trying to take this in.

Joseph: I get it. Can we agree that you avoided looking at yourself in parts and decided to do it your way? Can you see how much control you needed? There was no reaching you here; there were no possibilities of providing you a new experience because you already *knew*. You were all knowing; you knew how you were supposed to do this assignment and how you should have been affected by it. You did not do it the way it was assigned. Then you determined that it was something that could be liked or disliked. It's irrelevant whether you like it or not! Why approach this with that kind of filter?

Most of you block and stop experiences in your lives because they are funnelled through this *I like, I dislike* filter. My most profound experiences, if I'm going to value them, were shit I didn't like at all! So I don't stop myself and filter. I don't do things only based on whether I like it or not. It's so childish because it's just black and white; it's dualistic: like or not. This exercise can be, by far, more transcendent than like or not! That's equivalent to taking a work of art and treating it like something a child drew up.

So that's block number one.

Angie: I *know* I definitely do that.

Joseph: Block number two is . . . starting from the whole body. You do this because you don't want to feel what the parts, and the spaces separating them, have to say. There's a reason why we give this homework this way. You get it?

Angie: I get it.

Joseph: You'll need to do it again. Don't worry; there will be other things that we'll ask of you to do that will require you to look at it from a holistic perspective. But, you need to understand that if you continue to cling to one way of looking at things we won't be able to help you expand yourself.

Angie: Okay.

Joseph: Thank you for sharing.

We assume that the practice of wholeness is the most expansive way to do things. No, that's just you using the right side of your brain. If you lived that way only, you'd be living with half a brain. On the contrary, when we look at things through the left side of our brains we are able to see all the parts, and all that is hidden within them that make up the whole. So we need to practice both. We need both. If we were building a bridge we'd need the right side of our brains to show us how it could look and where it could be best placed. Then we would need the left side to fill in all the details to actually build it.

We were recently watching a documentary called *The Workshop,* and towards the end of the workshop everyone got completely naked. Now, you all probably think that getting completely naked is the ultimate form of exposure, don't you?

Group: Yes!

Joseph: But what you would have noticed, if you were really watching it with a keen eye, is that the physical nakedness didn't create as much exposure as one would have thought. It was easy to see that the participants, or *players,* were still hiding behind their drama and they were using their emotions and minds, rather than their clothing, to protect themselves. This is because once the shock of nakedness subsides, and because everyone was naked, they revert to the mind set they held before. The impact of nakedness gets neutralized with time and this allows the EGO to recoup its control.

Unfortunately for the players, nakedness did not decrease their bullshit and self-centeredness. There was one young woman, in particular, who stated towards the end, "Oh, I'm really facing myself here! I have this little bit of cellulite and I allowed myself to pinch it so you can see that I have cellulite." This was a woman who was in great shape but thought she was going to bless the viewer with her humility by showing what was "wrong" with her! Except that this was the same bullshit she had been running throughout the documentary, whether she was dressed or not!

Lynn: Their nudity became another wall. I've seen a lot of woman expose their breasts thinking they were being open when, in fact, they were disconnected from them.

Angie: I definitely don't do that!

Lynn: You did! You were raised to hide behind nudity.

Angie: What!?

Joseph: Okay just be aware of yourself, you're very defensive right now . . .

Angie: Yeah . . .

Joseph: . . . so just breathe, and be defensive, feel it, but see it! The key is to feel, "I'm defensive." So, clearly, you're protecting something, right?

Angie: Yeah . . .

Joseph: I'm not going to fight through your defensiveness. I'm going to use it as an example, so that we all can benefit, because we're all in this together! We're all trying to figure this out together. None of you are worse off than the other; believe me! So, whoever speaks gets the courage points . . . and, can go further.

Anyone else?

Nathan: I find myself like, kind of, just kind of neutral . . . not really uncomfortable; I mean it's my body, I've seen it, I see it every day. Like, for example the question, how do they look? I'm like, "They look like they're *supposed to*," was my response, you know? It is what it is.

Joseph: So you weren't present to yourself?

Nathan: I guess not!

Joseph: Because *supposed too* is past tense, right?

Nathan: Yeah . . .

Joseph: Hence, you're looking at yourself from the past, a past image of how you have seen yourself.

Nathan: This is why I'm sharing because I had a hard time with it. I was just like, "Why am I so blasé about it?" You know what I mean? It was just kind of . . . (Getting emotional) . . . it's bringing something up for me, right now, and I don't know what it is. Yeah it's just uh . . . I didn't care enough about myself to even look at myself.

Joseph: Excellent . . . excellent. Both of you are revealing the walls that are blocking you from true exposure.

Angie's wall was made up from the need to only see the whole and avoid the parts while Nathan created a wall/screen to project an old image of himself. He undressed, then he figuratively redressed himself. He got dressed, again . . . you get it? Nathan, you got dressed again . . . standing there naked, you got dressed, but you dressed yourself with your projection, you wrapped yourself in a hologram. This was a much harder exercise than any of you thought; anyone else?

Parisa: I can go.

Joseph: Okay.

Parisa: . . .umm I didn't do it last night; I did it this morning because I was so exhausted last night. So I took a shower this morning, and you want to know I've done this before . . . I already know about this, and I experienced the same problem I had the last time I tried this, which is why I'm here for this seminar, and that was . . . I could touch my body but not my genitals.

Joseph: What did you touch? Your knees, arms, shoulders? Did you touch anything that you thought was sexual?

Parisa: Yeah, my whole body!

Joseph: Okay, how quickly?

Parisa: One hour . . . I used body lotion . . . and I do it very frequently.

Day Two: *The Sex Seminar*

Joseph: Yeah okay, lotion's no good. Nothing in the instructions says lotion.

Parisa: It increases the sensation! But . . .

Joseph: No, no, no. That's you taking charge. You see, the lotion is another wall; it's another block. It's part of your routine. You brought the past in, and that's the problem. You brought the past in, so you weren't present to yourself! You began with "I've done this before." So already you had a preconceived notion of what you were going to experience.

Parisa: Maybe, but . . .

Joseph: No, absolutely! Not maybe. You just said it! "I've done this before . . . I already know." Did you do *this,* specifically?

Parisa: Yeah, I did this, specifically, but . . .

Joseph: No you added lotion!

Parisa: Well I applied it to the legs and stuff like that; I didn't apply it to the genitals! I did not apply it to the boobs.

Lynn: Where, in the instructions, does it say lotion? This is Joseph's point. What you do on your free time with your body is great. That's how you take care of yourself, but what we're talking about is the *specifics*.

Parisa: The sexual parts, to me, are the boobs and the genitals and I did not put lotion on them.

Joseph: Good, so you think your boobs and genitals are the only Sexual parts of you and not your whole body, as you said. That's interesting.

Parisa: You ask me about my knees, I put cream on my knees!

Joseph: I asked about your knees in order to determine if you experienced them as a part of you. They are not, to you, and that's fine.

Parisa: I applied lotion to take care of my body.

Joseph: So, why didn't you do that after the exercise?

Parisa: Why? I did it after the exercise! Yes . . . sorry I just remembered.

Day Two: *The Sex Seminar*

Joseph: Okay so I just want to hear about what happened during the exercise. I don't want to hear about what happened afterwards.

Parisa: I don't feel I'm good enough, in my genitals.

Joseph: I understand, so did you write that down, or any other findings?

Parisa: Nothing said to write it down . . .

Joseph: Yes, question number two did.

Parisa: I didn't see that question . . .

Joseph: That's called avoidance.

Lynn: Whether it's written or not, three times last night, I said to write it down.

Joseph: That's how we can see our own avoidance.

Parisa: I was half asleep, probably.

Joseph: That's an excuse.

(Laughter)

Now back to the experience, how did it feel touching them?

Parisa: I got horny . . .

Joseph: So you touched them!

(Laughter)

Parisa: Well, briefly.

(More laughter)

Joseph: Each time you touched them did you get horny, and I assume that what you are talking about when you say "them" are your breasts?

Parisa: Yeah . . .

Joseph: And did they look like they were a part of you?

Parisa: Yes. A rejected part of me. Not rejected. I wish they were better, that they looked better.

Joseph: Okay, but did they look like they were a part of you even though you didn't entirely like them?

Parisa: Yeah

Joseph: Did they *feel* like they were a part of you?

Parisa: Yeah.

Joseph: Okay, very good. What do you make of that? That they looked and felt like they were a part of you?

Parisa: I felt sexy.

Joseph: So do you think you felt sexy because the look and the feeling were okay for you?

Parisa: Yeah

Joseph: Is it possible to say that when we *see and feel* our parts and then see our parts as being us, we may be inclined to experience personal sexiness? What do you make of that possibility?

Tami: The exercise took me a couple of tries . . .

Joseph: I don't want to hear about you, yet. I want to know what you make of that.

Tami: Oh, sorry . . . um, I agree.

Joseph: What do you mean you agree? What does that mean?

Tami: I agree that would be sexy!

Joseph: What do you make of that, though? I didn't ask you tell me whether you agree or disagree. I'm asking what you think! Come on, think! What do you think of that? That's what I mean when I say "What do you make of that."

Tami: Uh, I dunno . . .

Joseph: Okay, think about it.

Tami: Okay.

Joseph: This is such a *Jeopardy* generation. You all think you have to answer immediately and correctly; but then there's no real thought given! You're all afraid of not getting it right. I'm asking a question you don't know the answer to, and, yet, you answer without taking the time to think about it. How is it that you answer so quickly?

Tami: Yeah . . .

Joseph: What does that mean?

(Laughs)

Tami: I don't know.

Joseph: So, why did you say "Yeah?"

Tami: Because I'm agreeing with you. I don't know the answer to the question.

Joseph: Okay, but my last question was "How is it that you answer so quickly?" to something you don't know the answer to? Ask yourself . . . don't worry about me. I'm not your parent.

Tami: I need to think about it.

Joseph: Yeah, there you go. Now you're being an adult with me. I'll get back to you. I want an answer, though.

Mercedes: I think that it's interesting that Parisa could still feel sexy and turned on and yet she holds this negative belief about herself. By the way Parisa, that isn't true! You think it's true and it's not, you're sexy.

Joseph: Parisa's ability to feel sexy, during the exercise, was a great accomplishment for her. All she has to work on, now, is this mistaken belief. The beliefs we hold creates the feelings we have. But a belief isn't a truth, otherwise, we'd call it a truth. So you have a belief . . .

Parisa: It's the truth to me, now.

Joseph: What's the truth?

Parisa: The belief . . .

Joseph: There is no truth *to you*. There's the truth.

Parisa: Okay.

Day Two: *The Sex Seminar*

Joseph: If one person here says you're sexy, then it's not the truth that you are not; it's a belief. You understand? If one person sees you naked and says, "Are you kidding me, you're hot?" Then your belief is just a belief, it's not a truth.

Parisa: Yeah.

Joseph: Because the truth cannot be conflicted by a belief. We can't negate a truth with a belief. Water makes you wet. You can't say, "No it makes me sandy!" And that changes the truth?!

(Laughter)

Parisa: Okay I understand . . .

Joseph: This is a wonderful opportunity to uncover whether what you think about yourself is the truth or a belief. If you want to know the truth you can question, challenge, confront, or prove your beliefs. You can run them past others for feedback. There are numerous ways to get to a knowable truth.

When you decided to experience your parts and touch your parts, you gave your body a chance to respond . . . and it did! You got to see that when you give attention to your body it will respond. Our bodies always respond to our attention to it. So, this was a large hurdle you just jumped. The only thing left is to work with the truth.

Some of you have trouble *truly* looking at, being with and feeling yourselves. In addition, you compound the problem by conjuring up judgements, which lead to beliefs that are not based on actual experiences with yourself. Amazing, you can't look at yourself, you can't feel yourself, but you have a belief on how you are! Like you know! You don't know! We need to expose ourselves to ourselves, and this exercise is a way we can begin to do this.

We cannot even talk about Sex without exposure. Why do you think?

Mercedes: Sex is exposure. It's the ultimate exposure.

Joseph: Very good. Not everyone will understand that, but maybe by tomorrow. (Smiling)

Mercedes: It's beautiful because we're compelled to do it. It's like we have to expose ourselves! It's like, you can't just not eat; you have to eat, eventually.

Joseph: You have to expose . . .

Lynn: We mentioned this yesterday, and I'm going to say it again: the only way that you're going to find out the truth is to not be so attached to where you think you're right. A lot of us do a lot of self work, just to validate that we're right. You're working for nothing, then. If you take the same approach this weekend then it will be a waste of time. We're here to begin exposing. Exposing what Sex is, and who you are in relation to it.

Joseph: As you expose, you expose yourself to you. As you expose yourself to you, you get more clarity on who you are. The reason why most of us are afraid to expose ourselves to ourselves is that we may not like what we see or feel, but that's stage one. You're not going to like what you feel or see most of the time, if not every time, you start this process. It's after a while, with the continual exposure, that you start seeing deeper and feeling more, just like you do in your relationships. As you expose yourself, in time and space, to the other, you inevitably get to see them more deeply, right? Why can't you do that with yourselves?

We need to do this, continually, with ourselves. Six or seven times, is not enough. That would be like getting naked with your wife or husband over twenty years, six or seven times only. It's like what? That's all? You exposed yourself six or seven times? That's what we do with ourselves! Now let us further clarify, when we say expose, we mean fully, consciously . . . expose yourself. Take your time, though, we need time to connect and see. That goes with anything in life.

So, look at the parts, see the parts, feel them, and once you've taken them a part . . . well, we'll have you answer that.

Why do we have you take it apart? What's the purpose of that? Why did we have you look at parts of you rather than the whole you? Why did we not have you take in *you* in your entirety so you could experience the oneness of it all? Why didn't we start there? Why do we intentionally say "parts?"

Alexia: Less opportunity to avoid.

Joseph: No.

Nathan: In order to know the whole, we have to know the parts.

Joseph: That's true, but that's not the main reason, that is the result.

Nathan: Alright.

Joseph: No, that's fine; you just jumped ahead a bit. I'll give you a point for jumping ahead.

Parisa: I've taken my parts for granted. I can see that what I can now do is experience them in detail.

Joseph: If you went to another planet, how would you look at the inhabitants of that planet, as a whole or in parts?

Angie: A whole.

Joseph: So you would go and you would see a whole Martian? You wouldn't notice his big giant eyes, or his skinny little legs? You'd just notice the whole?

Angie: No. Actually, that's not true.

Joseph: Yeah, when we go to another planet we look at it in its parts first. Why? We're giving you a big clue! Why do we have you break yourself up into parts? If they came here they would do the same. What's the purpose?

Nisha: So we can piece ourselves together?

Joseph: No . . . You missed the point Nisha.

Angie: Yeah, no kidding!

Nisha: To make us aliens to ourselves?

Joseph: Yes, to make you alien to yourselves . . . to *alienate* you from yourself. We intentionally want to alienate you from yourself!

You alienate yourselves when you see yourselves in parts. What you see is a loosely fitted group of parts which have space between them that make up the whole package called "you." And it's the spaces between the parts, the cracks, where you hide all the things you don't like about yourself; all your junk.

It's wild to me that we call our genitals "junk." We have "junk in the trunk," and we offer up our junk, "Come on baby, grab my junk."

(Laughter)

Day Two: *The Sex Seminar*

But there's a reason why we call it junk, Sex is where we hide all of our shit. It's in Sex that we hide all the things that we don't like others, or ourselves, to see about us.

The homework allowed you the chance to see what you've hidden in your body and it sounds like most of you missed that opportunity. But that's okay, because now you can do it again; at least you know where to go. That's why we call our Sexual parts junk! Could you give me another reason why you would call this magnificent part of you "junk?"

Kelly: From all the rap songs?

Joseph: Yeah. It is where we hear it, but we've chosen to adapt and accept it without question. As for the rappers, well, so you know, "What one represses, the other will express."

It's our repression of our junk, our garbage, which inspires others to express it for us! They're just labelling it on our behalf! And we've accepted it; we're not complaining about it! It's caught on because it does speak to how we treat our Sexuality; we throw a lot of garbage in it.

Sex is an empty space that we throw our garbage into because nobody goes looking in there! Except somebody you invite, and even the one's you invite won't be able to find it, if you hide it deep enough. They won't find it even when you have sex with them. It's such a big place; you can hide **all** your shit there! And it is not in the parts, but in the crevices of those parts, where you hide your shit.

The homework calls for you to be present and encounter your parts and the space between. When it's done correctly, the cracks and crevices will behave like ocean waves rushing in, and then being pulled back by the tide to reveal what's washed ashore, thus leaving behind the "junk" from the ocean that you dumped into. What does a magician do? They move one hand faster than the other and because we are genetically predisposed to follow and isolate whatever is moving, they are able to distract you and create the "illusion of magic" with the other hand. But, if you were able to go stiller than the slowest hand you would catch the trick. If you are still enough, when you practice being with your Sexual body parts, then you will see all the hidden "junk."

Let's say some of your crap was hidden in the joints of your knees and you weren't conscious that you hid it there, what you'd develop, over time, would be knee problems. Your sexual issues can easily show up, physically, in the knees. The knees are an erogenous zone that are sexual parts of you. Why do you think many of us are ticklish there and why do we measure whether we are being Sexual or not with skirts depending on if they fall above or below the knees? If you hide your junk in the knees and you avoided the knees during the exercise, I'd know that you're hiding it there.

Let's look at Parisa's experience again. What was she doing when she chose to lotion herself during the exercise?

Tami: Was she covering herself or protecting herself?

Joseph: Close. She was spackling herself. She was covering everything, so nothing could come out and so she didn't have to see it. That's the opportunity she missed. She didn't get to alienate herself. She went back to what was comfortable in being nude and whole. So try it again! There's some good stuff there! These are brilliant exercises! Once it is exposed, it leaves! And each time you do it you have an opportunity to get rid of more junk.

Mercedes: It's funny you use the word "junk" because I was really upset the other day before I came to the seminar because I know, consciously, one of the things I want to avoid is that I have a negative belief about being unworthy and disposable . . . that word, "junk," explains a lot to me. It's a huge thing for me and I understand now why I avoided doing the exercise. (Holds back tears)

Joseph: So do it at your leisure . . . It's an opportunity if you push yourself, but it's not going to be easy, it's going to be painful. But, once it's exposed it leaves, and that's the benefit of this exercise. You can do it long after you're out of here because each time you do it you give yourself the opportunity to rid yourself of more junk. So that's why we're suggesting you do it, "until." Until it's relieved, then you can go on to the other areas of pain. Finally, when you're connected and flowing, when the pain is minimal or gone outright . . . then, and only then, do you want to look at yourself whole.

Parisa: Can you give me an example of what's in these cracks you're talking about? Is it an old belief, is it an experience?

Joseph: It could be an experience. It could be an old belief. It could be religious beliefs that were instilled in us at a young age. It could be abuse, or simply misuse. It could be a big pain or something small and troublesome.

My aunt was sharing with me the other day that when she was younger she was told not to wash her hair when she was menstruating. That it wasn't good for her! So, that little idea stayed locked up in her and, eventually, grew into feelings of sexual shame. Because she hadn't questioned it, initially, it became a part of her, which led her to feeling dirty; a "dirty" that even a shower couldn't get rid of. Finally, it wasn't until she recalled and questioned this old wives tale, that she was able to release it.

Kelly: That doesn't make any sense!

Joseph: Yeah, exactly! But that's what we're left with when we live *an unexamined life.*

Lynn: My sister-in-law was not allowed to bathe when she had her period.

Joseph: Yeah, these are beliefs, and they get locked in.

Lynn: The belief in my sister-in-law's case was that she could die; she could bleed out.

Parisa: So is this exercise going to cure the memory?

Joseph: No, it will release it; as my old wise professor used to say, "To feel is to heal."

Parisa: I can do this with any memory? For example when I was toilet trained, I was a child and my mother . . .

Joseph: Wait, you know what . . . don't tell us. I want you to write it down. In fact I want everyone to write down their first experience with shit. Take your time and think back to your first experience with crap or shit. (Blank index cards are being passed around)

Don't put your names on it . . . A former student of mine, many years ago, remembered that the first time she came to her parents with her dirty diaper they made her put it on her head. That was her first experience.

Day Two: *The Sex Seminar*

Go back as far as you can remember even if the earliest memory was at 15 years of age . . . (Speaking while participants are writing) . . . doesn't matter when . . . The first time you had an experience with your shit, whether it was looking in a toilet bowl where you saw a piece of corn in it . . Your first experience with shit, and if there were other people involved, write down who was involved, but not by name . . . Just something brief we don't need a book. Then hand them in upside down.

(Group takes five minutes to jot down memories)

Okay, let's take a read here . . .

(Joseph reads them aloud)

I was on a camping trip with my uncle and cousin when I was seven. We were bugging my uncle about getting junk food, until he gave in. We ate as much junk food as possible because this was a very rare opportunity. Within two hours we both shit our pants. I remember standing on a rock in the middle of the camping ground being hosed off.

Joseph: I want you to begin to let yourself experience what that was like.

I shit on the toilet seat and the parents had to clean it.

I don't really remember but I'm sure it was good as I really enjoy a good shit.

(Laughter)

Now that was resistance, like I said, even if it was when you were 15 years old. You were to write it down. That's resistance, and it's not very funny to me because this person just missed out on an opportunity.

Seeing worms in my crap as a small child.

I remember going away to camp and holding it because I was ashamed to go to the bathroom.

I felt like I was the only one who went number two.

I didn't know what to do so I called for help to the bathroom to my mom . . . embarrassment.

I don't remember.

Joseph: More avoidance! You have to see the subtle ways in which we avoid not to feel, especially around shit. So those two people, you know who you are, you're avoiding your shit! And, it's only going to get worse. It's not Sex that's the problem. It's you, holding on to all this shit, and unwilling to take a deeper look at it.

One of the more positive things Oprah Winfrey did was to have people become comfortable looking at their shit. It was great! What a breakthrough, we now listen to Dr. Oz talking about crap, bowels, etc. and we look at our shit and we know "it's okay." We're becoming more comfortable with that part of us.

I used the toilet and forgot to flush; later my mom took me back in there and said that I had made her friend "sick" when she saw it.

As a child, while swimming in a pool, I pooped in my bathing suit and let it go into the pool. Felt huge shame.

I pooped in a baby toilet at my neighbour's house and brought it out for everyone to see. No one wanted to see it, and I was taught to put it in the toilet and flush.

In Kindergarten I peed my pants during prayer and I felt shame, fear, and anger.

My Mom doing the celebrating "pooh-pooh in the potty" dance with me, when I used the real toilet. That's the first and only thing that pops into my head, but I'm not sure if I really remember it.

Joseph: So that's something, it may not be this person's actual experience, but we can get a little confused about what's actually happened to us vs. what's been told to us. Nonetheless, it can still have a powerful impact on us.

I recall my stomach being upset a lot and running to the washroom at the age of seven or eight, painful and embarrassed. No memory before that point.

My first experience: I remember when I was being toilet trained, I was about two years old and was sitting on the regular toilet. The lights were not on and my mom was frustrated that I crapped in my underwear so she heated the chrome metal stick and burned my butt with it. So I learned.

Day Two: *The Sex Seminar*

My earliest memory of shit was not so much my actual shit, but a nickname I was given by my babysitters and family because, as a baby, I would poop so much they called me "Pooper."

Vague memory being in a car and shitting my pants, feeling shame and embarrassment, family was around.

I had no one to help me or teach me how to clean myself after; I was confused and uncertain but used toilet paper and felt like I used it the way it was supposed to be done.

Joseph: What do you make of all this? By the way . . . these are some of the unhealthiest experiences I've heard in all the years of doing this exercise. But what do you make of it? What do you think this "lab" is about? It's called the "Shit Lab."

Angie: There was a lot of embarrassment and shame.

Alexia: It's kind of reminding me of how our parents didn't teach us about Sex. They didn't teach us about going to use the washroom and what our body does to get rid of our waste.

Joseph: Exactly.

Alexia: So we feel embarrassed and ashamed.

Joseph: That's a big part of it, absolutely. Anybody else?

Simon: It's almost like Canada and the U.S. has got it worse. You guys can't even say I need to use the toilet, that you say I need to use the washroom. In the U.K. its like, "I need to take a shit," or "I need to use the toilet." And here it's like, "Where's the washroom?" or "Go number two."

Joseph: There's larger repression here, and it starts from very young.

Simon: People get embarrassed when I'm in a restaurant and I ask to use the toilet, they gasp, "How can you say that?" Yeah, I need to take a shit!

Joseph: Again, the repression starts young! The training to repress you starts very young. This is how you're trained to repress. Anyone else?

Nathan: A lot of people were punished.

Joseph: Yeah. What are we punished for? A natural human act.

Nathan: Yeah, everybody here shits, and everybody here has sex. Everybody here pisses, everybody breathes, everybody's heart beats, and it's like we're meant to feel ashamed for doing something that's perfectly natural that in the animal kingdom it comes completely natural. You don't see them getting embarrassed or feeling emotions about being who they are. Monkey's let their balls hang out all the time and it's not even a big deal. Look at us! We're having a hard time remembering a first memory of shit! It's so backwards to me!

Eddie: I've seen dogs look embarrassed. I remember watching my dog, while he was rubbing his behind on the grass because there was still some crap left on it, trying to avoid eye contact with me, looking really embarrassed.

(Laughter)

Nathan: That's because we look at them and laugh.

Joseph: Yeah, it makes you wonder what we impose upon them. Cesar Milan, commonly known as *The Dog Whisperer,* has opened the consciousness of many people about what dogs actually feel, understand, and get. So, it's almost like we've taught them to be ashamed, like the rest of us.

Simon: We do that don't we? We have strong feelings about when they shit or piss in the house. We'll spank them or throw them out of the house or something, so we teach them that. It's got to be a learned thing to be ashamed of that because, when they're puppies, they do it and they don't care. Same thing as humans, so I guess we're pretty close in that way.

Joseph: So, here's the big secret. What you've been taught in how to shit, how to handle your shit, and your perception of it, directly affects your view of Sex and your sex life! What do you think of that?

Alexia: I could see a pattern because I had a hard time remembering and then, when I did, I was kind of ashamed of it. The same thing happened with the homework, where I focused on all the negative parts and, right away, I wanted to throw roses on it and be, like, "Oh, but these are the good things!" It's like an internal battle of the positive, always having to look at what's good, vs. trying to avoid the shit.

Day Two: *The Sex Seminar*

Joseph: Very good. So how is your earliest recollection and experience of shit directly related to your experience of Sex, what you believe Sex is and what you've made Sex to be or to mean?

Simon: It's culturally acceptable, what we're taught from a young age.

Angie: Something not talked about . . .

Nathan: Can't do it in public, stuff like that.

Joseph: How is it that we could make the claim that your experience with shit is directly related to your **sexuality**?

Parisa: It's a natural process.

Joseph: Right, that's one reason.

Mercedes: We feel shame about just existing, basically.

Joseph: For many . . . Why else? It's simpler than that. Why else?

Angie: Something I learned from the Communication Seminar was that it's your first creation, right? And Sex is creative energy so it's like when you approach your parents with your doody, you're proud of it!

Joseph: Very good . . . It's the first thing a human being creates! The first thing a child creates, and a child is always proud of what he or she creates. Therefore, when they come with their creation, this is the parent's opportunity to help a child feel like they have something of value to offer. So, throwing a little poop dance is awesome! The child will absolutely begin to value what he or she creates! Also, as Angie mentioned, this first creation, which we suggest comes from *creative energy*, reveals a connection between itself and Sexual energy. How else are these energies related?

Parisa: They bring the same feelings . . . a turn on? People who are gay will feel the same feelings . . .

Joseph: The feelings are very similar in that area of the body. You're getting really hot now, you're getting closer . . . you're almost there!

Mercedes: It's a bodily function, it's a natural normal bodily function, and maybe it's the first experience of shame or embarrassment, if it's a negative experience, it's the first feeling of shame.

Joseph: Yeah if you start off negatively, it's not healthy starting that way, right? It's already setting a pattern that becomes part of the body . . . Come on, almost there!

Reese: It's a release; it's like a relief of tension.

Joseph: Well, again, that goes back to the type of feelings that taking a crap gives you. Like Sex, it gives you relief. What's the real connection here? Why does it have such a direct effect?

Nisha: Same body parts?

Joseph: Its part of the same body parts that we involve Sex with, absolutely. There are clear erogenous zones in the anus.

For most of you, you think Sex is just one or two openings, maybe three tops. *All* your openings are part of the sexual system that is you. So whatever opinions you form on any of the openings, even if it's about what comes out of your eyes and ears, such as mucus, wax, and tears . . . it affects your Sexual life.

We're being taught and acculturated about Sex from the first time we become aware of our poop, and its effects on others. It's our first lucid experience with Sex. Yet, it's only one of many openings that make up our bodies . . . openings that make up our Sexual selves.

Nathan: It's culturally embarrassing; nothing that comes in or out of our holes is something acceptable. That's what we're taught in society, from a young age.

Joseph: Absolutely! What do you think of that? We're always told to cover up our shit; the yucky stuff. As some of you may remember from our earlier seminars, we're taught to cover our mouths when we yawn. It's for the same reason we're taught bathroom manners. Your mother teaches you how to yawn. Yawning is natural, but covering your mouth is not. When mother teaches you to cover your mouth she's teaching you the rules of intimacy. She teaches how to handle your openings. Your early experiences with shit have also taught you about Sex and intimacy. Unfortunately, it's "taught" in an even more random and thoughtless fashion. And how you experienced it tells me more about you than you'd like me to know.

For instance, the share about when one of you forgot to flush and it made your mother's friend "sick," well, that tells me that you're obsessed with the opinions of others; especially women's. It also guarantees that you have trouble sharing your problems, "your shit." Lastly, you battle with constant feelings of shame around Sex and you probably create shameful sexual experiences in order to perpetuate this *crime* that was committed on you.

So, you think these sexual ways of yours evolved naturally? No, it was quite unnatural. From very early on, you are made to start disliking, judging, maybe even hating your sexual self. You're taught to repress your openings.

Simon: And those are the things that feel good, as well. It feels good to blow your nose . . .

Joseph: Yes, it feels good to cry! It feels good to sneeze! Though it's too advanced to talk about it now, sneezing is a highly sexual act. It's directly connected to your sexual process.

Kelly: What about cleaning your ears?

Joseph: What about it?

Kelly: I know it's weird but I love cleaning my ears! It feels so good!

Joseph: It can be part of the joy of clearing yourself.

Nathan: So, why did you say it's weird?

Kelly: Well I guess because no one ever talks about it . . .

Joseph: But yes, cleaning your ears can leave you with a great feeling afterwards, like a good shit, and you can hear more! After listening to this, you're going to tell me your ears aren't part of your sexual process? You're telling me your ears have nothing to do with sex!?

Parisa: Of course, they do.

Joseph: Yeah, but as far as you were concerned only your breasts and genitals were sexual to you.

Parisa: That was yesterday!

Joseph: Oh, she's got plans today!

(Laughter)

Joseph: How are your ears not part of your sex lives? Seriously . . . come on you're not *that* stupid. Are you truly *choosing not to see what's in front of your face?*

Mercedes: Hearing the voice! The smell . . . they can nibble on your ear a little.

Joseph: Yeah look at that, she's getting excited!

(Laughter)

Mercedes: It's hot!

Joseph: Yeah, do you see how much we omit? So you have to see, what did you choose as your sexual body parts? Did anybody include their ears?

Mercedes: I did! Yeah, I did.

Joseph: Good, how about your eyes?

Simon: Is every part of you, your ears, eyes, nose, all part of our sexual body? But you said you have to look separately, so this could take, like, four hours. That's what we should have been doing?

Joseph: Yes, it could, not should . . . but, you could. It depends on how far or how deeply you want to experience this.

Nathan: So, essentially, your whole body, not just parts. Like, I mean, I like the back of my neck being rubbed. That could be Sexual, and so whatever it is, for whomever?

Joseph: Yes, if I took a magnifying glass and zoomed in, all we'd see is pores! Openings, the entire body! See what you're missing? Could you imagine how different your Sex life could be if you did this as a practice? This exercise will begin to make you more sensitive to touch, to smell, and to how you see things. You will feel sexier, more energized. People will experience you, saying, "Wow, something's different about you!" If you just did this exercise a little, every day! But consciously, not Parisa conscious; Parisa conscious is, "I've done this before, and I know all about it." NO, you have to do it as if it's brand new, every time, because every day you can experience something new with it. If you approach something like you've done it before, then you can't get the NEW because you're being with what you KNEW, so you miss out on the NEW.

Lynn: Not to mention that you're shedding this old body, anyways; you're always getting a new body, so really it is new! Literally, every seven years, every cell in your body has been replaced. Literally! Almost your entire body is new every seven years.

Angie: The more in detail that we're getting about this exercise . . . well, a lot is coming up for me. I had this experience on psychedelics once, where I was just fascinated by every little thing! I was with a partner, too, but we spent eight hours in my tent exploring like fingertips . . .

Joseph: That's what you've been missing out on, because you can't take psychedelics every day, I've tried, and it doesn't work.

(Laughter)

But this is a natural way of reaching that state of consciousness people have been talking about for centuries. These and other types of practices of this kind are designed to help you, naturally, find a transformative or even transcendent experience of yourselves. They leave you not only feeling good about yourselves, but also more sensitive to *your* internal and external worlds.

What you want to take note of, though, is that, at first, these practices are likely to leave you feeling heavy, or what you call "bad." The reason for this is simple, when you turn on a faucet that hasn't been used in a long time you will find that the water is always dark in color. But, as you let it run it, gradually, turns lighter and lighter until it is running clear. The same will happen with you as you begin to allow the backed up shit to flow out. It's going to feel crappy, at first, but with time, it will get clearer and it will feel so good! But, you've got to expose yourself for this to happen.

Some of you now see that you have had a limited view of your *Sexual body*. So imagine how much more you're missing if, in fact, Sex is more than the body?

Parisa: So you're saying that if we do the exercise every day, we don't have to think about our beliefs because by only appreciating and digging deeper and deeper, it will resolve by itself.

Joseph: It helps to question our beliefs, but when you speak of appreciation you're adding a whole other component to the discussion. It would be great if you could practice appreciation along with this exercise. But to actually appreciate, well, first you need to know that appreciation doesn't mean approving. I appreciate my hand, but I'm not approving of it when I'm appreciating it. Of course, appreciation can enhance any of these exercises and labs but it's not necessary for our purposes.

We're just saying be with it, touch it, feel it. So yeah if you want to advance it, since you've been *doing it for so long*, (smiling) add the appreciation. It will accelerate it, absolutely.

Now, Tami, would you like to answer my earlier question?

Tami: I don't even know what it was?

Joseph: Okay, I'll repeat it. Why did you answer quickly, a question you were clueless about?

Tami: I guess I thought I knew the answer . . . I was trying to make up the answer. I was thinking too much as opposed to just feeling.

Joseph: Okay I want you to get clear and give me a clear answer because now you've added two or three different reasons . . . okay, narrow it to one answer, and we'll get back to you.

Tami: Okay. (Embarrassed laugh)

Joseph: What do you make of all this? The homework, the shit lab . . .

Nisha: How is yawning connected to sex?

Joseph: We're taught from childhood how to yawn, and it's taught differently to females than it is to males. Men are allowed to go (demonstrates big yawn) where women are like . . . (demonstrates meek, covered up yawn)

Nisha: So you start learning all of that?

Joseph: You're taught, you don't learn, you're acculturated.

Lynn: Look how you're sitting and look at how Nathan's sitting.

(Laughter)

Nathan's spread legged and you're . . . oh look! You're clamming up as I speak!

(More laughter)

Joseph: Girls are taught to cover up or close their openings! Remember, parents teach protection!

Nathan: Is that why girls don't fart or, at least, that's the myth?

Joseph: They're taught not to show their shit. Again this is acculturated, absolutely. Unfortunately for me someone forgot to teach my aunt's that . . .

(Laughter)

Simon: I remember in a rugby photo, I think it was under ten's, where all the boys were sitting with their legs open and I had my legs crossed and my mom said, "In the next picture you're gonna have to open your legs!" I remember I was the only one sitting like that!

Joseph: There you go. We are taught the rules before we can even think about it. We're taught how to behave around our "private parts," as they like to call it. No explanations! What do you make of all this?

Angie: I just think of this little girl that I saw a few weeks ago in a donut shop and she came out of the back screaming, "I went pooh! I went pooh!" Talking to everyone walking through this cafe and people were just staring at her strangely, so I high fived her! The cool thing was that her dad wasn't shutting her up. And I remember when I was a little kid, my mom used to potty dance for me. She would bring the whole house down, stoked! It was a celebration!

And this little girl, to me, well…it was really cool because I've seen a lot of shame attached to crap. And it's sad.

Joseph: Exactly. So what do we do with our shit when we have too much mental, emotional, or psychological shit going on? We either handle it the way we were taught or we don't handle it at all. And you want to know that when we aren't handling it, we are actually using learned avoidance tactics. We are trained ahead of time on how to handle issues. Therefore, if you make an effort to teach a child effective ways to resolve conflict or practice healthy self expression and communication, you'll be forming an individual that won't have any resistance to

Day Two: *The Sex Seminar*

handling their shit. With these types of skills, the child won't be so afraid to look at theirs and other's issues; they'll be courageous. So cut yourselves some slack here, give yourselves a break! Look how you were taught. Don't be so hard on yourselves just because you're having trouble dealing with your shit. What do you expect?

It helps to know this. You can relearn to handle, understand, and manage your issues. This knowledge makes it easier to embrace the work that it takes. Yeah, we got shit. And it needs to come out. Just like when you go to the toilet.

Lynn: And for some of you, maybe you can now begin to understand why you're so defensive and protective of your shit; especially if you were punished for it. How scared you might feel when something shitty comes up for you?

Joseph: So can you see how this relates to the junk in the trunk? Where else should you put it? Of course, you're going to put it in the "back or the front." But is that how you really want to continue to refer to yourselves and your Sexuality, as *junk*?

Simon: Can I just share a very quick story? I think it explains how far this goes. I was on a date with this girl and I liked her for about a year and, finally, we went out on a date and had a nice dinner and everything. We got to the end of the night and we were standing outside of her place and she was like "my place or yours" and all of a sudden I needed to shit really badly. I was about four or five blocks from my house. I was so worried about taking her back to my house and taking a shit that I told her I'd catch up with her another day. I was so desperate that I just gave her a kiss on the cheek and ran. I ended up shitting my pants on the way home.

(Roar of Laughter)

And not only was I ashamed of my shit but it actually got in the way of my sex life, as well.

Joseph: You said it best; our shit gets in the way of our Sex.

Kelly: That was really shitty!

(Laughter)

Joseph: There is a natural course we travel, a continuum if you will, that has our relationships grow from an informal one to a formal one. This includes our relationships with ourselves. And it best serves us when we travel it with care. So, I'm not saying just go fart and shit with a person as soon as you meet them. No, you do need to wait till you get comfortable with them. But you have to find comfort with it, first. That's the challenge here. Can you be comfortable with your Sexual parts, and can you be comfortable with what comes in and out of them. You see, because one day you'll have to. One day you'll be too old and they'll have to change your diaper for you and you'll shit your pants and need something to help you piss and by then you'll say "Fuck this shit!" But, by then you'll probably not be having sex and it won't matter.

Can you begin to embrace this? It's hard, absolutely, but that's why we're taking the time to explain it. For us to understand the bigger thing called Sex, we have to start where you're at; I mean you, individually. Most of you, if not all of you, think you **are** Sex. That's why we say, she thinks she's 'the shit,' he thinks he's 'the shit' . . . you think you're the Sex. You think you created sex. You think you're doing stuff that was never done before. No one can do it like you. You couldn't be more wrong. You can't even embrace your own shit, so how do you know what you can or can't do. But this is great, we're beginning to experience you for who you are, and if we can see what's within, we can see what's outside. Insight can bring better out-sight; as out-sight can improve your insight. One of the most profound out-sights, ideas from the outer world, came from a man named Sigmund Freud. What did Sigmund Freud believe?

Simon: That mother is our first Sexual contact.

Joseph: Is he saying . . . or are you saying, there's some kind of incestual relationship between us and mom.

Simon: Everything I do is based on trying to find someone that's like my mom. So if I'm looking for a girl, I'm going to find someone like my mom, everything's related.

Kelly: Is it like a pattern?

Simon: Yeah it's more in depth than that, but that's kind of the gist.

Joseph: Does this also apply to women? Is mother their first contact with Sexuality?

Susan: I'm not sure, but, we do come into the world through our mother's vaginas.

Joseph: True . . . Anyone else?

Angie: Penis envy?

Joseph: What about it?

Angie: I don't know a lot about it . . . its pop psychology for me . . . but women have penis envy and men are fixated on their penises; everything's about dicks. Like, everything comes back to dicks. Which country has the biggest missiles? Who has the biggest car? Who has the biggest flashiest apartment? And, it's all related to . . . dicks!

Joseph: Okay, let's take a look at the first idea . . . Freud says we are all repressing incestual urges. Let me suggest that all the sex you have is incestual. If this is so, how is it so? How could he make such a statement? What is incest to you?

Alexia: Being sexual with a family member?

Joseph: Yes. Anyone else?

Mercedes: Something familiar? Within the family . . .

Joseph: Good!

Lynn: How's this for a definition: *Incest is sexual activity between two people who are considered for moral or genetic reasons, too closely related to have such a relationship.*

Joseph: Again, I'm suggesting all sexual relationships are incestual. How can I make that claim?

Simon: I guess some people look for their parent figure as their partner.

Joseph: Recent studies suggest that we tend to be attracted to people who look similar to our parents. Therefore, if this is true, we are more likely than not to form a parent-child relationship with these individuals. Why do you think there's such an emphasis, sexually speaking, in labelling and addressing our partners in child-parent terms?

Here are some of the classics: "Who's your daddy?" and "Who's my naughty girl?" Oh and, of course, there's "Oh, baby" and in Spanish, "Aye, Papi" which translates into "Oh, daddy." and Then there's the mommy stuff, "Come here, big boy" and "Let mommy take care of that" and "Make mommy cum" . . . getting creepy, right?

(Laughter)

Day Two: *The Sex Seminar*

I suspect all of you look to form a parent-child relationship because the only way you know how to do it is incestually, at least till you've resolved some of your more significant childhood issues. Most of what you're initially attracted to in a mate is *caused* by your unresolved family issues. Remember, life is always trying to resolve itself and it starts to do it at the beginning: at the roots.

This is all very common, more common than you think. We are attracted to people we feel a familiarity with, as Mercedes was getting at. FAMILiarity . . . family; we are sexually attracted to people we feel this familiar thing with. It's not until we're together with someone for a while that we realize, "Oh, my God, he's just like my father," or "She's just like my mother." It may show up at the beginning, but our issues block our view of it.

Brennan: How do we catch it in time?

Joseph: I see you haven't really been paying attention. So, for you, the answer is through self work and self awareness; through practices like meditation and reflection.

Through the fractals of today we can see the past. Let me give you an example of what I mean by that. Let's start with the internet. The internet has revealed what I saw years ago.

I used to work in a porn shop in Times Square, New York in the early 80's where I helped in ordering films; they were mostly 8mm at the time. Within months the VCR came out and everything changed. This brought porn into the home and as its popularity increased so did the number of "regular people," men and women alike, who walked through our doors. Since I was the one who worked the counter, I had to keep track of which type of genre of movies sold best . . . and incestual movies were right up there at the top. Especially when a movie called *Taboo* hit the shelves. *Taboo* and then *Taboo 2* were two of our constant and biggest sellers. These movies were about incest. People seemed to have no problem coming in and plucking down $69.99 for these VHS tapes.

Group: $69.99!?

Joseph: Yes, they were extremely expensive at first . . . That's when I realised we were more incestual than we wanted to admit.

Now you go on the internet and there's websites galore, father-daughter, father step-daughter, mother-son, mother step-son, my friends' daughter; there's just hundreds of thousands of websites, just for that.

So that's good, it's getting it out at least. We're beginning to see that there is an incestual energy that runs through our society. Now, I'm not saying we want to have sex with our relatives, but I am saying that we are consistently forming relationships with people that tend to nearly duplicate the mental and emotional relationships we've had with our relatives. And until we take a closer look at this, until we begin to resolve our early childhood issues, we'll be stuck recreating our past. Sex, then, is just a by product of this. As long as we only work with what we know, we are going to create incestual relationships . . . What do you make of this?

Susan: My husband tends to act like a child, most of the time, and even when I am being an adult with him instead of a parent, it still doesn't work. Why?

Joseph: Because the best you can have is an adult to child relationship. It takes two adults to have a *real original* relationship. In addition, as long as one of you is a child it will still possess components of emotional incest. At the end of the day, you're having sex with a "child" who you're related to through marriage.

You don't create the world when you come into it. It's already here. You adapt to it. You form to it before you can think for yourself. Your frontal lobe, the area of the brain that helps make decisions, isn't fully developed until about 21-24 years old. By then, you're filled with information on how to be and think. You're out of your mind if you think you're deciding and choosing from a conscious mind.

Simon: Isn't it partly genetic, carrying on our genes from our parents, you know like this is what we should look for, for the survival of our genes?

Joseph: Yes, genetics plays a big part. Genetically, we are programmed to increase our gene pool and incest would stagnate that. But, we also have a tremendous genetic need for safety. So, apparently, we compensate for it by trying to recreate the mental and emotional *comforts* of our earlier family lives. We "look" for people who resemble our families; we recreate mental and emotional replicas that we carry on relationships with. But this "looking" is not a conscious one as Freud explained. It is an attraction that is sourced by the unconscious mind. We don't look for mates; we are drawn to mates based on our earlier childhood experiences.

Parisa: What if we grew up in an orphanage?

Day Two: *The Sex Seminar*

Joseph: Good question. Aside from the influences that foster parents or authority figures may have had on the orphan, genetics also plays a big part.

You want to, first, understand that if we, as people, do something over and over again for generations, it will, eventually, become part of the genetic pool. This is easily seen with alcoholism. After prolonged use of alcohol a family will, in time, develop a predisposition to alcohol abuse.

To understand and to go forth with Sexuality, we always need to understand the origin of things. Now, today we are looking at the origin of body care, "waste management,' and how we were taught our sexual boundaries. Once we become aware of these trainings we can finally choose. You'll have the ability to look and **consciously** say, "I don't have to do that anymore, I want to try something else or look at it from another place."

Hugh Hefner, like him or not, has had a profound effect on our sex lives. He was quoted as saying . . . would anyone like to read this out loud?

Susan: *"If you want to know what Sex is all about in current affairs, look at history, because it repeats itself over and over again and you will find the roots of anything today in the past."*

Joseph: What do you make of that?

Reese: It supports what we were talking about yesterday that Sex goes in a circle.

Joseph: Yes, for Hefner, it's cyclical. If that's true, then it's possible that we're not necessarily advancing, we're just moving in a circle: from expression to repression, expression to repression. Are we advancing or learning anything new? Are we moving forward?

Let's look, again, at some history or more accurately, "Our story." It's not his story or not her story, it's OUR story; but I digress . . Let's go way back, to the Mesopotamians.

The Mesopotamian civilization existed, starting about 3400 years ago. To understand how far back that was, you'd have to think of it in terms of maybe . . . when Christ was born, which was about 2100 years ago and then you'd have to add another 1300 years to get an idea. You can also look at it by going into the future. Let's say we are the Mesopotamians existing in the year 2011, add 3400 years to that and you'd be in the year 5411. Suffice to say, it was a long time ago. So let's see if there's any insight they can offer us. (Group watches a video on the Mesopotamians)

Joseph: So what do you make of this?

Mercedes: What stuck out for me was the female poets love poem to her *brother*. It was clearly Sexual. Was she really speaking about her actual brother?

Joseph: No. Like today, the title "brother" was meant to show the familial closeness of their relationship . . . This has been going on for a long time ladies and gentlemen. Again . . . we commonly use, and apparently have used, these family titles as expressions of love and Sex. What do you make of the Mesopotamian's view on Sex?

Angie: Sex was something you could, like, own; wives were considered property.

Simon: There's a use; it has its purpose.

Susan: It was a business transaction between husband and wife.

Mercedes: I feel like they almost partitioned it, like there was transactional Sex, and outside of that, it was for pleasure and procreation.

Joseph: What do you think about the openness that existed around prostitution?

Susan: Yes, that was another area where Sex was a business transaction.

Joseph: Yes, but men also went to prostitutes for healing purposes. They talked to their gods for sexual favours. They viewed Sex as a large force. Granted, they tried to own parts of it as we do today. But unlike us, they spoke clearly about how Sex was a transcendent power. To them "Sex was mightier than the sword," and that's saying a lot, considering how life was lived back then

Simon: Sex has started wars.

Joseph: Sex has stopped and started wars, hasn't it? What do you make of that? They had the belief that it was a larger power, 3400 years ago! Can you wrap your minds around that?

Mercedes: So the priestesses were prostitutes!? Sex was religious. Religion today, wants it kept secretive.

Joseph: Well we're starting to recreate that. There's a reason why we call porn stars, porn *stars.* You see human beings have always followed the stars, to know where they're at and where they're going. We still do that today, except there's so much more light. There's so much manufactured light in this world that we can't see the stars anymore. So we've created stars that we can see--movie stars, porn stars, sports stars, and super model stars; all kinds of stars. And we use them to know where we're at, where to go, and how to behave. We haven't changed at all. The only difference, today, is that stars are other people.

We all can't help but look at stars and go towards stars. Whether it's up in the sky or down on earth, it's what we do. We look to stars to know how to dress, how to act, how to have sex, how not to have sex. Therefore, it's not surprising, but rather a natural progression, that we eventually called pornographic workers "stars." Back in the '80's, before they were stars, pornography workers were looked completely down on. But today, they've become the stars who teach us how to do sex. Pornography has become one of the major sources of Sex education for kids today.

A civilization's belief about Sex determines how children are taught Sex. In Mesopotamia, Sex was a transcendent power, therefore, children were taught Sex from a spiritual standpoint. Today, we believe we are larger than Sex; that we can control and overpower with it. So, Sex is taught by sex workers and pornographers.

How far do you think we've come since the Mesopotamians?

Simon: It's pretty frustrating that we haven't learned our lessons from history. And, on top of that, you've piled all this on us . . . it's just fuckin' ridiculous.

Joseph: Yeah, sorry about that. (Smiling) But that's the way we're going to get this. By knowing where we're at and where we are going. This will give us the opportunity to enrich and enhance our sex lives. Everybody wants that.

Let's shoot ahead, another 500-1000 years, to the ancient Greeks and see how they handle Sex and what Sex was like for them, compared to the Mesopotamians

(Group now watches video on Classical Greece)

Joseph: So, this was about 1000 years after the Mesopotamians, about 2500 years ago and about 500 years before Christ. The ancient Greeks, our sexual ancestors, are credited for birthing western civilization.

Kelly: Why for so long . . . like, lesbian and gay men . . . they seem much more open back then, than it is now.

Nisha: It's almost like we suppressed what they left behind. It's, like, they knew more back then than we know now.

Alexia: Yeah there weren't even any categories. They had no distinction between heterosexual and gay.

Tami: They were just people and it was all feeling. It didn't matter whether it was woman, man, young, or old.

Joseph: How much have we actually progressed?

Nathan: Even the young were informed about Sex and Sexual energy.

Mercedes: I see they used the term Pedophilia but it obviously wasn't used the way we do today. They took care of the young without taking sexual advantage of them.

Joseph: It seems as if they were Sexual explorers. Are we explorers today, or are we just starting to explore? Where are we compared to them?

Angie: Today, we define everything. I hear people saying all the time, "Hey, are you gay? Or are you straight? Bisexual?" And I mean it just seems silly to have to put a label to any of this!

Joseph: Think about all the labels today, all the letters to describe gay, straight, lesbian, transsexuals and so on . . . it's like alphabet city. But labels are necessary, to a point. It's when we over think it, or over label, that it becomes a problem.

Simon: Everything is a category now.

Joseph: Yes. Why is that, do you think?

Simon: It makes it easier to control . . . you can make generalizations about behaviours; by saying this group of people is more likely to act this way . . .

Joseph: What else do you do to control something?

Simon: Suppress it.

Joseph: How? What do you set up?

Alexia: Rules, barriers . . .

Joseph: Barriers, boundaries, boxes, categories, walls, should or shouldn't, that's how you suppress and control; you UNI-form it. You put things in a single form of some kind so you can work within it, in order to experience it. In and of itself, this process is neither bad nor good. But, we need to put the things of life in some sort of container. Otherwise, we'd have no ability to experience it to any degree. We've done this with sex.

Sex is in a *contained space* created by our collective consciousnesses, and there are several of these contained spaces throughout the world. We've added rules, laws, and regulations to these containers and they are capable of expanding and contracting, depending on the level of our awareness. Suppress awareness and the room shrinks, expand it and it grows. This goes on from era to era.

Reese: Are you saying that the sex box of the Greeks is the same sex box we use today?

Joseph: Yes. Imagine the box as a house that has been passed on for generations. It has been used in different ways, by different people, and it's been decorated and rearranged many times over. Sometimes, it's had extensions added to it and, at other times, it's been made smaller due to limited resources. But what stays consistent is the house itself.

Nathan: So the Greeks had sex in the same house we now have sex in.

Joseph: You can say that.

Nathan: . . . and while the Greeks lived in the house, they didn't apply labels to homosexuality as we do.

Joseph: So it seems.

Nathan: My dad's gay, and I know as a kid growing up, when I first found out . . . it was fuckin' horrifying. But, as I get older and as things evolve, and because of the labels we put on it, it has actually gotten easier for me. So now it's gone full circle, the label thing.

I recently asked him, "When did you know that you were gay?" And he gave me a pretty profound answer; he said he doesn't think he's gay, he just thinks he's a sexual being. He could be a sexual being with anybody, it doesn't matter what their gender is; it just so happened that he found a man . . . That was almost a relief for me; he took that word out of it.

Joseph: Do you love your father?

Nathan: Yes!

Joseph: Who better than one's own parent, your first teachers, to open your mind and expand your awareness of sexuality? Nathan, you want to see that your love for your father had you question him. You wanted to know more about him, and that opened up the possibility of deeper awareness--of not just him, but of yourself.

Lynn: And Nathan, if I may ask why, as a child, did you think it was horrifying?

Nathan: Well . . . to be honest, my dad wasn't always the greatest father. So, like, we would visit him in the summer and he always had *roommates,* and I was just a little guy. I was probably, like, ten or younger and I would witness stuff going on. My dad was an alcoholic and he did a lot of drugs and was not very responsible with the kids. So I grew up watching guys giving him blow jobs, messing around in the bedroom. I'd wake up in the morning to gay guys naked, everywhere. I didn't understand what was going on and I was confused whether it was right or wrong. It wasn't what was going on in other people's houses.

Lynn: Do you think you blamed Sexuality for his bad parenting?

Nathan: Possibly . . .

Joseph: Do you think if he wasn't gay he would have been a better father?

Nathan: No . . .

Joseph: How about as a teen?

Nathan: Yeah . . . kinda. I was really angry as a teenager. I'm not sure.

Joseph: What was done to you was abusive, to say the least. Because you love your father, and needed to continue to, you had to find something to blame his behaviour on. So you need to look at what you may have linked this experience to. You want to begin to look at it from a sexual perspective. Sex was used to abuse you, even as a witness. Could it be that you blame sex for what your father did to you?

Nathan: Maybe. I have a lot of anger and mixed emotions around sex.

Joseph: Understandable. We're going to look at this further, Nathan, but for now I'd like you to consider that maybe you've connected his fathering with his sexuality . . . and he was just a bad father, who happened to be gay.

Nathan: Today, I could say I know that.

Joseph: So there was a time when you probably didn't.

Day Two: *The Sex Seminar*

Nathan: There was a time when I thought I was gay because my dad was gay, and I looked just like my dad!

Joseph: I get it . . .

We were watching *Modern Family* the other day and part of the episode centered on the gay couples young adopted Vietnamese daughter. She was carrying on about being gay and her parents were frantic, trying to figure out why she believed this. They understood from their own experiences that one could know this about themselves at a young age. So when they finally calmed down and asked her about it she shared with them that her friend just found out she was Italian. She was Italian because the rest of her family was Italian and since her parents are gay, she must be gay!

This is the misperception of an innocent. That's also what it was for you; it was your *innocence* trying to figure it all out. Sex is an infinite force that is difficult to understand for an adult and nearly impossible for a child. Fortunately, it's not too late to look back and re-perceive it from an adult's perspective. The approaches we are taking this weekend will help to uncover these misconceptions and to link events with their proper causes.

Simon: Can I ask one more thing about the Greeks? Everyone says they were some of the greatest free thinkers in history. How much weight did they place on feelings?

Joseph: Some say we are a combination of three parts: intellectual, emotional, and sensual/physical, and that the key is to find a way to live in the middle of all three. That way we can access a balanced and centered approach to life. With this in mind, let us suggest that maybe the Mesopotamians were heavy on the sensual and the Greeks on the intellectual. So, if life is truly trying to resolve itself, then there must be a group that would need to represent the emotional part of humanity.

With that being said, let's take a look at the Romans, and then we'll stop for a break.

(Group watches video on Ancient Romans)

"We demand that sex speak the truth . . . and we demand that it tell us our truth, or rather, the deeply buried truth of that truth about ourselves which we think we possess in our immediate consciousness."

Michel Foucault, *The History of Sexuality 1*

Joseph: Welcome back! Why are we having you watch videos on the history of western sex?

Simon: Because we live in the western hemisphere and this is part of our history.

Joseph: Exactly. Again, in order to understand where we're at, sexually, in our society and why we are where we are, we need to look at ourselves from *within* a context of something larger than ourselves. Therefore, the best way to do this is historically. We need to look at ourselves from an historical context. Now, tell me what comes up for you about the Romans.

Angie: It surprised me that the Romans were *aware* that they learned sex from the Greeks.

Joseph: Yes, they borrowed the concept of Gods being the source of Sexual energy.

Nathan: Yeah, but they seemed to have done that for selfish reasons, not spiritual. They practically worshiped their penises.

Joseph: More than practically.

Mercedes: It was as if they used the Gods, rather than serve the Gods.

Joseph: Well, that goes to show you that it will not be enough to leave this weekend knowing that Sex is a force larger than us all. We'll also have to learn how to find sacredness with it.

Simon: It seems as if the Greeks and Romans were a lot less repressed than us.

Joseph: Yes, it does seem that way. To understand what sexual repression causes, all we have to do is consider your common garden hose. Now, if you have a garden hose and you turn the water on, what happens?

Group: The water shoots out of it.

Joseph: Right, and if you were to put your hand over the top of it, what would happen then?

Group: It would back up.

Joseph: And what would eventually happen as the pressure builds?

Group: It would begin to leak out.

Day Two: *The Sex Seminar*

Joseph: Right again. The built up pressure would begin to force the water out through the sides and cracks of your hands. Its natural flow, which you have repressed and obstructed, is forced to take a deviated path out. The same goes with Sexual energy. When it's repressed, it eventually manifests itself in a deviated form, or *deviant* form.

We'll speak more about this later. Who else?

Simon: I was struck by the Roman woman who had written the book that's similar to today's *Fifty Shades of Grey*.

Joseph: How many people do you think thought *Fifty Shades of Grey* was unique or even earth shattering? Such a big deal was made of it. But, what I think you're seeing is that this type of writing and sexual exploration was done before. It's really no biggie, especially if we go back just under 300 years ago to Marquis De Sade. Today's book was actually quite tame compared to the things he wrote. Very tame! What do you make of this?

Angie: Well, you've mentioned how we almost believe that we invented it; like it's something new.

I remember being in Pompeii when I was 16 or 17 with a bunch of friends and we were walking around and there were penises carved on the ground, pointing in the direction of brothels, and when we got to the brothels there was porn there, it was painted on the walls. It was just wild to us! I mean, this was a little bit before internet porn had really taken off and most of the exposure that I and my friends had had was through Playboy Magazine and that sort of thing. But finding that there was, for some reason, shocking that that existed; it felt almost like it was crass. It was like, "Nooo, they didn't do that, *then*!?" It was pretty graphic porn on the walls of these brothels. It was painted there, and even though I knew that and had seen that, going over it again and seeing it in that video, was like "Oh yeah. Shit, maybe we didn't invent it."

Joseph: Are many of you, at least, surprised and, for some of you, shocked in seeing some of the things that went on thousands of years ago? How are you looking at sex, now, with just a little historical context?

Nathan: Just looking at it from my job, I work for the parks department and the things I see happening in parks is pretty extreme. In areas of the park where people can avoid the police, lots of sexual things happen.

There's one particular park where I'd go and cut trees that blocked all these trails and that included "lover's log." It was called that because men would go and park in the lot and wait for someone to *back in* with their cars; to back in was code for sexual interest. And perfect strangers, just walked up to each other and they'd go off for some knicky knacky, and that was it.

I'd see some old white guy with a young Asian guy and, as we're working, they'd be like "Hey, how you doin'?" No hiding. This became so commonplace that the city had us clear out a path so the cops could have a clear line of sight, so the people that were rendezvousing could get caught. It happens!

Joseph: A lot of this is caused, once again, by repression.

Nathan: Well like you said, if you "close the hose" it's going to squirt out wherever, and whenever it can and it's happening in parks. People go to these places with their families. Meanwhile, in these same parks, sex is happening.

Angie: It's awful that the cops have to come and stop people from having sex!

Joseph: Like he said, people go to places to avoid the police. This was not the case in ancient Greece, as you saw in the video. Greeks were able to do it in a more open fashion. They designed places they could go to for sex: baths, and so on. This lent to a greater opportunity for full expression and exploration of sex in Greece.

Understand, repression will **always** lead to deviation.

In the '60's and '70's, there was a secluded area by the water on the west side of Manhattan, New York, that was called "The Meatpacking District." This area, by day, was where New York housed its wholesale meat markets and meat packing businesses. By night, in its emptiness, it was documented that homosexuals would congregate there for sex.

(Some laughter)

Yes, ironic . . . but it was a sad irony, actually. Because what these men were "forced" to do was to pack themselves, in large numbers, into these oversized trailer containers to have sex. Where else could they go? They were constantly repressed. They couldn't go to most hotels because they wouldn't be rented a room if they registered together. They were forced to live in certain sections of the city if they wanted to try to live openly. Lastly, they were always in a precarious situation when it came to their bars and clubs because the police, especially in the 60's, would

Day Two: *The Sex Seminar*

come and raid them on a whim. This continued repression and uncertainty caused some of them to go into sexual hiding, in a most undignified place, the meat packing district's trailer containers. Strangely, the "Meatpacking District" today, is a highly renovated trendy section where people, from all over the world, come to experience all the upscale bars, clubs, and restaurants.

Now, what does this say about a society that forces its citizens to revert to these types of primitive conditions? How sexually liberated is a society that forces its citizen's to go into hiding? How are you going to know Sex if you're repressed? You can't! How can you explore Sex with even the least amount of repression?

What we're doing this weekend is exploring it. Again, it will be painful, at times, boring at others, and it will require you to take risks. We are going to look more deeply at history, which will tend to be boring for some of you, because it is absolutely essential in understanding Sex.

Yesterday, we asked you where you are at and you basically and obscurely answered, "Main and Vine." By tomorrow, when we ask again, "Where are we at sexually?" you'll be able to give a clearer answer, one which is context filled. You will leave here tomorrow with a different perspective, period. What do you make of all this? Why do you think we search and try to understand our families? It's for the context; it's to better understand us.

Simon: Seems like the more civilized we get, the more repressed we get because there are more rules.

Joseph: The fact is, the more civilized a society is, the more prostitutes it has.

Simon: So, I was just thinking, what if we go even further back to Neanderthals, where there wasn't verbal communication? I just wonder what their sexual habits were back then. If they would just be "anything goes" because they hadn't created any taboo's, yet.

Joseph: Well, you have to assume that rape was a part of their sex lives. All you have to do is look at the animal kingdom and you'll see that even animals rape! Civility is necessary, boundaries are necessary, and they are neither good nor bad, in and of themselves. We can set them up any way we choose. The problem is that, after a while, we stop choosing and we begin to live an "asleep civility" or a civility that was chosen for us. A civility we are too asleep to question.

For most of you, your sex life was chosen for you! It was chosen for you to feel bad about your bodies, it was chosen for you to think that you are a dish rag. It was chosen for you to think that you're superior. It was all chosen for you to feel that you're free and full body, or just body parts. It's all chosen for you, because like I've said, it's not until you're about 24 years old that you can really think for yourself, fully.

Parisa: So, we are victims?

Joseph: No. It's just chosen for you. You're victims if you decide not to take a look at it. Then, you're a victim of yourself--of your own ignorance.

Lynn: If you get stuck in your beliefs, then, you are a victim of what society did.

Joseph: Yes, hence, a victim of your own repression. But none of us are victims, we can go out there and explore. We've been victimized, yes, but are we victims? No. I refuse to say I'm a victim. That's not a self description I use. No. Some asshole touched me the wrong way when I was a child and I was victimized! But fuck you if you're going to make me a victim! Fuck you if I'm going to live like a victim.

Lynn: Then I've allowed you to squelch me for the rest of my life! Fuck that!

Joseph: Yes. You don't get to do that to me.

Lynn: Fuck you that you think that I'm not going to live with dignity, self love, and self esteem just because you touched me! Fuck you! You don't get anything else, hope you enjoyed that touch.

Joseph: What do you make of all this?

Nisha: It's interesting to me that infidelity was throughout history. Why even get married? I don't know why anyone would bother getting married to one person, because it's a transaction. I wouldn't have thought back then (during the Roman and Greek period), that infidelity was that prominent.

Joseph: That's because you don't understand a basic thing about us human beings. There's a reason why we have to **work** on relationships. What's the fundamental reason we have to work on relationships?

Reese: We're animals.

Joseph: No . . .

Simon: Because it's not natural.

Day Two: *The Sex Seminar*

Lisa: Because we're not monogamous?

Joseph: Right . . . we're not monogamous!

We are not monogamous by nature. It takes a lot of work to be monogamous! You have to build a bond with someone, so that you can say, "I choose to stay with you!" But everything in us says, "NO!"

Parisa: Absolutely.

Joseph: We're not monogamous, and that's why relationships take work. They don't just happen easy-peasy. If you are insisting on easy-peasy relationships, you're avoiding a fundamental flaw in that approach. We're not monogamous by nature! We're not!

Mercedes: So why do we do it?

Joseph: When two people, who have their own unique experience and views of the world, get together it's like two circles joining and interlocking together. They're, basically, forming one large circle that has an interlocked middle. When they join, they get to share each others' experiences. And it's within that interlocked section that they get to build together. It's in this section that they get to grow and bond through mutual experiences. This makes the circle stronger. In turn, this action creates a space where intimacy can flourish. Finally, as this interlocked area is solidified, the couple can increase the size of it by sharing more of their personal lives, hence, more of their personal part of their circle. How much or how little they share is up to them. A large interlocked area is not necessarily better for some couples. It all depends upon how much the couple wants to synchronize. But, what works against this bonding is the fact that we're not monogamous by nature.

We have to choose to work against our natures, and that's the way we improve ourselves. It's like physical exercise--let's say lifting weights. It's hard to lift weights, but when we choose to do it, it opens up opportunity for growth. In addition, you want to understand that bonding with another doesn't mean you have to lose yourself in the process; there's a whole outer part of each circle and that's each of your separate lives. So, even when you're apart, you're still connected through the interlocked section of your two circles, thus, never losing the sense of support you provide each other when you're together. But again, we have to work at it because having sex is not enough.

Angie: Yeah, bumping uglies is not enough.

Joseph: Well actually, you're bumping circles, not uglies! As Chris Rock says, "There's no bad pussy . . . If you think you have a bad pussy let me check it for you after the show and I'll let you know . . ."

(Laughter)

Is it because of this thing called SEX that we can actually experience intimacy? When we decide to just go further past the intercourse we can begin to build a different kind of sexual experience together. An experience that makes a caress, a kiss, *everything* become sexual . . . sensual. It's through deeper sexuality--through the power of this Sexual force--where intimacy is established. But it's not achieved by the act alone. This thing called Sex is a multi-faceted and multi-dimensional force which we cannot control, but can only surrender to. It's not as simplistic as you would like to think.

One could argue that ancient Greece was more advanced around its sexual expression and freedoms than we are today. I'm not saying we should return to the ways of the Greeks, but how cool was it that they had, for instance, no categories for homosexuals. Homosexuals and their supporters are presently battling for rights in court that, in Greece, was inherently theirs. Remarkable! What do you make of this? How does it feel having a historical context, before we look at our own recent history? Does it help and if so, how?

Tami: Well this gives me a whole new perspective that didn't really exist for me before. I can see, now, that I was so narrow-minded . . . so sex was more like a how-to or what-to, or questions or judgment and I was so wrapped in my own shit that I didn't see and just thought, "Oh yeah, sexual energy, that's lovely. I can feel something between me and someone else in the room," but it's, like, so much bigger than that!

Joseph: So many of you had quick answers around some of our earlier questions, especially yesterday. Why did you answer so quickly?

Tami: . . . I don't know . . .

Joseph: You're taking your time now, as we are beginning to explore Sex and Sex in its context. Your responses are more thoughtful as your experience of Sexuality has grown. What does answering quickly cause? How did you rip yourself off by answering so quickly?

Day Two: *The Sex Seminar*

Tami: It caused me to not actually think about it and I just spoke from judgment. I feel foolish now.

Joseph: So you ripped yourself off by answering quickly. That's what you want to look at. Why do I answer so quickly? Am I afraid to look stupid? What are you afraid of?

It's a gift to feel weak. It's a gift! Thank God we can feel weak and be weak. Weakness is one of the greatest gifts life has given us. It's where we find our compassion and humanity, humility, and our forgiveness for each other. Because we're all weak! By accepting our weakness we can grow. We can ask for help and **that** brings us together, it has us ask the other "Can you love me?" rather than "Can you want me?" So, we're afraid to expose ourselves as weak. Because we think we'll be unloved and unwanted. But when we are, the opposite happens.

So, if you're courageously exploring this thing, you'll be exposing yourself, your weaknesses, and your lack of understanding to you and to others for what might be the first time. You will leave here, on Sunday night at 9:00 p.m., changed to varying degrees. And you will have an opportunity to actually find some humanity in all of this, some compassion for one another and, most importantly, for yourselves; maybe even forgiveness for yourselves. Sex is all taught before we have a chance to figure it out. Before you can say no, it's all imposed upon us.

It reminds me of an old routine that, actor and comedian, Martin Lawrence did. He says, and I paraphrase "If I go to jail, nobody's going to mess with me; I'm going to just walk in there and dare someone to mess with me. I'm just gonna confront them and say, Yeah, NO WAY! You're not going to do anything to me . . . and . . ." And, next you see him bent over getting raped! We're all weak! Nobody's that big and bad . . . but with knowledge and understanding there is no subject matter that's too big for us. What better way to find humanity than the way we came into this world, through Sex! What better way to find out who are we? . . . Let's break for lunch.

* * * * *

Joseph: Okay, welcome back. What reflections have you had? What do you make of all this?

Simon: I feel like my brain is on overload.

Joseph: That's why we take breaks.

You see, boredom is a feeling that takes over when we are under-loaded. When we are overloaded we become especially vulnerable to boredom.

Simon: How's that!?

Joseph: When we are overloaded with new information we need to process it, otherwise we're forced to do a data dump. The pressure forces the information we've just acquired to be expunged. It's a safety mechanism. At that point we're empty again and susceptible to boredom. If you haven't processed the earlier information, why would you want to refill with more info? Therefore, you start avoiding the new information until "you're bored." That's why we take breaks AND ask that you reflect on your experience. We say reflect not analyze.

You're overloaded, Simon, because you're pushing the mind. You're being stretched, maybe a bit too far, and you're pushing back. Therefore, you have to rest in between sets, like a workout, because the important thing right now is getting the historical context. Then, we can do the easier exercises, and the more fun stuff. But we have to get the context because, without that, you have nothing to stand on. At least, if you know where you're at in terms of where you're standing, it becomes easier to continue exploring this enormous subject.

So, what thoughts, what reflections?

Simon: Well, I feel I'm worried that I'm not getting enough out of it because I enjoy watching stuff like this. So, I'm worried I'm watching it for enjoyment rather than work.

Joseph: And what does this have to do with your father?

Simon: My father? . . . My father's dead.

Joseph: Of course . . . for you, the future is uncertain, so that's where the worry comes in. The plights of our parents are not ours; the destinies of our parent are not ours. So when we create an unnatural association to any parent, we pay a price. This association, in Simon's case, is life expectancy.

Day Two: *The Sex Seminar*

When a parent leaves our lives at a young age, we tend to "force" a physical relationship with them, which is impossible to maintain because they're no longer in a physical state. So, Simon, you overcompensate by taking on your dad's destiny. Obviously, this is interfering with **your** natural desire to enjoy life. That's more natural to you. Work and learning comes after you've enjoyed; you learn better that way. That's how you're built. Unfortunately, because of your father's passing, you've switched it. You are afraid of dying young like your father so you're trying to get in as much learning and work as possible. Now, would you worry as much if you knew you were going to live to 150?

Simon: I'm not worrying about it; I'm just saying I'm enjoying it too much.

Joseph: No, actually you said you were worried; but again that's all in the context of time. If we suddenly decide to stretch this seminar over a week, you wouldn't be as worried. You're just anxious of the pending end, or *doom*, of Sunday's imminent arrival. It's about time for you, that's why you worry. You want to help yourself? Stretch out time; give yourself 150 years.

Lynn: Is that common for you, worry? Is that a new feeling or an old one?

Simon: (Sheepishly) It's common.

Lynn: A lot of that is in your nature to want to constantly explore. Just know that you're always going to be exploring whether you're here for another 20 years or another 80 . . . That is who you are. You're always going to be hungry.

Joseph: There is no, "Did I get enough?" There is no "enough" because that implies that you get full. Proclaim, "I'm willing to drop dead when I'm full! When I'm full I'm going to drop dead!" Think of it that way. "I'm going to give everything I have so that when I'm out of here I know I've spent it all, given it all. I've perceived and given so I can leave satisfied." By the way everybody, this is how he lives in his sex life. (Simon nods in agreement)

Everything that's going to come up we are going to relate it back to your sex lives; your approach to Sex. This is not random, it's all related. This is just Simon's personal context. This is about how he imposes time upon Sex.

So how does time and Sex work for you? What's the relationship between you, time, and Sex?

Reese: I can totally relate to that, as well, and it relates back to my homework because I did it so seriously and structured. I went number one, do this, check, number two, and so on . . . and it relates to time. I'm always in a rush. There's just this pressure that I feel like I need to lighten up a lot more and not take it so seriously.

Joseph: Your both being over male, over *yang*. You know . . . yin and yang?

As discussed earlier, we have the left side of the brain, which analyzes and breaks down, and the right side of the brain which forms, reforms, and gives an overview to our experiences. They are equivalent to the ancient Chinese yin and yang symbol. The right brain is the yin, the female principal, which provides space and overview, while the left brain is the yang, the male principal which provides the measurable, like time. Yin is space and yang is time; female and male. It is genetically observable that we are both, as mentioned before. We have 23 chromosomes from our mother and 23 chromosomes from our father. These two, seemingly, opposing forces are what have us experience **true** oneness when they have blended properly together within us. For a more expansive understanding of Sex, we need to start looking at how these two parts of ourselves have formed our relationship to Sex.

To accept that there are two parts to us allows us to seek assistance for one or the other. For instance, in Sex, if you're being too linear, more right brain, you're being too yang so you need yin. You need to apply a more *female* approach. So, you can take your time; give it more space . . . and apply the yin part of you. When a woman says to her lover "Hey, take your time . . . go a little slower," all she's saying is she wants some yin, a little bit of the female side of him . . . the side that goes softer and slower. In reverse, there are times where it's too soft and too slow and then "Okay, give me some male, some yang; harder please. Suck me harder!" We can *play* with that balance in Sex, individually and together. When a couple understands this, they can help each other. They can take turns until they cease to know where one ends and the other begins.

I remember in the '70's, there was a common perception that if you had anal Sex, you had homosexual tendencies. Then in 1972, I read a book by Xavier Hollander, called *The Happy Hooker*. It was a New York Times best seller that playfully explored Sex from the perspective of a woman who was a hooker turned Madame. She continued her writings for Penthouse magazine in a monthly advice column where she said in response to a question about anal Sex that, "Any Sex between heterosexuals is heterosexual Sex." Well, that comment, for many like me, debunked that idea permanently. This myth is hard to buy today with all the openness there is around anal Sex, yet it was a once widely held belief . . . or fear.

We are beginning to break some of these boundaries down, while seeking more expansiveness. People like, *and we suggest you look them up*, Xavier Hollander, Masters and Johnson, Alfred Kinsey and Shere Hite, among others, brought us a wider perspective that helped us redefine Sex for this new millennium. The rigidity of the last century needs to continually be readdressed. That's why we started with Freud and what we believed he was suggesting when he said "We're all incestual!" . . . Let's take a five minute break.

* * * * *

Joseph: Okay? Prove to me we're not incestual. All of us!

We pursue sex more from a need for comfort, safety, and security than we do for love. How many of you and how many times have you had sex because you were lonely, needing comfort, or needing a feeling of security?

(Everyone in the group raises their hands)

Group: Many times.

Joseph: Aren't these needs part of our basic needs as a human? Basic needs that we may have not fully received in our childhood? The first place and people we get these needs filled are from our home and family. So it's no small wonder that we turn the people that we wind up having relationships with into our parents. And we complain in essence saying "Can you be the parent today and I'll be the child . . . hey, I was the parent yesterday . . . it's your turn . . . Why am I the one always taking care of you!?" This is just about our fundamental needs. It's still incestual.

Simon: Does that have something to do with the dominance and submission of the Romans that we have adopted?

Joseph: Again, a lot of what people get from dominant and submissive roles is a sense of security. It's a sense of being taken care of, even to the point of having a desire to be taken. Sex is all about power, at this point. It's the relationship between parent and child. It has more to do with having to feel safe and secure than loved. Safety and love are two different things. They run parallel, they exist separately. When we stop seeing the other person as family, when we stop seeing our mates as family, we can finally begin to have a relationship that's not incestual. Then, and only then, can love flourish.

Mercedes: You're not **using** the other person for your own needs.

Joseph: Good.

Mercedes: So it's a choice.

Joseph: Exactly, keep going.

Mercedes: Not expecting or needing that person to prove to you that you're lovable, you already know that you're lovable. You're not expecting them to heal those wounds of your childhood anymore.

Joseph: Right, when you are no longer placing the responsibility upon the other to fill your void, you're finally able to have a natural adult Sexual relationship. But, as long as the other has to take care of you in any shape or form, or vice versa, then you're having an incestual relationship, because it's still parent-child. Also, don't think you're bypassing incest when you're both being children in the relationship, that's just *sibling* incest.

Simon: Is there anything wrong with a relationship being formed in this way?

Joseph: No, there's nothing wrong with it. It's how we start. But, it's not how we have to continue. Freud wasn't saying it was right or wrong, he was saying this is what it is! This is where you're at. To progress further, requires our awareness of *what* we're in and *where* we are at. You see, the Greeks and Romans didn't struggle as much through this because marriage was not about attraction, as much as it was about economics. They married for position, money, and power. But, that didn't mean they were better off than us. The inherent childhood issues remained and still had to play out. What probably happened was they played it out with their children and paramours, initially, and then their spouses, after time.

Angie: What's a paramour?

Joseph: It's the equivalent of a mistress, a lover, but it applies to both men and women alike.

Susan: You're saying that since women were considered property back then, that the family thing didn't kick in till some time later?

Joseph: Yes, it's easier to project on others and cast them into a role, after you've gotten to know them.

Day Two: *The Sex Seminar*

Lisa: This happens in places like India, where they arrange marriages and the wife is expected to take a lowered position.

Joseph: Historically, we've traditionally gathered together for safety and protection; it was safety through numbers. We built our homes practically on top of each other, not unlike today. But unlike today, the living quarters were smaller and shared. It wasn't uncommon for parents and children to sleep in the same room or even the same bed. As a matter of fact, when parents had sex it was often done in the *family bed* after the kids were, hopefully, asleep. In addition, it was reported that when suitors came to visit, it was not uncommon for them to spend the night and sleep in the family bed; of course, with a partition between the daughters and themselves.

Throughout history it can be found that sex in the household was far from hidden. Between the family beds, or thin walls, or materials that separated the rooms, for those who were able to afford such luxuries, Sexual energy was experienced to varying degrees by all. Forget about six degrees of separation, how about one or two degrees?

Eddie: So, parents had sex while their sons and daughters were in the same bed?

Joseph: Yes, glad to see you're listening.

(Laughter)

They were exposed to Sexual energy in a pretty direct way.

Think about animals. We don't always remove them from the room when we're having sex. Don't you think you're exposing them to Sexual energy? I'm not implying whether it's right or wrong. Just don't be naive; they are being affected.

Mercedes: Why is it so taboo to even talk about it? If incest is everywhere and always has been . . . what fear is there that causes us to want to put up the walls and not look at it?

Joseph: It is widely known that inbreeding weakens the gene pool and that, genetically, we are programmed to be attracted to those who will strengthen it. Nature assists us with this task through smell.

Genetically, we are predisposed to be repelled by our immediate family members. I watched a program some short time ago that tested this theory. In the test they collected sweat filled tee shirts from various men who had just finished working out. And as I remember, they had a handful of women smell these shirts to see if they liked or were even attracted to the smells. What the women didn't know was that the shirts belonged to family members, boyfriends, and other men. And what they found with each woman was they were repelled by the shirts that belonged to the men in their families and attracted by the ones belonging to their mates! This is genetics at work.

In answer to your question, Mercedes, in the big picture, physical incest is rare and usually explainable. We are afraid of that which we cannot control. And in the case of incest, most believe it should be easily controlled. But, when extenuating circumstances occur such as extreme sexual trauma in childhood, a missing gene or a genetic mutation, separation at birth or childhood from family members, or even the "Desert Island Syndrome" or DIS, it causes the protective mechanisms that stop incestual urges to either be bypassed, overcome, or stopped completely.

Angie: What is Desert Island Syndrome?

Lynn: DIS occurs when individuals of a group are cut off from other individuals outside of the group over prolonged periods of time and eventually are left with little or no option of Sexual expression other than through their immediate group members. This problem could be found with closed cultures, religions, or power systems such as the old British monarchy.

Susan: How does "separation at birth" as you put it cause incest to happen.

Lynn: There have been multiple reports where parents who were reunited with children they gave up for adoption, or siblings who don't meet till adulthood, have experienced Sexual feelings towards one another and on several occasions consummating these feelings. The term for this, which was coined by Barbara Gonyo, is called: Genetic Sexual Attraction or GSA.

On the GSA website (as cited in *The Guardian*, 2003), it is explained ". . . that romantic love and erotic arousal may be the delayed by-product of missed bonding that would have normally taken place between a mother and her newborn infant, or between siblings had they not been separated by adoption." This unfulfilled childhood missing is, apparently, so powerful that it allows some to cross the natural boundaries against physical incest.

Joseph: You can now see what happens to us when our childhood needs are denied us.

Children are ill equipped to lead themselves in matters of Sex. So when they're left to their own devises they will always make a mess of things. When parents fail, or opt out, at guiding their children through the Sexual terrain of life, they inadvertently create an environment that fosters GSA. For instance, if you have two siblings, who are basically taking care of themselves and each other, they will eventually be tempted to Sexually experiment with each other. And because nurture has overcome nature at this point, it doesn't feel entirely wrong to them. It's not until they move closer to adulthood that they begin to feel the shame and guilt usually associated with these actions. What happens next is that their shame and guilt becomes the very walls that stop them from resolving this issue as adults. As for the rest of us, because of our lack of knowledge around the subject matter, we put up walls of fear. Hence, everyone winds up with walls and all we get is a stalemate. Get it, Mercedes? (Mercedes nods yes)

For those of you interested in exploring this further, we would recommend you watch Steve McQueen's movie, *Shame*. . . . Let's take a ten minute break.

* * * * *

Joseph: Welcome back.

Simon: I'm glad you gave us this break . . . I can see how I needed to process all this, again.

Joseph: So, what did you come up with?

Simon: Can I ask a question?

Joseph: Okay.

Simon: What keeps going through my mind is how do we get past all the guilt and shame of sex, or *my* guilt and shame?

Joseph: Good, you took ownership.

Education is the key; it brings clarity and light to our confusion and ambiguity! In addition, it provides objectivity, which allows us to approach the subject matter with limited or, hopefully, no judgment.

I learned very early on that judgment has no place in self work. The early teachers of the '60's and '70's, such as Vernon Howard and Ram Dass, preached the need to practice objective observation. This is the practice of seeing oneself from an objective point of view, thus, eliminating judgment. This approach is especially necessary for the study of Sex. There probably isn't a topic that elicits more judgment than Sex.

I don't judge the things I'm feeling or the things I think of. I'm already convinced I can be the most disgusting human being I've ever come across. My thoughts and feelings can range from the sublime to the ridiculous. But, what sets me apart from most is that I don't judge myself; I just observe. I watch the thoughts I'm having. I understand that these thoughts and feelings that run through me . . . are not me! It's just what pours through me and I have the option to pick and choose which I'll accept or follow. I make my own choices and decisions. Not from what's based in right or wrong but what functions in my life and what doesn't. So, I don't judge anybody's sexual inclinations, preferences, or what have you, because, "Yeah, I can get it."

With objectivity, we can begin to see and understand how incestual our relationships are. At which point we can start to cut away the aspects of them that are co-dependent. This opens the door to an independent relationship, one that is no longer incestual. Finally, we get to see what it's like to have Sex with an adult rather than a relative. This is easier said than done, though. It's especially challenging when we've married because it's family now.

This is why people have no trouble cheating. It's an opportunity to get out of this family thing, even if it's just for a little while. There comes a point in all incestual relationships when we are no longer able to maintain this deviated attraction, unless we are extremely deviant. It's then that we begin to pursue affairs, go to prostitutes, or separate. It's the way we break out of it. Granted, it's not the most functional way, but it's what we do to cope with this overbearing incestual pool we're in.

Jeremy: I'm getting a little confused on how I'm supposed to look at incest.

Lynn: How about we call it *energetic incest?* In other words, we don't mean sex with an actual blood or relational relative but a sexual relationship with someone who carries or represents the same energy of a family member. Does that help?

Jeremy: Yes.

Susan: I find I judge myself harshly around sex.

Lynn: That's because you're not looking at yourself clearly.

Up to now you were barely willing to look at what you do sexually, let alone think. So, how could you judge yourself accurately? You judge harshly because you're asleep to yourself. And that judgmental voice you hear is likely the voice of one of your parent's.

Day Two: *The Sex Seminar*

We just do things from a sleep state, we are not really aware of the components that go into having, let's say, an affair or doing things that leave us feeling shameful or guilty. We rarely, or hardly, reflect back at our actions. I guarantee you there were a lot of events that happened before you found yourself in a compromising sexual situation. There's no such thing as "It just happened."

We need to observe our thoughts to see how we got into what we're in. As Joseph said, he's not his thoughts, I'm not my thoughts, and you're not your thoughts. So you don't have to be afraid now of what passes through your mind. Joseph and I think a lot of things and we crack each other up constantly sharing our thoughts with each other. And yes, he's one demented puppy.

(Laughter)

Joseph: Let me give you an example on how I manage **my** thoughts, or more precisely, thoughts.

The other day, I'm watching the news coverage of the Boston Marathon bombing and my first thought was about how horrible it all was. My second thought was . . . "Wow, two of our clients are there. I hope they're ok!" One had gone to run the marathon and the other went to support her. Then my next immediate thought was "Oh my God, the Boston Celtics are playing *my* New York Knicks and they're going to be so fired up because of all this, they might beat the Knicks!" That was the thought! As you can see, my humanity lasted for all of one or two thoughts before it became personalized, into my own stuff. And what do you think I did next? I just laughed . . . so what? I had this thought! And I returned to what mattered, I called my clients and made sure they were ok.

I had that thought and so what? Who cares? This is an example on how I, personally, laugh at myself. It's all choice, "my" feelings, "my" sensations, "my" thoughts, I don't take ownership. I say *my* but they come and go. I just watch them. I'm the witness.

Nathan: I have a hard time understanding that every relationship that comes together is going to be incestual, till a shift happens. So, it's EVERY relationship?

Joseph: Every.

Nathan: Every?

Joseph: Every!

Nathan: Holy shit!

(Laughter)

Mercedes: Is that even with friendships?

Joseph: It can be. Friendships are often referred to in family terms. It's very common for a friend to say, "Oh you're like a brother to me!" My response to that is, "No, thank you. Please don't start treating me the way you treat your family. I'm not your brother."

But that's what we do. "He's like a brother to me." "She's like a sister to me." We turn everybody into family, because that's what makes us feel safe. This is especially challenging when there wasn't a sense of safety in the family in the first place, or when there's a loss, as in Simon's case when his father died. Fortunately, we are all driven to remedy this. A classic approach is trying to do it with our own spouses and children. But, all too often we take rather abstract approaches to safety by joining gangs, clubs, associations, teams, and work associates. Ideally, providing ourselves with a sense of safety through ourselves is the best cure.

Now, Nathan, there was no chance for you to become gay. No chance, psychologically, because all you can think of is "Look at the disgusting things men do, why would I want to go with them?" You looked, and look for safety from women. You trust a woman much more than you would a man. You feel more comfortable with women much more readily and, in the meantime, you hate yourself . . . because you're a man.

Nathan: Oh, fuck.

(Laughter)

Joseph: Because the abuse you experienced was predominantly sexual in nature, and Sex is one of the most powerful forces in this world, you were impacted by that much more powerfully. It has affected your life more deeply because it had the *Sexual energy* behind it.

The power of Sexual energy can transform or even transcend you, but it can also stunt you and destroy you. It's POWERFUL. For you, Nathan, it created a powerful shift in your life. It's challenging you to see that your childhood experience was just a tiny part of your life. You're judging all of *man*kind from what only a small group of men did. It's inviting you to take a look at men from another point of view. Sex is trying to teach you! It didn't abuse you. Your father did, and he used Sex to do it. Sex wants for you to stop judging men . . . to stop judging yourself. To stop hating yourself!

Day Two: *The Sex Seminar*

Lynn: Nathan, you may want to consider that maybe you're a man hater?

Nathan: Well, the next thing that pops into my head is, I look at the other side of the spectrum and I have friends who are just the epitome of dogs. Constantly running around with their dick in their hands trying to put it in any hole they can. And I'm not like that and I look at them like "What the fuck is wrong with you? How could you treat a woman like that?"

Joseph: What you're witnessing is men responding from their base animal needs. What you're not seeing, because you're over focused on finding what's wrong with men, is what women do when they are responding to their base animal needs.

What is a woman's basic animal need?

Nathan: Same thing?

Joseph: No.

Women: Security? Security!

Joseph: Yes, SECURITY! SAFETY! At their worst, women will fuck you over and around, every which way, until you give them a sense of security and safety.

(Laughter)

... "Make me safe ... make me feel secure." And you're like "Oh yeah I'll make you feel secure." You don't get it; you don't see it because women don't do it the way men do. You don't understand that they're reacting from their lowest animal nature when they obsess about safety and security. It's from the waist down!

A synchronized body is a body that you run rather than it running you. It includes all of the body. But for most of us we live from the waist down. So from the waist down, the yang in us pursues "conquering and dominating" for a temporary sense of power while the *yin* lures others in to be consumed, which when digested, leaves *it* with temporary feelings of safety.

Nathan, do you think keeping women and their children safe makes you a good man?

Nathan: ... Yeah.

Joseph: You poor dumbass. (Says smiling)

Women who function from basic needs would like you to believe that, especially if they're not your kids. Meanwhile, you believe they're functioning from a higher level because they are taking care of their family. Well I bet you **she** didn't take care of you. No, **she** took your money and used you, **she** wasn't with you because **she** loved you, **she** was with you because you fit into her slot, a slot left by the last man. You're just a man she plugged in. That's the lowest animal nature of a woman.

Nathan: You talk about it as if you know this happened to me already!?

Joseph: It did!

Nathan: (Smiles sheepishly) Yeah . . . it did.

(Laughter)

Joseph: And it will happen again if you don't get this. You need to MAN UP . . . or yang up! (Smiles) . . . I'm doing for you what your father failed to do.

The good news is that we all have higher natures, but you have to first get in touch with the lower nature before you can incorporate the higher. You haven't recognized what a woman's lower animal nature is. If you had, you would not have been so hard on men . . . Don't get scared Nathan, I said hard *on* men not hard *for* men.

(Laughter)

Once you see both, you'll realize, "Oh, that's just who we are."

Lynn: Many of you find your safety in women because you couldn't find it in men. You don't understand that just because she feels safe with you, because of your money or power or what have you, doesn't mean she cares about you. The minute that you don't provide safety for her, if she hasn't developed herself within, she's fucking your best friend. We will go to whoever makes us feel the safest, when we have not developed ourselves.

Joseph: Understand, a woman's number one drive is to keep her and her family safe. It's genetically built in. All women are like this until they develop themselves beyond their basic animal needs. We are ALL like this. So, if you're unaware of yourself it will run you. If you're aware of yourself you can make other decisions. I can think "Oh, the Knicks might lose to Boston" and on the next beat go "Yeah, whatever" and move on beyond my animal nature--the part of my animal nature that wants to conquer and destroy. Even if it means being heartless; that's part of my lower animal nature.

Day Two: *The Sex Seminar*

Lynn: Nathan, you've been hearing the truth from women; you've just chosen not to listen. But you've been listening to your mother and sisters, and you've heard it all. Unfortunately, you're all man haters and you support their ideas . . . It's time for you to get to know men *fully* and to find out what healthy male sexuality is all about. It's a beautiful thing.

Simon: That's the best thing I've heard. It all makes wicked sense to me now. Thanks for using your example Nathan, because it's helped me understand . . .

Nathan: Then maybe you can help me.

(Laughter)

Joseph: By all means, ask for help.

Tami: My father wasn't present so, when it comes to abandonment issues, how does that play out sexually?

Joseph: Well it's going to leave you with a hole that has to be filled. Whether you fill it with penises or you fill it with money, security, or attention, it will not be enough. It can be healed Sexually, but not in the way you think.

Lynn: This urge to be filled is already inherent in being a woman; abandonment just exacerbates it.

Joseph: Yes, so we have to find a way of filling ourselves. But before you can do that you have to be with the emptiness.

It's only by experiencing the emptiness that you're able to figure out how to properly fill yourself. We need to *embrace* the emptiness. What we do instead, is run away from it. When you've embraced the emptiness fully, you'll know it because you'll find yourself crying *so hard*, you won't be able to stop. And when the crying finally does stop, when the hole that was once filled with tears goes empty, you'll experience "emptiness" as nothing more than *free space*.

Now, what you do with this free space is up to you. It's, officially, out of your parent's hands. You will have the freedom to keep it as is or fill it with whatever feels right for you. But, again, this cannot happen unless you go into it and

experience it fully. It could take three thousand years or it could take a week, it depends on how deep you're willing to go and how much you're able to endure. Let me forewarn you, this is no easy task. I've had countless people proclaim "bring it on!" and "that's what I want." But you need to know that wanting it is not enough. It will take muscles--physical, mental, emotional, and spiritual muscles. You'll need a guide and training such as reflection, contemplation, yoga, and meditation.

Parisa: I have gone six years without sex and I can please myself but I don't need to be in a relationship. I don't need anyone in my life. And I feel maybe there's something wrong with me because everybody is in relationships except for me. It's not a NEED anymore.

Joseph: Then you're in free space and you can actually have a relationship for its own sake; not out of need.

Parisa: But there's no interest.

Joseph: Okay, when there is there is.

Parisa: So, this is the freedom that I'm going through now, I'm experiencing the emptiness.

Joseph: I know you'd like to think that but, no.

What's actually happened for you, Parisa, is that you're living on top of your pain. Your quasi-spiritual work has taught you how to lay a floor over it. It's like sweeping it under a rug, except it's more solid. So, after six years, you've convinced yourself that you live in a free space when in reality you're only occupying half of it and there's no room for anyone else in it but you.

You're not complete with your pain *of emptiness* but as soon as you're finished, you'll experience more space; space that was there all along. At this point, other people will show up. It's your pain that keeps others away. Pain that has filled the space which others could normally occupy. You get it? But remember, the path to heaven is THROUGH hell.

Eddie: You said earlier that affairs just don't happen, then how do they happen?

Joseph: The kind of pain that is in Tami and Parisa are the types of pain that fuel affairs. That being said, there are very specific reasons and elements that *create* an affair.

It seems that everyone that has an affair goes "Oh, I don't know, it just happened" That's like saying, "I just happened to be walking and somehow my penis slipped out of my pants and I fell right into that vagina." Let's pull back the covers and see the anatomy of an affair.

Lynn: Here are some of the elements necessary for an affair:

Limited or no authentic communication in a relationship.

1. *When the sex is repeatedly driven by only one of the partners.* This is when only one of the partners controls the where, when, and how of their sex life without the other's buy in.
2. *When there is no mutual fulfillment.* This can be caused by selfishness, entitlement, or simply by being oblivious to one's own, or the others, needs.
3. *Distrust.* Many individuals show up in relationships already distrustful, based on their own unreliability or because of a previous experience of infidelity. By the way, in relationships where there has already been an affair, the couple have to work even harder on trust because now the distrust can cause it to happen again, by either partner.
4. *Not filling your own needs.* When there is an over reliance on one partner to fill the needs of the other, this ultimately leaves one of them unfulfilled and discontented. Thus vulnerable to outside "help."
5. *Our natural need for intimacy.* This makes us all vulnerable to affairs because if we're not getting enough warmth, closeness, and connectedness we cannot function well in life.
6. *Lack of relational skills.* Many of us are highly unskilled in relationships. We learned from our unskilled parents and have not gathered any additional information on our own. This often leads us to repeating our parent's mistakes.
7. *One sided awareness.* This is when only one of the partners becomes self-aware and the other hasn't. It changes the game and an affair becomes the method of protest. The awareness comes in the experience of becoming lucid to their mate, a re-stimulation to life, or simply growing tired of the "family incestual approach to relationships."
8. *An inability to be intimate.* Often, due to traumatic experiences, individuals find themselves incapable of giving or receiving real human contact. They eventually revert to their base animal needs; which means getting their needs met by any means possible.

9. *When things become unfair.* When things become **unfair** in a relationship it becomes easy to have an **affair**. It's the feeling of *injustice* that gives us permission for an affair. We feel *justified* in seeking out our needs through others in order to balance out the *unfairness*.

Joseph: Affairs are not cut and dry, they are very complex. How do you blame someone, for instance, who has trouble or is truly unable to experience intimacy for having an affair? What if their life is so empty that an affair gives them at least a glimmer of life, of feeling, that keeps them from killing themselves? Would you deny someone that?

When we've allowed a relationship to become old and routine and everything we do is mechanical, then even a dumbass could stimulate us. People often wonder "How could he go with her and why would she go with him?"

Kelly: Is this why men have sex with prostitutes?

Joseph: No. These are affairs we're talking about. As long as there is a money transaction, it is not an affair. Prostitution is a whole other thing. Prostitution has to do with anything from healing to getting your darkness out, and everything in-between. Many choose prostitution as a way to deal with their pain without having to get it all over their relationship. Now, I know that sounds ass backwards but for some, that's the only outlet they see available to them. But we're talking about affairs here; what do you make of that?

Mercedes: According to this list everyone's having an affair. I mean, I can't think of a single relationship I've had where some of this wasn't pertinent.

Joseph: Yes, because affairs are not just physical, there are mental and emotional affairs also. Emotional affairs are very common and we don't think that's cheating. Anytime you're not giving your partner what you **could** give them, you're cheating. You're cheating when you remove your attention from your partner; when you aren't giving them attention, time or care. We're all cheaters! I've accepted this, and because I accept it, there's no repression and I can actually have space to choose. What do you think of this?

Mercedes: I have emotional affairs all the time, but I never considered it an affair. Now I can understand why my partner was getting upset.

Joseph: How about now?

Mercedes: I understand but, I still feel entitled. Like, why not?

Day Two: *The Sex Seminar*

Joseph: Entitlement comes easy.

If we've been under or over indulged by our parents or a parent, we will come to feel entitled or owed. For an under indulged individual, they will feel owed. They may strategically over care for the other in order to obligate them; at least in their eyes. I've done that more times than I care to remember in my life. I've had sex with nothing but daughters in most of my youth. Granted, other men's daughters but I played father. It was incestual. Now I had no problem with that, not at all. The energy in my family was highly incestual.

My step-aunts who are eleven and thirteen years older than me would periodically change their clothes in front of me, for as long as I could remember. Now granted they were not biological aunts but I had been in their lives since I was three, so I was family. When I turned 13 my parents moved and I was allowed to stay behind to live with my grandparents and aunts so I could finish my last year of junior high school. So, here I was living with these two *women*, who were in their 20's, occasionally exposing themselves in front of me. Eventually, because of lack of space, I wound up having to sleep in the same bed with my 25 year old voluptuous aunt for almost a year; and there weren't any *genetic smells* to repel me. It was excruciating. And since I wasn't abused directly, it took me many years, well into my adulthood, to realize that this was a form of sex abuse. Abuse born from ignorance.

Now, I don't blame them, because that's how they were raised; there was a large amount of sexual illiteracy in my family. It was thought that these types of actions were actions of *free spirits*. But, it's not free spiritedness if it's conducted without the understanding of the power of Sex. Therefore, because of my experiences with my aunts, playing father with my girlfriends felt natural and correct.

Simon: If a young teenage male is abused by a woman it's almost congratulated.

Joseph: Yes, we are just starting to understand that this is damaging. Men generally look at sex physically, first; they don't realize the damage inappropriate sexual contact can have on an underage boy. Just because we want it physically, that doesn't mean we can handle it mentally and emotionally. We're starting to wake up to that mental and emotional sexual abuse is a *thing*.

Now, when we speak of marriage we mean it as any union that seeks to form a lasting connection between two individuals that may or may not include children. Okay? (Group nods) Good!

We come into this world through Sex and we're born into a pool of mental and emotional dependency called *family*, and it's in this pool that we are formed. When we leave home and go into our lives, it becomes preferable to work out our childhood issues before considering marriage. This is because then we'll have a greater chance to actually marry an adult; if we marry at all. This doesn't mean that childhood stuff won't come up, also; it just won't play out half as hard as it will for those who go straight into marriage. But, if there's no break between leaving home and getting married, then we'll definitely marry a parent and recreate our childhood; and you'll be surprised to hear me say that can be a good thing!

It's when we get to understand our childhood, from an adult perspective, that we can become free of it. So, if we get married as *family* and we grow conscious within it, we can help each other resolve our primary issues together. Then we can re-marry, as *adults*, with a new found respect and gratitude for the soul who helped us through our journey. This is what relationships can offer us. They can accelerate our personal growth.

Nathan: Now we can finally choose each other.

Joseph: Right . . . now you're choosing each other.

Susan: How does our childhood stuff play out in marriage? I'm trying to imagine what that would look like.

Joseph: It looked like seeing my mother, and feeling my mother's behaviour in my wife. What you, first, want to understand is our mates come from their own systems, their own *puzzle boxes*.

When I was a kid I loved playing with puzzles and I owned quite a few of them. I would play with them for hours upon hours and when I became bored I would start another. I'd go continually back and forth putting them together and since my room was rather small, I'd eventually mix up the pieces. What would always happen next was I'd find myself putting together two pieces, which fit perfectly together, that came from different puzzle boxes. And I didn't always notice that they were different. Sometimes it would be because they were the same color or a similar object. So if you asked me where these two pieces came from, I'd swear it was from the same box. This was what I experienced in my marriage.

We showed up with our separate puzzle boxes, inadvertently mixed up the pieces and then became insistent that the pieces were from the other's puzzle box. My anger became her fault and her sadness became mine. In reality, we just happen to fit together but we were never the cause of each other's problems. When we finally realized this we were able to begin resolving. We started going through the pieces and figured out which were mine and which were hers. It was easier than going alone, by this point. That's how it plays out: it starts with us projecting on one another.

Eddie: Then the incest stops?

Joseph: Absolutely, we have to remember that we come into relationships with our own lives; our own puzzle boxes. Until you realize this, all you can do is project on one another. But when that becomes clear to you, the projector shuts down and you can distinguish your stuff from your mate's. One of the things that can assist us in all of this is Sexual energy.

Sexual energy can stop the projector because it separates us before it bonds us. When we experience sexual energy as something larger than ourselves, it becomes easier to see the other. The other is no longer the source of this energy but someone you're blessed to share it with.

Susan: I see it as two people standing side by side taking it in and using it for sex.

Nisha: Wow! You go Susan!

(Laughter)

Lynn: It's in Sex . . . because of Sex, we get to experience the transcendent. We get to experience ourselves leaving our bodies for a little while, don't we? La petite mort, the little death. It's what happens to us upon orgasm. We leave our bodies and we get a glimpse of what it's like to die. And an orgasm is much more profound with another person; we can't quite do it the same by ourselves.

Joseph: All hail to masturbation! But, like Lynn said, it's not the same without the extra energy of another. That's more transforming, but if you use this energy to perform the mechanical then it's no longer Sex, it's what we call, "**Man-made sex.**"

Eddie: What's Man-made sex?

Joseph: Glad you asked! (Smiling)

Man-made sex is sex that is predominantly controlled, operated, and manufactured by men. We draw a distinction between human sex and Man-made sex because it is chiefly practiced by men. Let's look deeper into what Man-made sex is after a short break.

Day Two: *The Sex Seminar*

Group: Ahhh, noooo!

(Laughter)

* * * * *

Joseph: Welcome back! Man-made sex is so small and controlled and mechanical, it has no ability to provide us with access to pure Sexual energy. It doesn't have the power to change anything or anyone; it can't even change a light bulb. Pornography is a perfect example of man-made sex.

So, let's look a little closer at man-made sex in your lives . . .

Lynn: Put your books down, put your feet flat on the floor and let's begin to clear your minds . . . our minds.

Now, close your eyes, keep your hands apart and just let yourself breathe easily and effortlessly.

Continue to breathe in, and out . . . in and out.

Can you now allow yourself to begin to relax in your seat, while breathing in and out . . . in and out?

(Lynn guides the group, body part by body part, into full relaxation)

Now keep your eyes closed . . .

In a moment I'm going to ask you to open your eyes and pick up your books. I'm going to ask you some questions, and I'd like you to just write down the first thing that comes to mind for you. Again, just allow yourself to write the first thing that comes into your mind.

And now, I'd like you to allow yourself to go back as far as you can go, into your childhood . . . as young as you can remember . . . the younger the better.

Back, back, back . . . and now, from that point forward, I'd like you to allow yourself to remember all that you can . . . Now, slowly and comfortably, allow yourself to come back into the room, and when you're back you may open your eyes.

Okay. Grab your books and write down the answers to the questions I will be giving you. (Lynn instructs, thoroughly, on how to format it on the page.)

Day Two: *The Sex Seminar*

Lynn: Are we ready? . . . Title this section General Sexual Environment or "**Sex Mapping.**"

Question 1: What was the general sexual environment like at home when you were a child? . . . Write down whatever you recall. Don't worry, if it makes no sense. Just take what comes to mind.

1A) What was your mother like, sexually?

1B) What was your father like, sexually?

1C) What were your siblings like, sexually?

Question 2: How did you play out sex? . . . Just write whatever comes to mind.

2A) How did you play out sex between the ages of nine and 14 years old?

2B) How did you play out sex between the ages of 14 to 20 years old?

2C) Lastly, how did you play out sex between the ages of 21 to the present?

Okay, everybody stand up and put your books down on your chairs.

(Group is brought to an open space in the room)

. . . Now, you're going to keep breathing through this entire lab. You're going to mill around, you're going to see and be seen, and you're going to make eye contact with everyone you pass by . . . and there will be no talking. Begin . . . see and be seen, and breathe. *(Group mills around for 1.5 minutes)*

Now begin to partner up. Pick one person you'd like to partner with. Then take your chairs and go make space for yourselves throughout the room.

(Group pairs off)

Listen up! What you're going to do is share your answers. First share with each other your answers and then discuss your findings and whatever else comes up for you.

(After sharing, group members continue to speak with one another engagingly)

Lynn: Okay, everyone, let's return to the circle and discuss what's come up for you.

(After much discussion and some sharing, most participants conclude that they were "set up" for sexual issues)

Day Two: *The Sex Seminar*

Joseph: . . . So is there any wonder, after looking at your childhood map, you're left with so many sexual challenges? Many of you have thought there was something wrong with you or that there was something you needed to do to change yourselves; that you were broken. No, this is what you were born into. This was **your** *sexual childhood environment* and it's making clear to you where you're at and why you do what you do, sexually.

This situation we are in is like that of a child who has broken his arm and is expected to set it himself. We're asked to fix something, but we don't know the first thing about it. That's what we're like sexually, and we can't let anybody know because we're afraid of being seen as stupid or being judged. Why are we so afraid of being seen as sexually stupid? . . . Why?

Nathan: Alexia and I, in our discussion, only got as far as the first series of questions. I couldn't get past the first ones. It's pretty clear, I fuckin' hate men. I'm still struggling with that, trying to figure it out. But it's like okay, so I hate men. But I'm seeing there was a lot of negative energy on my mom's side of things too. My whole sexual energy experience as a kid growing up was very hostile on my mom's side and way fucked up on my dad's side, and I feel like I have no fucking idea right now. I'm just so lost.

Joseph: As I heard Anthony Robbins once explained, "We gravitate towards the lesser pain." So the lesser pain would be around mom because she's *there* and it's tangible and supportive. You also gravitate towards that pain because it's a familiar pain that you find comfort in. Hence, it's easier for you to be in a woman's arms, even if she's "crazy." Because it's a lesser . . .

Nathan: Ugggh, Fuck!

Joseph: Well, that's what your father said, right?

(Laughter)

It's a lesser pain than the one you experienced with your father.

What you don't get is men are a gift to you! What if men are the vehicles through which you get all this crap out? That it's through this very struggle with them that you find yourself? And that, maybe, you could eventually love men and see them as part of the same team--your team. Everything that you're upset at me about . . . *look at how he's looking at me* . . .

(Laughter)

Day Two: *The Sex Seminar*

. . . It's not in the present!

Nathan: No, it's from the past.

Joseph: So, what if it's not only that you use men to project your past on, but that men are *allowing* you to project it on them. Whether, you project it on them when you're walking around and they bump into you, or when one of them cuts you off on the road, or when you get into a fight with them at a bar, they're helping you get all your pain up and out. They're helping you get your rage up. They're helping you bring it to the surface . . . they're helping you bring it to the surface until you realize that they have nothing to do with your pain. That *it's* from your past and that, maybe, you're the one who's being abusive.

This process, that life is putting you through, is intended to help you see your past, through men, from an adult perspective. So you can experience your childhood pain in the present, where you are better equipped to handle it, to feel it, and heal it. Wouldn't you like to help the child, you once were, with these issues?

Nathan: Yes.

Joseph: So, this is your chance. But, you won't be able to until you see that they have nothing to do with your pain. Now, there is a limit to how long they'll do this dance with you. Without some work on your part, men will eventually give up.

You'll experience it like you've pushed them away when, in actuality, they'll have given up on you.

When you've become conscious that the person or people you are projecting your past on have nothing to do with it, you can begin to do some real self work. This is where meditation, reflecting, and self observation come in. These are tools and methods that allow us all to process the *images* of our past. Because, after you've stopped blaming others and are no longer projecting on men, you'll be able to see men for who they are. At that point you'll probably wonder . . . *"What right did I have to take my pain out on all these guys?"*

Nathan: Well, I think in, almost, a way I cheated myself.

Joseph: Of course.

Nathan: Like, big time!

Joseph: If you were a woman, you would have cheated yourself less, but because you're a man you cheated yourself from yourself.

Nathan: I did. All it's been is "Watch out men, or else!"

Joseph: All that is, is the angry little kid in you who's been taking his issues out on someone who looks like daddy.

Nathan: I'm not even talking about that! I'm talking about . . . I think I've cheated myself on not allowing myself to be a man, in a sense, because I hated it so much. I came to hate the lower nature of man. I've never allowed myself to be a man!

Joseph: Have you been violent in your life?

Nathan: Yeah.

Joseph: Towards men only, I presume?

Nathan: Yeah.

Joseph: Okay, then that's where it comes out.

The way men tend to take out these father issues is through violence. That's how we do it, we get violent. Now, it's not always against women, we get violent towards each other. We do it all the time in sports. There are a lot of men with daddy issues who play it out, violently, against each other. We try to punch it out of each other to try to get past it. Believe me, you've allowed yourself to be a man, the lower nature of man, as you put it, because you've been violent.

Nathan: Well, I'm talking sexually . . .

Joseph: What's the difference? What's the difference between violence and sex? It's hard to tell the difference right? There's a lot of violence in sex, isn't there?

Lynn: If you were an alien from outer space and you came upon two men wrestling and two men having sex, or a man and a woman having sex . . .

Nathan: There wouldn't be much difference.

Lynn: Right!

Joseph: We have to ask if there is a difference and if so, what's the difference? We have sex and violence tied together, especially in this society. So where's the sex in your violence?

Nathan: Wow . . . thanks.

Joseph: You're welcome.

Anybody else, what did you get from your mapping?

Parisa: My dad was a womanizer, and I've always attracted womanizers. But, when I was two my mom left and I was stuck with my stepmother who didn't get enough sex. My dad never slept with her and she was constantly angry and depressed. She talked to anyone who would listen about the lack of sex she was having.

Joseph: So you've recreated your childhood, except you're the one not having sex now.

It's important to recreate your childhood so you can witness and make sense of it as an adult, from an adult perspective. As an adult, you can easily see why your stepmother was angry, can't you?

Parisa: Yes.

Joseph: And, do you think it was her choice not to have sex in her life or was it imposed upon her? I'm asking because, according to you, for you it's a choice.

Parisa: I think she wasn't aware enough for it to be a choice.

Joseph: Okay, so now you can understand it can be a choice or it can be imposed upon you. These are the two sides. When we live an unexamined life we, effectively, give up choice. It's only through awareness, which **can** come through recreating to our childhood that we get to actually choose.

Parisa: Oh, nice, thank you.

Joseph: You're welcome. So this is good stuff, this sex-mapping; it reveals a lot.

Lisa: For me, I noticed there was a lot of shame and repression in my "map." I'm kind of freaking out right now because, I had a breast reduction ten years ago, and I always thought it was because they didn't suit my body; they were too big. Now I think it was because I was trying to become less Sexual. I didn't feel comfortable with the attention.

Joseph: Let yourself feel all that you're feeling, fully. I know it's hard, but it is worth it. Remember, *the path to heaven is through hell*. It will free you . . . and by the way . . . what you just saw in the lab, was spot on.

You're a product of what you were born into and you responded with all you knew, and it wasn't enough. You didn't mutilate yourself, thank goodness, so it's okay, but . . . you want to be with the reality of where it came from; where your movements and actions came from.

Lisa: Well, I didn't mutilate myself, but I have scars.

Joseph: Know I'm not being heartless when I suggest that you embrace these scars. Think of them as battle scars that you've received through your family wars. The war of Sex is not between women and men, because men and women are more alike than not. It's rather between your misconceptions of Sex and *Sex* itself.

We battle against the nature of Sex, whereas animals and plants don't. We all do, you're not alone in this.

You know what? Let's watch a video on labiaplasty in Lisa's honour. We need to know we're not alone in this war against Sex. This suffering is being perpetuated, in the world, as we speak. Let's attack this before you all sink back into comfort.

(Group watches a video on a young woman's painful experience with labiaplasty)

Joseph: What do you make of that, Lisa?

Lisa: That was painful and degrading for her. She didn't even realize how degrading it was to have her labia cut just because of what others thought. And just because of pornography, women do this because that's what pornography says we should look like!

I can now see that I didn't love myself . . . and I still don't.

Joseph: That's great; this is a start. You're now clear about where you were at and where you are now.

You can see from your *sex mapping* that you were informed about Sex, by someone who was informed by someone else . . . who was informed by someone who was informed by someone else, and so on. Through your personal sex mapping you can see the cause and effect of your sex life.

We can paint a pretty or ugly picture of our sex *ourstory* (history) or we can look and accept it for what it actually is. We can say, "Okay this is where I'm at and it's in my hands now." We can go forth, from this point, and explore and discover what it means to "*love myself.*"

When Sexual energy is repressed, like any energy that is repressed, it becomes combustible; hence, violent. That's all violence is, it's repressed Sexual energy. If

Day Two: *The Sex Seminar*

you leave dynamite sitting for too long, it becomes unstable and can blow up at anytime. It's the same thing when we repress Sexual energy. In the case of the young woman in the video, it manifested as self violence . . . as it did in your case, Lisa.

If women were to begin to inform themselves better, do you think there'd be as many of these operations as there are now? Lisa, if you had a group of women supporting you at the time, do you think you would have made a different decision?

Lisa: Maybe . . .

Joseph: Yeah, maybe. It's something to consider because you would have had more information to draw from. Just about all of us are uncomfortable speaking about Sex. That's the main problem here . . . we're uncomfortable speaking about Sex!

Parents need to make a concerted effort to overcome their discomfort in order to teach their children about Sex . . . and these conversations have to be practiced. Practice creates comfort. Parents could practice with each other and, in time, they'd find themselves speaking about it in comfort and with clarity.

Children need to be informed. If you leave your child to figure it out on their own, they're bound to do something reckless or violent. They don't know what they're doing. They're playing with fire.

Sexual communication is an issue. Even mates have trouble communicating about sex directly to each other versus other subject matters. It's a difficult subject to speak about for us. But, the more informed you are, the easier it is to talk about. The more informed you are the more options you have in your sex life.

(Looking back to Lisa)

You took the proverbial bullet, for everyone in your system who repressed Sexual communication. You understand? But the good news is that you're still ticking, you can redirect the misdirected hostility and find a way to grow from this, so something like this doesn't happen again. No one will have to take this bullet, again; especially your children, but only if you continue to reflect on this. You follow? I'm sure you'd take a stand if you saw your nieces encountering anything like this, right?

Lisa: Yes. I'd definitely give them my opinion.

Lynn: The amount of sexually based operations that women are having is growing exponentially. And men aren't immune to *toying with their penises* in a similar fashion.

Day Two: *The Sex Seminar*

(Laughter)

Penile surgeries have skyrocketed in the past five years. Men are having all kinds of procedures, some quite dangerous, on their penis for the strict purpose of sexual enhancement. Between what men see in porn, and what they think women want, men are doing some drastic things to increase their penis size.

Simon: Women do want large penises.

Joseph: That's true. Scientists have explained that the reason men have, proportionally to their size, larger penises than other mammals is because women want large penises.

Angie: Really!?

Joseph: Yes, Angie. You didn't *really* think that all those nights you stayed up wishing for "a big one" didn't have an effect?

(Laughter)

 . . . It's all your fault we can't fit it into our jeans. Why else do you think we grab on to our penises so often through our pants? We're just rearranging it because you've wished it too big.

(Laughter)

Lynn: Yeah, you wish!

(More laughter)

Group: Oooh!

Joseph: Okay, okay! Wow, I walked right into that one. (Smiling)

But, in all seriousness, it seems as if sexual insecurity has increased for men as well. Men appear to be so sexually hyperconscious that they're undergoing all sorts of penile experimentations and operations to improve their penises and performances. And they do it because they don't feel they're *enough*.

There's this commonly held belief that your sense of *enoughness* should come, or can come, from Sex. Rather than being grateful that it flows through you and you can experience it and **create** with it; you also want it to define you!? Why limit yourselves so? Is that the main thing in the world you're going to use to define yourself? When we're defined by what we create and less by sex we, naturally, become sexy.

To me, Betty White is so damn sexy. She's 91 years old and she's sexy. She's just a hot old broad. She's awesome! This is because she's created herself to be a work of art, and she never repressed her Sexual energy. She's performed two sexually extreme roles, to a tee. In *The Golden Girls*, she played a sexually naive woman, and in *The Mary Tyler Moore Show*, she was a nymphomaniac. She played them so well because she was in touch with her sexual self. She's so alive!

Because of her vibrancy, her life force, and Sexual energy, she's allowed to say things that even someone 20-30 years younger than her could not say. Take any random 61 year old who has repressed themselves, sexually, and have them tell a Betty White joke and I'll bet you'd be grossed out.

So, why don't you get grossed out with a woman thirty years older than that? That's because she owns her Sexual power. She has a relationship to it. It flows through her. And she flows with it; she surfs it. People who are not afraid of facing **Sex**, expressing it, and confronting it become sexy. They will not gross you out, unless you're repressed.

Another perfect example was Joan Rivers. She was relevant and had more cache with the young generation, than most women her age. She would say all kinds of shit and you'd crack up at it without caring that she was older. That was because she had confronted repression her whole life. She had informed herself, she had challenged herself and had grown because of it.

Once we decide "I'm gonna THINK about Sex, I'm going to feel it, and I'm going to let myself be in all of it," we'll find our sexiness. And, for those of you like Lisa, who went at it from a repressive direction, know that these unfortunate events and decisions often are what are needed to have us begin to question ourselves and our beliefs around Sex. Then, these events become gifts in disguise. Every challenge has a gift at the end. You just have to find it.

When we insist that our only identity is sexual, when we're only interested in whether we're "fuck-able" or not, well then . . . we've diminished ourselves tremendously. Sex hasn't diminished us. We've diminished us! We've diminished Sex. Sex hasn't diminished us! We've taken this amazing power and said, "Come here and let me shrink you, control you so I can get everybody to look at my ass, or my tits, or my cock, or my muscles. Come look at that, don't look at me! Look at that. Because that's who I am!" That's *not* who you are! At the end of the day, if we continue to insist on identifying ourselves through Sex, we lose the time that could be better spent discovering who we truly are and are becoming.

Alexia: You know this makes me think about work. I've identified myself, a lot, by my jobs and if I'm really being honest, I see that they've all exploited me sexually, in a way.

Lynn: More than ever, if you look beyond the surface, you'll find that the majority of females out in the world have jobs that are sex driven or implied. We're not saying that having a small aspect of sexuality in a job isn't okay, but that's not what's happening. Sexual energy has become a necessary component of most jobs available to women. The same can be said about the jobs men hold. They're, mostly, based in violence, which is sexual energy in one of its rawer forms.

Joseph: Let me say before we go any further, thank you, Lisa, for taking the bullet for the rest of us. The bullet called "self condemnation." And thank you for the gift of your share, which opened up, not just your pain, but our hearts and us.

What do you guys make of all this? Like every other seminar, we go where you take us.

Mercedes: I wonder what's going to happen now, to that girl in the video who just had her labia chopped off. Because the labia wasn't the problem, and the problem will still be there. Now that it's chopped, it's going to be something else for her.

Lynn: Well, humiliation will still be there. Her sister, being the spiteful person she was in teasing her and telling all her male friends about her large labia in the first place, will now tell them "Oh guys, now she got it chopped off!" So, there will be a whole other level of humiliation. Again, that's why we say go *into the feeling*. It's not the "thing" we project our issues on that's causing our pain, it's the feeling underneath it.

Joseph: If she cut her labia down for aesthetic reasons, because it would have been aesthetically pleasing to her . . . that might have been alright. But since she did it from pain, from believing she was less of a woman because of its size, well that's where the problem lies.

Mercedes: Right. So, she did it to please others instead of herself.

Joseph: It's where you do it from. If you do it from a clear place, it doesn't matter what you're doing, entirely.

There's an old story of a monk who went up to his Zen Master and asked, "Is it acceptable if I were to smoke while meditating?" The master looked at him incredulously and said "Get away from me, stupid." So the monk thought about it, and thought about it, and a week later he went back to the master and asked this time " Is it acceptable if I meditate and smoke? " The master looked at him and said, "Of course."

Lynn: I remember the master actually said at first, "Of course not" rather than "Get away, stupid."

Joseph: Well, yeah . . . he did, but he should have said it.

(Laughter)

What's the difference?

Tami: Meditation comes first.

Joseph: Why? What's the difference, besides the order? Why was it okay for him to meditate and smoke and not smoke and meditate?

Kelly: If you meditate and you still want to have a cigarette, then go ahead. But, maybe your meditating will stop you from having a craving . . .

Joseph: No.

Parisa: It's because the second time he didn't actually stop because he rejected him...

Joseph: No.

Nisha: Different energies, the act of smoking versus meditating?

Joseph: No.

Tami: Being versus doing?

Joseph: What do you mean?

Tami: When you're meditating you're being, being still; but when you're smoking you're doing.

Joseph: Not exactly.

Simon: The reason over the action.

Joseph: How so?

Simon: By meditating . . . you focus on the reason . . . why . . .

Joseph: No.

Kelly: Spit it out Simon!

Joseph: Yeah, you know as soon as he starts with his reasons, he's headed in the wrong direction.

(Laughter)

Angie: I think it's where you place the importance. So, it's like if he was smoking, as, like, the first and foremost thing, and then meditation came afterward he'd be saying that smoking was more important . . .

Joseph: No, that was what Tami was getting at.

The human body and the human mind have an incredible capacity to turn the worst of events--the worst of things--into something useful, and even healthy, when the mind is in the right place. If you're stranded in the desert and your urine is all you have to drink, and you drink it to survive, you'll be just fine. Also, I've seen people eat so healthily--vegetarians and vegans--who tend to be sick most of the time. While in contrast, I've seen others who eat much worse than a vegetarian, but who are playful with their food and joyful of their food, be healthier.

What this story is saying is when one is in a meditative state, a state where one is clear and still in their center, then whatever they do from that place will be correct. Their actions aren't going to affect, one way or another, their being-ness. They will operate their lives within a context of peace.

Once you *Be* in the creative woman that you are--I'm speaking to all of the women directly at this point--you will naturally *be* sexually expansive and explorative. You will know you are more than just sex, even though you are a major conduit for it. Then it won't be harmful if you decide to jump on a stripper pole, because it's not defining you. But if you jump on a stripper pole to be defined, that's going to be problematic for your self-worth and esteem. Again, we have no judgment. We're just explaining what it is; its effects, and how it costs you.

Lynn: And where you're at.

Simon: That thing you just said with the food that you had told me during a session, it really worked and I was getting really stressed out . . .

Joseph: Well, share. Give them the inside information!

Simon: I just became vegetarian about eight or nine months ago and I was really struggling to find food that I liked because salads were boring and bland and I'm used to having steaks and stuff. I told Joseph, so he suggested I try eating whatever I wanted for six weeks. "If you want to eat donuts for six weeks, do it." Eventually, I got so sick of eating that stuff that I realized I have a choice and that I can eat pizza two days a week then the next day I'll just eat salad. So it balances and I can follow my cravings more naturally instead of worrying about it because it was actually making me sick. I worried about my food choices all the time. I worried whether I was getting my protein or this and that. So once I relaxed and ate what I wanted, I was much happier. I realized that the sickness could have got really bad, to the point of an eating disorder. Today, there's no more pressure. I don't have to eat perfectly, just balanced.

Joseph: What do you guys make of that?

Mercedes: I used to have an eating disorder, and this is just my opinion, but if you're watching what you eat and trying not to eat certain things, you have an eating disorder. If you're not just eating what you feel like when you want it, you have a mild eating disorder. Animals in the wild are never thinking, "Oh, I need this much protein, this many carbs." They just eat what they want to eat and there's no obesity . . .

Lynn: When you have so much emotion tied up in food, as you do in sex, and you don't know where you're at, then there's no choosing what you want to eat, healthy or otherwise. What I'm getting from you, Simon, is that you freed yourself from the repression and didn't over think it; that's what made you sick! It made you sick to over think. You were doing that with food and you would do that with Sex, too, if you over thought it, it would make you sick.

Joseph: When I suggested that he not take it seriously his mindset changed, basically putting him in a meditative state of acceptance of *what is*. In this state, the body regulated itself for the reasons Lynn just mentioned. There was no emotional *charge* around it.

Lynn: Whether it's eating vegan, or eating whatever you want, when it's an emotional charge it's still an eating disorder. It's not so much the food we eat but

Day Two: *The Sex Seminar*

the emotions that we place into it. So I could eat only nuts for the rest of my life, and be completely healthy and vibrant if I'm doing it meditatively.

Joseph: Hear that? Nuts!?

(Loud laughter)

Lynn: Picked the wrong food group?

(More laughter)

Simon: Don't say meat, now!

(Eruption of laughter)

Lynn: Anyway . . . I've lost my train of thought . . . do you get where I'm going, here?

Joseph: She's like, "Save me!"

Tami: You were saying you can eat nuts and still be vibrant!

Lynn: It's to find the balance wherever you're at, with Sex or food, and they're linked.

For some people it's to eat a steak every day, and that is what they *need*. For others, it's a vegan diet. But as soon as you put your emotions, guilt, and shame onto food, you're fucked! As soon as you place them in Sex, you're *fucked*! When these feelings are misplaced onto these primal areas--Food & Sex--there's no room, no freedom to see who you are, or what you need! Maybe I need a woman to eat me out; maybe I need a man to do that. Maybe I need to make love to a woman and that would fulfill me; maybe I only want to be with men. Maybe I love women and can see everything about them that's beautiful and just luscious but I don't want to have sex with them. I'll never really know if I've inundated my Sexual self with guilt, shame, rage, or other such feelings. . . . I do like nuts, though.

(Laughter)

Mercedes: I had an experience that really drove home how powerful it can be. Whether it's food or sex, when you're *not supposed to have it* and how charged up it makes it; how much more you want it.

I took some medication a few months back and I had to eat 40 grams of fat three times a day. At first, I thought that should be easy, eat a cheeseburger. But, there's only like 13 grams of fat in a cheeseburger. So I soaked my food in butter . . . it was disgusting. It was at the point where I started hating butter, ice cream, hating olive oil. I started hating these things because I thought they were so bad for me, and the craziest thing was that I lost five pounds! My fear had always been that if I ate so much of these types of foods I would gain weight, and actually the opposite happened. It was shocking to me, because I had to have it, whereas before I wasn't allowed. Now I could have more than I wanted, and it totally blew my mind!

Joseph: A balance can be struck.

I remember in the '90's I did the controversial, yet popular, Atkins diet. The Atkins diet was a high, high fat diet that required you to eat high quantities of fat and hardly any carbohydrates. What is supposed to happen, if you do it correctly, is that your body goes into ketosis and it starts burring fat for fuel causing dramatic weight losses. It felt so imbalanced, eating all this fat all day long, every day. But, when I returned to a regular diet, it turned out to be the perfect blend. Oddly, going to such an extreme had me create a balance; I didn't even have to try. It became so easy to eat healthfully!

It was the mindset of extremes that created so much pressure. And the pressure to stay at these extremes created more problems than I had originally started with. But, what I never imagined was that when I finally let go, I fell into the middle and my body started regulating itself.

Now, don't think we're advocating going to extremes. There is an easier way. What we're saying is when you have misidentified yourself as, say, being only your body, you leave yourself vulnerable to going to extremes. It's easier to find the middle, the *happy medium*, when you haven't repressed your self-identification to such extremes. There's a lot of time to define who you are. Wouldn't it be better if you just explored who you are? You'll experience less pressure if you do it that way. Christopher Columbus discovered the Americas in 1492, but it took us about another 400 years to *uncover* the Americas. The same goes for us, we were born when we were born but it takes a lifetime to uncover who we are. So, sexually speaking, the key is to avoid identifying yourself with anything in particular. That will keep you from going to extremes.

If you identify yourself as a sexual object, then you become an object, not a person. When you take Sexual energy and use it to only form yourself into the person that everyone else wants, then you're just creating yourself as a product. You're selling, or presenting, yourself to the world to be *consumed*. So, you become consumption; you become something to be consumed. That's the stuff Hollywood dreams are made of. It's taught to us and is propagated daily through media. . . . We'll take a closer look at that when we get back from our break. But in the meantime, is there anything else you need to know to help you put all this into perspective? Are there any other thoughts about it?

Angie: I had an experience about four months ago. It was related to food and a lot about sexuality, actually. For most of my life I was a vegan, and very concerned with eating as healthfully as possible, but the crazy thing was that my weight blew up to the point where I was not at home in my own body. I was nearly 300 pounds and, now, I'm in the middle of the hard process of shedding that and getting rid of it. I made a big change in the food that I ate, and a month later I wasn't noticing any physical changes but, instead, really intense emotions came up. I had always, even at my highest weight, felt good and sexy and I think I was kidding myself.

Joseph: Do you know why these emotions came up?

Angie: Why?

Joseph: When you started to lose weight you released emotional pains that were previously covered by fat. You were spackling the cracks with fat. You want to look at what was happening in your life right before you started to gain weight. Was there a painful experience that happened prior?

Angie: Yeah, maybe!? I had this crazy insane "aha moment," where I went out one night, and I was all dressed up, with my girlfriends and, normally, I would feel really good, yet I felt so insecure; I almost cried. It wasn't a feeling that I was familiar with. I had never known that intense insecurity, but that was a result of changing the food I was eating. And I guess whatever it was . . . obviously I was stuffing down something with the old food that I consumed. It was interesting that it related to my sexuality. I was so uncomfortable sexually. I felt so exposed at the bar, out in public. It was the first time ever feeling that way . . . I had to go home and . . . I sobbed. Joseph: Yes, and again we swing till we find that middle

Angie: Yeah!

Joseph: . . . and if we stay on one side then it's just a matter of time before we swing back to the other side . . . to pay.

Angie: Yeah . . .

Joseph: It's to find the middle. So, for those of us that have cheated and clung to safety, it has forced others to feel unsafe--the unsafe you don't want to feel. The pendulum has to swing to its opposite side until it finds the middle.

Day Two: *The Sex Seminar*

If we cling and attempt to control Sexuality then there's always going to be someone who's completely out of control in their sexuality. We have to begin to understand this energy and what we're doing and trying to accomplish with it.

We're finally communicating and sharing. The fact is, when everybody's sharing, it makes our experience this weekend, like Lynn said, much more profound. This is different than a one-on-one session with a therapist. This is us exploring and utilizing everyone's stories and experiences to create a bond of humanity. A bond that says, "Hey, we're all in this together." And, when human beings come together like this, it always accelerates our understanding and seeing. This is the power of communication. We are witnessing some courageous people, this weekend, putting it all on the line for the sake of communication. We **all** move forward with these types of individuals.

Back in the '60's there was this comedian by the name of Lenny Bruce, who was one of *these people*. If you were to ask any comedian over 40, who his major comedic influences were, one of the first names that would come up would be Lenny Bruce.

Lenny Bruce's comedy was confrontational and alive. He sought to expose the sexual hypocrisy of his time and paid dearly; ultimately paying with his life. He was arrested multiple times for obscenity and fought feverishly in the courts where he eventually lost everything; dying penniless. Yet, because of him, comedians such as Chris Rock, Louie C.K, and Howard Stern give him full credit, at every turn, for allowing them to be able to fully express their thoughts and ideas; especially around sexuality.

This is from a Lenny Bruce stand up routine performed at *Cafe Au Go Go* that was used as evidence against him in an obscenity trial. (*Joseph proceeds to read out loud*)

"To is a Preposition, Come is a Verb"

"To is a preposition.
To is a preposition.
Come is a verb.
To is a preposition.
Come is a verb.
To is a preposition.
Come is a verb, the verb intransitive.
To come.
To come.
I've heard these two words my whole adult life, and as a kid when I thought I was

Day Two: *The Sex Seminar*

sleeping.
To come.
To come.
It's been like a big drum solo.
Did you come?
Did you come?
Good.
Did you come good?
Did you come good?
Did you come good?
Did you come good?
Did you come good?
Did you come good?
Did you come good?
I come better with you, sweetheart, than with anybody in the whole goddamn world.
I really came so good and I came so good 'cause I love you.
I really came so good.
I come better with you, sweetheart, than anyone in the whole world.
I really came so good.
So good.
But don't come in me.
Don't come in me.
Don't come in me
Don't come in me, me, me, me, me, me, me.
Don't come in me, me, me, me, me, me, me.
Don't come in me.
Don't come...in me...in me in me.
Don't come in me, in me...in me.
I can't come.
'Cause you don't love me--that's why you can't come.
I can't come.
I love you, I just can't come; that's my hang-up."

I can't come when I'm loaded, all right?
'Cause you don't love me.

Just what the hell is the matter with you--what has that got to do with loving? I just can't come that's all.
Now if anyone is this room or the world finds those two words decadent, obscene, immoral, amoral, asexual-- the words "to come" really make you feel uncomfortable--if you think I'm rank for saying it to you; you, the beholder, think it's rank for listening to it, you probably can't come. And then you're of no use, because that's the purpose of life, to re-create it."

Joseph: We are taking great strides here to fill our needs to communicate about Sexuality. We need to question and ask and explore. We need to stop thinking we

Day Two: *The Sex Seminar*

already know. We're beginning to see what sexual avoidance is causing the youth of today. What the lack of communication is doing to us. How ignorance is causing us to mutilate ourselves. And then there's the violence we're committing against each other.

It's time to take the power back that we've handed over to the few who have used it for monetary and control purposes. They've monetized Sex. Do you want pornographers, government, or religions to be your primary teachers? Why are you following what others have come up with, without thinking about it yourselves? Individuals like Lenny Bruce have given up their lives so we can, today, freely speak about and explore Sex.

So, thank you for taking a stand by participating in this journey this weekend, we **will** continue to explore.

We will now take our one hour break Enjoy your dinner.

* * * * *

"One must feel sorry for those who have strange tastes, but never insult them. Their wrong is Nature's too; they are no more responsible for having come into the world with tendencies unlike ours than are we for being born bandy-legged or well-proportioned."

Marquis de Sade

Joseph: Welcome back everyone; we hope you had a good dinner. So what's come up for you? What thoughts or reflections have you had?

Susan: I can't stop thinking about Lenny Bruce. I can't believe that they arrested him for something that, by today's standards, would be considered so mild.

Nathan: Yeah, wow! I have trouble with the little repression my job gives me . . . I can't imagine what I would do if the whole world . . . or the government was trying to stop me from talking.

Angie: All I can be with is, like, how repression, from one extreme or the other, can cause such pain . . . I'm seeing that as free as I thought I was . . . like, what I've been actually doing is just going to extremes. Even when I'm rebelling, it's still a reaction to the pressure from the other side.

Joseph: Excellent, Angie. As we've said before, extreme repression creates deviations.

Day Two: *The Sex Seminar*

Okay, anyone else?

Eddie: Why do I get exceptionally turned on by soiling women, is it because of repression?

(Laughter)

Joseph: No, that's because you **are** a pervert.

(More laughter)

No, actually, that may have something to do with it. Why do we give up our power?

... Let's take a closer look at this.

(Index cards are handed out to each member as Lynn leads the group)

Lynn: *Everyone close your eyes and take yourself to a sexual event, act, or situation that you have participated in, that nobody else knows about except you and the other; if there was another person involved.*

Look in your body ... what are the feelings and thoughts you have regarding this experience?

Was it pleasure full, exciting, shameful, guilt filled, fearful ... wonderful?

Now, open your eyes and write down the experience on the index cards we've provided.

When you're finished, please place the cards face down on your desks.

(All the index cards are collected and Joseph adds several cards to the pile for all to see)

Joseph: As you can see, we've added other cards to the group to assure privacy and anonymity. *(Joseph shuffles the cards extensively)*

Okay, we're now going to pass the cards around, **face down**. Please take the top card, place it face down on your laps and then pass them to the next person.

(Joseph is handed the remaining cards)

Day Two: *The Sex Seminar*

Good, now we're going to go around the room and read them out loud and I'd like you to say "I" first, as if you were reading what you wrote. At the end, our assistant will read the remaining cards. . . . Let's begin.

(Each member in the group proceeds to read, out loud, the content of the card)

I sometimes fantasize about having sex with animals.

I masturbated thinking about my sister. I was fifteen.

I had sex with my husband's brother. I've never told anyone.

The last time I had sex was against my will, and I haven't had it since; that was four years ago.

I was eight and I would have a reoccurring nightmare that caused me to sleep with my parents. One night they thought I was sleeping but I heard weird noises and now I know that they were having sex.

I love rough sex, the angrier the better, I like to be flipped over, fucked hard and strangled, hair-pulled, smacked. All of it! But I've only found one man who has been willing to go there with me. And we're no longer together.

I had sex with my sister when we were younger.

I don't get stimulated unless my asshole is played with and my fiancé refuses to do it. I'm afraid my married life is going to SUCK!

I can remember taking showers with my father when I was five and feeling aroused when he would wash me. I still feel shame.

I love when men talk dirty to me during sex, especially the words that degrade me.

When I was thirteen I had a sexual experience with a boyfriend and a couple of his friends. I was too young and regret it all the time.

I tried anal intercourse for the first time because I had heard that it's what guys wanted. It was a horribly painful experience because neither of us were educated on how to do it properly, I needed stitches and have been scared of sex ever since.

I let my dog lick my vagina till I came.

Day Two: *The Sex Seminar*

I had a threesome with my boyfriend at the time and another woman, I was surprised by how much I liked being with the woman but was too embarrassed to speak about it with anyone.

When I was 15, my mother walked in on my boyfriend and I in the "69" position. Our relationship was never the same and we've never talked about it.

I was in high school and I had sent a naked picture to my boyfriend at the time. When we broke up, he betrayed me by sending the photo to all of his friends which ended up spreading around the entire school.

(Several more were read out loud before the assistant read the rest)

Joseph: Okay, first let's take a minute to feel whatever is coming up for you.

. . . so, what was that like for you?

Alex: Holy shit . . . its fuckin' heavy in here!?

(Laughter)

Tami: I just stared at the ground right when everyone was reading. It was hard to be with it.

Alexia: There's a lot of feeling in my body.

Joseph: Yeah. There is going to be more feelings with this particular lab because it causes you to go deeper, to the hidden or repressed. In addition, as you begin to become more aware of what's there, the heavier it will get. We are pushing, unplugging, and unclogging. This needs to happen before the heaviness is released.

So what was it like reading these, hearing other people's situations?

Angie: I judged myself a lot more than I judged anyone else. When I was writing mine down, I was like 'Holy shit! You're disgusting!' Then I finished writing it and I almost felt like I (was) separated from it; when I saw it on the page. Then when everyone else was reading them out, I realized I didn't judge them. Why do I judge myself?

Joseph: It's a benefit, there's a payoff in judging yourself. What's the benefit?

Angie: I guess making yourself better . . . like improving.

Joseph: No, quite the opposite.

Day Two: *The Sex Seminar*

Angie: Oh, like staying stuck in my shit . . .

Joseph: So. What's beneficial about that?

Angie: It's comfortable . . .

Joseph: What else? What does it cause others to do if you judge yourself?

Nisha: They won't judge you . . .

Reese: They don't have to.

Joseph: They don't have to! "Let me kick my ass, so you don't," AND then you get them to take care of you, so you don't have to grow up. Judging yourself is a good way not to grow up.

Angie: So if it's super hidden, I guess if it's something that you never share . . .

Joseph: What's super hidden?

Angie: Well I mean the act of judging yourself and as a result never having to grow up and people taking care of you. It's not like it's something that, you know, I or any of us have obviously ever been really super open about. If you say to somebody, "I hate my boobs!" They'll be like, "Oh, your boobs are great!" or something like that, you know it's like fishing for compliments, it's just something that you don't talk about.

Joseph: Stop telling me about "we" and "us." Tell me about **you.**

Angie: Something that I don't talk about, something that I've never spoken about before. It's like, if I can be . . . yeah, if it's something that I've kept that suppressed and that hidden, then I can stay comfortable in that . . . and I can stay stuck in that.

Joseph: Yes, and it's hard to stay stuck, now that it's out there and on paper; out in the cosmos. Anyone else . . . what was is like hearing these and speaking it as if it were your own?

Nathan: I found it interesting that everyone had a tremble in their voices. Every single person's voices were trembling as they were reading it. And I had a hard ass time reading it.

Joseph: Why, do you think?

Nathan: Well probably because they know that it's hard to expose their darkness; their darkness that nobody knows.

Joseph: In that moment we are all in the same boat, aren't we?

These experiences are **all** of ours. We need to share these experiences whether we are scared, hurt, or excited about them. This is **our sex** . . . and we shared it.

Nathan: Yeah, it was pretty obvious. Like everybody's voice was trembling . . . I was so fucking happy mine was like four words!

(Laughter)

I don't know if I would have gotten through it, because watching everybody, and they were like, "I can't read this, I can't read this . . ." and I was like "Oh my God, am I going to be able to see?" But we went around the room and Alex expressed the heaviness of the room and like, hell yeah, it's fucking heavy in here! Let's open a window!

Joseph: Can you see that it's not just a figure of speech when I say that this belongs to all of you? We are connected in all of this, your shame is my shame and I accept that, and I'm sorry that you've had to live that shameful experience. I'm sorry that we have to be set up in a situation, cosmically and historically, that has us be in so much shame, guilt, and confusion before we can wake up. It belongs to all of us. And, today, we've alleviated a lot of it for each other . . . anybody else? What was it like, hearing it, reading it?

Kelly: I didn't want to read it because I didn't want to embarrass anyone. The caretaker in me showed up and I didn't want to hurt anyone's feelings. I didn't want them to feel sad, or ashamed, or embarrassed . . .

Joseph: Quite the opposite, if they're here and they're in this healing process, then you are actually doing the best thing possible for them. It's as if you're a nurse assisting a doctor. The real hurt is that they've been sitting with this their whole lives, that's what hurts. By the way, know that's what's underneath your *caretaking* is that you don't want **your** feelings hurt.

Kelly: Yeah, I was going to say that. But I feel a bit lighter because there's something that I did get off my chest!

Joseph: Oddly enough, even though you don't know who said what, you feel more connected. You don't need to know all the bullshit of the story to connect. All you need is to stop hiding and be honest. When we do that, connection naturally happens. And with that connection, feelings increase. Like with Alexia, you are stimulated and invigorated just by connecting with each other's experiences and pains.

Lynn: Why don't we need to know the story?

Tami: In regards of who was reading what, it didn't matter. My heart was palpitating and I wasn't even worried about what I wrote, it was just the feeling. I was feeling anxiety . . . I could feel the intensity of the emotion in the room.

Lynn: So when you look at each other, can you see what feelings are already there? You don't even need to attach the story to it. That's what we're all feeling. The heaviness, what you call heaviness, it's the shame, it's the guilt, the fear . . .

Joseph: Again, 93% of all communication is non-verbal. You are always reading each other's non-verbal signals. You take it in like you're reading a book. You take it in through all your five senses. You are all capable of getting each other's experiences, to some degree.

What else does this bring up for you? Can you tell us what question provoked this lab we call "The Deviance Lab?"

Claudia: You asked us why we give up our power.

Joseph: So, what answer did you come up with?

Alexia: We feel shame?

Joseph: You're answering a question with a question; it's not an answer.

Parisa: Keeping a secret?

Joseph: You're doing the same thing.

Parisa: Keeping a secret.

Joseph: Keeping a secret . . . what about it?

Parisa: People keep secrets because they are shameful . . .

Joseph: Don't tell me about **people**, tell me about what you think! Speak in the first person. We avoid our feelings and ourselves when we consistently speak in the second person. Think about it. Why do you want to speak in the second person? That means you have just *once* removed yourself. When you say we, us, them, or people you're speaking in the second person. So you're not communicating to me directly. You're not! Know that about yourself. When you say we, us, them, or people, you're no longer communicating directly. It's like you've attached a splitter to your communication . . . which weakens the transmission of your information.

Recently, we were having trouble with our cable and the first question the cable technician asked was "Do you have a splitter in the house; is there a splitter where your cable is hooked up?" As long as there is something in between your direct communication, you will experience a loss of power.

When we, something, or someone moves us from direct communication, we lose power and our communication diminishes instantly. That's how we hide; we go into the second person so others don't think that we're talking about ourselves. Can you take a chance of owning your opinion, your feelings, and your thoughts? We all laugh when someone does it in the third person; don't we? You would laugh if I said, "Joseph thinks you guys are trying to hide behind the second person. Joseph really thinks that you should think of communicating more directly." You'll smile at this just like I do when you speak in the second person; it's funny to me. Lynn and I know instantly, you're trying to hide. Know that! When you choose not to speak in the first person we get less of you. Why would you want to do that? I want to hear from you! What you say truly matters!

Lynn: You've all been doing that quite a bit this weekend, as you speak of Sex.

Claudia: Kids don't do that.

Joseph: No they don't, they're not hiding yet. They *play* hide and seek but they don't do it seriously. We do it seriously; we've forgotten to play!

If you're doing it playfully that's a different story. But you're not playing; you guys are serious about this. You're so habituated; you don't realize that you're producing a muffled communication. You don't realize it is hindering and depleting your message, and when you add a mumble on top of it, or a swear word under your breath . . . then you really cut off communication. This is *how* we give up our power.

Now, *why* we give up our power can be easily traced back to all the shame, guilt, embarrassments and uncertainties we carry from past experiences, lack of education, and ignorance. This leads us to feeling incapable, which in turn, causes us to get scared and run to some form of mommy or daddy, some form of authority. There are plenty of people who want to take power and they'll swoop right in if you give them the opening.

Day Two: *The Sex Seminar*

There are religions and governments that would like nothing better than to absorb your power. They represent themselves as parent figures offering you security and safety at the cost of your freedom; and if you feel incapable you'll gladly comply. This is what we do, historically, in times of wars, illnesses, and plagues; in times of any crisis.

What do you make of all this? What do you make of the lab . . . and what does all this have to do with Sex?

Nisha: I'm seeing that since Sex is bigger than us, any repression of it causes us to have distorted experiences. To make matters worse, we then lock them away!

Joseph: Very good!

How much power can you lose with this type of sexual repression; holding back these sexual secrets?

Susan: Too much!

Joseph: Though these shares were done anonymously, was there any sense of judgment from the group? Is anybody here judging anybody harshly? Did you feel, if you can be honest, any judgment towards anything you heard? What did you feel about the things you heard; anyone?

Susan: Compassion.

Tami: Empathy.

Mercedes: Big fuckin whoop!

Joseph: What do you mean by that? Like, "You poor thing" or "It's not such a big deal?"

Mercedes: So what? Get over it!

Joseph: Get over it?

Mercedes: Yeah . . . it's no big deal

Parisa: I understood them all except for one, the one with the angry sex . . . it scared me. I don't remember it fully because it's something that I don't wish to experience.

Joseph: What were you scared of?

Parisa: Uuuh?

Simon: The anger or the violence?

Parisa: Yeah, something like that.

Joseph: The violent sex?

Parisa: Yeah, that is something I don't wish to experience, so this is the only one where I had a hard time listening. I hope I never experience something like that.

Joseph: I'm sorry that you have . . .

Simon: I felt sad that most of these things happened to children that didn't know what was going on because of lack of education, or people were doing things to them, and they couldn't defend themselves. So I felt compassion for those people. It's a shame that happened to them, and they didn't have any knowledge.

Joseph: Exactly, and for those of you who continue to have these types of experiences, you need to know you're only carrying on what you were taught in childhood.

Claudia: I felt the same way as Simon because having a son, if something happened to him and he felt he couldn't come to me, I would hate myself.

Joseph: Right, because if you have the *door* wide open and you make it really easy for him, then he should feel like he could come to you. But if you're blocked, repressed or worse, then it might be hard for him to approach you.

So what would it take to remain open? What would you have to do, or what are you doing this weekend, to help you stay open?

Claudia: Well, I'm here. I don't really have the pieces together yet . . .

Lynn: Well what have you been doing here?

Claudia: Just here to feel it . . .

Joseph: Not, why are you here, what have you been doing since you've been here?

Claudia: I've been listening a lot, sharing a little, reflecting a lot . . . and, uh, starting to feel.

Day Two: *The Sex Seminar*

Joseph: That's great, that's how it's done. You share, you reflect, you listen! Hopefully you'll start learning, you'll get different perspectives, and you'll focus on this single subject to increase your knowledge and your IQ. That's where new options are born. Each day offers an opportunity to grow so you don't have to live and die with what happens today. **This** is the process, and you're spending these two and a half days, accelerating your growth.

The other thing that you're doing is working in and through a group. When you engage in this type of work with others it, naturally, accelerates your growth exponentially! Everything you process is processed together, whether you're aware of it or not. So, even those of you who sit here and say nothing, know that you are affecting and being affected by the group.

Cesar Millan usually works with the dogs he trains in the comfort of his client's homes and neighborhoods. But on occasion he'll come across a highly troubled dog that necessitates additional external assistance. So what does he do? He takes these dogs to his "dog pound." This is a place on his property where a collection of his dogs, who he has trained, live together. He places these dogs into "the pound" and what you see next is remarkable. The dogs themselves begin to naturally confront, discipline and bond with these troubled animals until they fall in line. The same thing happens to us *animals* in a group setting.

You guys make our jobs easier by just being together. Your spoken and non-spoken contribution to each other's processes is immeasurable. Yes, fear, guilt, shame, anger, and sadness all come up, and it's difficult, but we're all going through it together, aren't we?

Alex: Yeah, I feel more connected to the group, now, than since we started.

Joseph: Well you look more awake now. You looked petrified up till now.

Alex: Oh!?

(Laughter)

Joseph: And you might just be reflecting the group, you follow?

Alex: Okay.

Joseph: Because we're more connected then you think. This is your stuff, this is mine, and everything that we're talking about and going through this weekend is ours; it's us. I would do what you do in your life, if I were in your shoes! Why? How can I say, with such certainty, that I would have done what you all have done in your lives . . . if I were in your shoes? Why can I say that? I would do EXACTLY the same thing.

Jeremy: Because you weren't prepared.

Joseph: No . . .

Angie: Because if you were in my shoes you'd be me.

Joseph: Exactly, and I'd have your perspective, and your insight, and your lack of insight and I could only do what you do; so how the hell can I judge you? If you're judging me, you're not in my shoes. So where are you? And where are you when you're *self judging.* You can't be in your own shoes in those moments! Whose shoes are you in then? . . . It might turn out that you're wearing your mommy's high heels.

Let's take a break.

* * * * *

Joseph: Welcome back! So tell me more about the lab.

Mercedes: It felt like, it was too much like, a pity party at times. Like, "Oh that's horrible," but I don't think a lot of us would even be here or be interested in taking a Sex seminar and doing things to better ourselves, in exploring this, if our sex lives had been, you know, "perfect." What's the *use* of even doing this then?

Joseph: Ton's of use! Ton's of use if your sex life was great, because then we could explore where else Sexual energy could take you!

Mercedes: But if there's nothing wrong . . .

Joseph: We're not here for right or wrong, we're here to grow!

Mercedes: If it ain't broke don't fix it, right?

Joseph: That's limited. So if I've come this far . . . don't tamper?

Mercedes: Well, some people do that.

Joseph: We're not talking about "should" or "should not" or "right" or "wrong." We're saying there's capacity for growth--*always*. I'm not going to put a bullet in my head because I decided "I've gone far enough, let's end it now! Why fuck around, it might be bad tomorrow!" Isn't that what you're suggesting? Or to hold on to the status quo since you've reached a certain piece of contentment. And when I say piece I don't mean P-E-A-C-E. I'm saying "Why stop there, we can keep growing."

The point for most of us is to get our awareness out of the basement and onto the ground level so we can finally function in a healthier manner; then you can grow something! The presumption is that all your stuff is stopping you from reaching the sky. No, it's stopping you from even starting! In other words, what's pitiful about all of this--and it deserves pity--is that many of you haven't even started living sexually yet! That's absolutely pitiful for us! Because you have to see that life is like a structure with at least seven possible levels, three below ground, ground level and three above ground, and we haven't even come up from the underground, yet. Until we do that we cannot live in any of the upper floors.

So even if we were on the second floor, well you can still grow yourself to the 19th floor. Why place limits on an infinite energy? The sad part is that the majority of us still live underground, sexually. We have to hide in the dark, we hide our Sexuality . . . do you get it now? We live underground, all of us! If one of us is below then we all are below. Some of you might think you're above ground . . . that won't last because, eventually, we'll drag you down with the rest of us. We're trying really hard to come above ground but there are forces opposing this. These forces include our animal nature, institutionalized religion, the righteous and government, to name a few. These forces, which appear to suppress us, actually help us to strengthen ourselves through this very fight. And once we've strengthened ourselves, once we've come above ground we will see, and come to the realization that, *we've been fighting ourselves the whole time*!

Therefore, we haven't even started because we're tied together like two people in a three legged race. And, if we're in opposition then we'll wind up only going in circles. We're not advancing, because "as long as you are stuck in anything I'm stuck with you, and I'm not going anywhere until I get you out of here." What good is it for me to go to heaven if I can't take you with me? So, when I look at all of you, I see how shitty it is that you've had to go through what you've gone through because of ignorance. We devote our lives to helping uncover this shit for ALL of us. It's not enough for me to be born, achieve a certain level of consciousness, and think, "I'm good now," and leave the rest of you behind. What fucking good is that? Didn't I build myself upon your shoulders and the shoulders of our ancestors? And I'm just going to now cut and run? Noooo . . . I can't turn my back on you; Lynn can't turn her back on you, because we ARE you. We've been through the same or worse, and now we're doing it together. I started this sexual exploration with little help and Lynn experienced the same. Then we got together and helped each other and now, years later, we're all working together. How wonderful!

I understand that feeling that wants to *cut it off so we can move on*. It's born from a feeling that is capable of making us stop from going forth. I'm also completely compassionate to that. So when Mercedes, said "Get over it," I'm with her. I appreciate it for her. That's where she has to be now; maybe not in a year from now, but now. I wouldn't suggest, otherwise, until she can build some muscle to take on whatever she needs to *get over*. (Addressing Mercedes) When you're saying that you're not speaking to us . . .

Mercedes: . . . I'm speaking to myself . . .

Joseph: Right . . . and we are you and we're here with you, and we want that for you, too. We want you to get over it . . .

Mercedes: But that's the only way for anyone. I mean, that's the gift of having the experience. You feel ashamed and then you get over it.

Joseph: There is no "That's the *only way*." There are many ways. There are infinite ways, and there are many additional ways that we are learning and experiencing daily!

We are finding new ways of healing, growing, sharing, and overcoming things. Thank goodness we live in an infinite universe, with infinite options and infinite directions to be lost and found in. But, if I were to follow your line of thinking and box myself in by proclaiming "This is how the world is," then there would only be finite ways in which I could work things out. But if I keep growing and expanding, more ways will show up! More ways to deal with cancer, more ways to deal with poverty, more ways to deal with hunger and homelessness, with our . . . ignorance; our options grow as we do. I've increased the ways I deal with and resolve my emotions.

When I was younger, I would *handle* my anger by punching walls. Finding holes in the walls of my apartments was commonplace. I would convince myself that it didn't matter because "I'll patch it up before I move out." And my excuse was, "I'm not punching you!" I would say that to my girlfriends! Meanwhile I was scaring the shit out of them . . . and I was oblivious to that. I even did it when my oldest daughter was young not realizing the true trauma and violence that I was imposing upon her.

Today I communicate, I express my anger and frustrations in words before they get past the tipping point, or I simply *feel* them and *release* them. These are just some of the ways I've discovered to manage my emotions. I no longer get it all over everyone. There are options other than what we've learned and experienced in childhood. If there weren't, I'd be dead today.

I've been in some very dark corners at times in my life, with no one there to help, wondering why I should stay alive. And then I'd remember what I experienced and learned from my meditations and reflections. I'd remember as long as this world, which I was a part of, was infinite and had energies in it that I could access to help me heal and grow, I could then . . . *hang on for one more day*.

Sexual energy is one of those energies. It's an energy that I first used destructively before I discovered how to surrender to it constructively. First I *used* Sex for validation and control through women; then, I used sex for relief through drugs. Don't kid yourself, drug use is fully sexual. When I was inhaling drugs or sticking them in me, it was no different than intercourse for me. And, like intercourse, it was orgasmic. Like intercourse it relieved me, till the next time. I found that drugs gave me the same thing I was getting from women, which wasn't much since I had no idea how to connect other than from a place of self indulgence, without the hassles. I was able to experience the high I got from intercourse without having to deal with another person's problems. Drugs became my woman; and it was sexual! Since I couldn't control Sex through women I decided to do it through drugs. That was the only way I knew how to cope then; it was a viable option from my childhood. And if I hadn't looked further, if I hadn't chosen to grow with life, if I hadn't surrendered to Sexual energy . . . creative energy . . . I would not be standing here today.

I keep growing, Mercedes, for not just myself but all of us. And as we continue to explore Sex, as we continue to share our experiences, as we continue to join together, we will grow and we will leave here *larger* than when we came in. Insights and perspectives, through the eyes of others can only expand and grow you.

Lynn: For most of us, the only way we've known how to deal with our pain is either through repression or deep self-pity. So, I understand that you're tired of the self-pity; but it has its place. And we promise that we will continue to look at better alternatives.

Firstly, we have to re-experience the pain and repression that has placed us where we're at, then we'll be able to move to the next stage, which is releasing the pain.

Joseph: It's in deviances that we play out our pain. It's in these deviances where we hide many of our unresolved issues and it's the repression or over indulgence of these deviances that have caused our issues to remain unresolved. So, as we get them out we can begin to resolve them, and sometimes they resolve themselves just by getting them out. We haven't even remotely, figured out all the wonderful uses of Sex. We only engage in Sex, superficially.

Lynn: Most people who come to Joseph and me with sexual issues find that their problems rarely have anything to do with Sex. Sex is just the symptom.

Eddie: How about fetishes . . . are they deviances?

Joseph: Fetishes and deviances go hand in hand. All fetishes are a result of repression which causes deviances. We're not saying they're bad or good, they can be great fun . . . great FUN

(Laughter)

. . . but they are a result of the repression of Sexual energy. The purpose of fetishes is to release and balance repression and deviances and there are healthy and unhealthy ways of going about this.

A healthy way of exploring deviances is with your lover. You could play your *fetish games* with a person you trust and or love. It relieves so much, and starts the healing! Or you could do it in an, ultimately, unhealthy way, which is with a stranger. Because of the natural lack of care and love we have with strangers, it can worsen our challenges. We think that playing out our fetishes with strangers immunes us from judgment, when in fact . . . it exacerbates our own self judgment. There's no healing going on, because there is no real care to help in the healing. Care is the prerequisite feeling needed for healing to begin.

As our relationships grow, and we begin to share our fantasies, we give each other the opportunity to unlock sexual energy. This, in turn, helps the lovers to help each other heal and grow. Their bond then perpetuates the energy and desire for greater sexual exploration. The mutual utilization of this primal energy is one of the greatest gifts relationships offer us! Fetishes are wonderful tools that help us unblock the hidden and the painful . . . in a playful way. What do you make of this?

Simon: I've never thought of them that way, I thought they were wrong in some way and that's why they excited me.

Joseph: Thanks for speaking in the first person.

Day Two: *The Sex Seminar*

You know about heart bypasses, right? Well it was recently found that there were some individuals who had clogged arteries who, upon surgery, were found to have had additional channels out from the heart. In other words, they found that the heart . . . the body created, for lack of a better word, other arteries. The body built other ways to stay alive, to manage, until help arrived. We do the same, sexually, through fetishes. We create other outlets when we can't do it directly.

So by all means, play out your fetishes; just look for healthy ways to do it. Look for people who care and can share your passion with your particular outlet. When we choose strangers to do this with, we take the risk of compounding our pain. Just play! Whatever it is, you want to do fluffy, furry sex, put on giant rabbit suits, you want to be in a giant crib with diapers, go right ahead! Play! Who cares? Play! We don't even know what is causing us to want to do that! That will come later, don't worry about it. Play! Find someone who you can trust and play with, just like you did as kids. It's like you said, "Kids don't do this, kids don't hide," they play. That's what we need to begin to do in our sex lives to heal this. Like kids, we need play!

Let's take a break.

* * * * *

Joseph: Welcome back. Parisa?

Parisa: I'm not very playful. In fact I'm usually quite serious in my approach to sex. The lab showed me that. I think for me, the lab made me feel a lot heavier and it was actually pretty overwhelming. I couldn't even hear the stories people were reading about after a certain point.

Joseph: Ah, very good, so just notice that. Don t build a story around it. Just be present to that; just notice that when you've reached your pain threshold your attention shuts down.

You see, what's good about this is you now have proof that your psyche will protect you; it will shut when it gets too "heavy." Therefore, you can take risks; it's safe. Because you know it will shut down if you go too far, anyway, so then you can invite into your relationships, more conversation. You can trust your psyche to protect you! It just did, when it became too much. Your bottle was overflowing with information and you shut down, that's okay! That's normal. Don't worry. So, now you know for a fact, people can tell you anything and it won't destroy you. Whether we are sharing it or receiving it, we think it's going to do something to us. No. You'll shut down at a certain point if it's too much.

Day Two: *The Sex Seminar*

Lynn: Do you know what the feeling was before you shut down?

Parisa: I felt a lot of anxiety.

Lynn: Fear?

Parisa: Yeah . . . physical, very physical.

Joseph: Okay, so just breathe, don't make a story about it. The anxiety is from what you wrote about on the card. And it's bringing up and out . . . stuff. Know this is **you** beginning to heal!

You shut down because you have something else to do, you have to take care and heal this. That is the best you can do, for now. The rest of you are helping Parisa; you're holding the fort so she can be with what's she's in. That's what we do; we hold the fort for each other until the other is strong enough to join in.

We all come here in different grades; most of you are preschooler or kindergarteners . . . first grade, tops. This earthly plane is elementary school. If you knew that you were actually in preschool or first grade . . . if you knew the truth . . . you'd be laughing right now and you wouldn't be taking yourself so seriously. You'd just think, "Oh fuck, okay . . . let me have some fun. Yeah, I don't know. I want to know. Maybe I can get to second grade before I die." This is pre-school, kindergarten stuff!

Lynn: Whatever everyone is feeling from this exercise, know that it's exactly what you need to be feeling. And as it passes, it expands you a little more so that, the next time, you'll be able to take in even more. This is the process of building and expanding your consciousness.

Joseph: You're growing your emotional muscles, and the next time you'll be able to take in things much easier and process it much faster. You'd speak up five minutes earlier and if it continued, we would be talking about things that wouldn't normally come up till the end of day three.

It takes work to build emotional muscles and that's what we're doing here this weekend. Those who **are** communicating are building a little faster. Those of you that are silent and haven't said anything all weekend, you're building also; just at a slower pace. But it's okay, because this is still pre-school. You're not going to talk that much, you're a little afraid, mommies not here; you're trying to get adjusted to being with the other kids, and you're just waiting for naptime.

Parisa: Hmm!

Day Two: *The Sex Seminar*

(Laugher)

Joseph: So once we get that, we'll realize that it's okay. We don't have to be a graduate student, we are kindergarteners. If you realize this, you'll suddenly have more compassion, more understanding; you'll be more chill. We'll be more open to what we're doing and not doing. "Oh, you shit your pants? That's okay, let's get you washed up! No biggy!"

Just look at the things that we've experienced, that we've heard today, and we wonder why we feel all this pressure? We have good reason! Look at what we were born into, the ourstory that we were born from. Main Street and Vine . . . now you know a little more about where Main and Vine is. Now we can see "Oh okay, I'm being a bit hard on myself here. There's a lot to learn and understand, still." And I understand those of you with children are in a panic about ruining their lives; don't worry about fucking them up! Like we always say, "*It not about whether we're going to fuck up our children or not, but about how badly we're going to fuck them up.*"

(Laughter)

We keep telling you that you're going to fuck them up; we're just trying to learn how to do it as little as possible. That's all, because we're not perfect.

Nathan: I find it interesting, the whole thing about Sex being infinite . . . I really like that because there's no pressure, then. I always have things to work on. I just have to not limit myself to the box.

Joseph: Well put. You see, we're not even told when we're going to die, at least not most of us. Not knowing helps reduce the pressure we place on ourselves. If we knew exactly when we were going to die, we'd be like the characters in the movie *In Time*. We would be panicking, trying to steal back some time and acting just plain crazy!

Simon: The movie, *Big Fish*, actually says the opposite because the main character knows how much time he has to live, so he can just relax.

Joseph: Well, there was more to it than that but Tim Burton's *Big Fish* did, reportedly, give actor and writer, Spaulding Gray permission to commit suicide. He was very, very ill, physically and mentally but couldn't bring himself to ending it all until he watched it.

We all have a terminal illness, we all **will** die; but we don't allow ourselves to think about it in order to live without panic. It's very difficult to inspire **ourselves**, knowing time is running out! We'll just harden our arteries with this worry and we'll start draining the *hour glass*. But don't confuse this with taking a laid back approach; we're talking about taking an expansive approach.

The more expansive, the more I breathe, the more I breathe . . . the slower I age. I start actually expanding my life when I breathe more slowly and deeply. I take in more life. I get wider and, ultimately, I live longer. So when you worry, you're cutting your life short just like when you're smoking cigarettes. Both have us shorten our breath. So breathe! Know you have time and do your thing; and know that we're all in this together.

When you do this you slow up thought; your thoughts deepen. You become able to see the repression and the fears that imprison you. It's not until you realize that you're in prison can you know what imprisons you. At that point, you can begin to call out the systems that have entrapped you. You can call out the parents, the culture, and the governments. What happens after that depends on what stage of ourstory you're in.

Let's take a listen to this Lenny Bruce audio from a show he performed immediately after returning from being arrested on obscenity charges.

(Group listens to audio as Lenny does a routine on oral sex using the words "blah, blah" in place of cock sucking and cocksucker)

Mercedes: I thought it was brilliant how he countered their repression with his "Blah, Blah" routine. It just shows how we put too much emphasis on the word rather than its meaning.

Angie: What the fuck! Why can't we just speak, why can't we speak what's on our mind?

Joseph: You can. You just have to take a stand.

As far as we are concerned no one's going to stop us from communicating. Your deviances, your unfortunate situations, and your pains don't have to stop you from communicating, either. Sexual energy needs to flow like water and we can help ourselves by assisting it. You can count on this power to provide you the strength to do it; to give you the strength to stand for your own Sexual expression, and that of everyone else. When it doesn't flow, again like water, it erodes whatever is in its way, including us. Anyone or anything that represses our Sexual expression can only do so with our permission. We give repression room to grow when we are afraid to confront, to question, and to look.

But we're creative, we'll find a way. It seems crazy today, that Lenny Bruce couldn't say cock sucking . . . insane right? But it's because of him that comedians can speak their minds today. As we said before, he died miserably. He died penniless, going to court and fighting the institutionalized repression which eventually took the life and comic genius right out of him.

There have been many who have sacrificed for our Sexual freedoms. Even individuals like Hugh Hefner and Gloria Steinem, who didn't see eye to eye, paved the path for greater Sexual communication, expression, and exploration. It has become our inheritance and birthright!

Mercedes: We don't have as much care for men as we do women around sexual abuse. What do you think that causes for men?

Joseph: Well, anyone who is uncared for, who's given less compassion eventually becomes a problem for all of us. If you don't take care of the uncared man then he becomes the abuser, an abusee always becomes the abuser.

Nathan: So, how do you do that?

Joseph: You care for him, you listen to what he has to say, you set up systems of healing, meetings, seminars, and you give them outlets to grow beyond these crimes. Presently, it's pitiful what is offered to men, especially since they are the ones who commit the majority of sexually related crimes. We need to attend to our boys like we are now doing with our girls.

Lynn: I was just reading a story of a man who voluntarily went and asked to have his penis cut off because of his uncontrollable violent thoughts. He complained about how he couldn't stop thinking of wanting to rape and even murder women. So that was his only outlet.

Kelly: What happened?

Lynn: He went and had it cut off.

Simon: I watched a documentary about a similar thing as well; it becomes their only option after a while.

Joseph: Yes, unfortunate that we haven't come up with enough options, or support for the proper options. We still haven't gotten to the point where we can make sense of this type of thing.

I was a single parent for 19 years and I was extra watchful and careful as I gave my daughter love. Because it was just the two of us, I made sure that her physical boundaries were well protected. The problem was I never considered her emotional boundaries.

Because I was a single parent, and it would work the same way if you're in a loveless marriage or sexless marriage, I became emotionally attached to my daughter. I would speak with her, at times, about my relationships and other emotional issues, as if she were a mate. I made her my emotional spouse without realizing it. Since my mother had done the same thing with me I never saw anything wrong with it. *Also know that the gender of the child doesn't make a difference; mothers marry their daughters, not just their sons, and fathers marry their sons, not just their daughters.* It wasn't till her late teens that I realized I had caused her emotional damage. I had made her my emotional spouse and I had to divorce her emotionally. This painful process of separation, for both of us, took years to resolve.

Children need two parents, if for nothing else, to get two different primary perspectives on life. A single parent can only supply one primary perspective. We're doing basic math here. Two is better than one, assuming, of course, that we're dealing with two halfway decent parents.

We turn our kids into emotional buddies rather than be their parents. I was being her dad when it came to everything physically, but not always emotionally. Not when I was inundating her with my problems. A lot of you here know what it's like to be that child, and a lot of you know what it's like to be that parent. All of it is from lack of education, lack of knowledge, and lack of awareness. We are just beginning to understand that sexual needs aren't just physical. When we avoid or don't take care of our *sexual-emotional needs* we leave ourselves and our children vulnerable to an inappropriate emotional marriage. Sexual energy has to move and flow. It's not going to stop just because you're not managing your sexual-emotional requirements.

If you try to hide from Sex you're going to start dying because Sex is what keeps us alive. Sexual energy, or creative energy, keeps you alive, whether you get it directly through another human being, or you source it from everything around you. Creative energy allows us to keep growing and creating our bodies and minds. It supplies us with new ways of thinking . . . new alternatives. That's why most relationships **do** have a chance to grow and heal if they want. We just have to do the work!

Nathan: That's where the choice comes in.

Joseph: Right. So we have to become aware of our deviances, we have to bring them out; you need to know the ourstory that created the deviance. Our most recent ancestors were the extremely repressed Puritans and Victorians. In their society, illegal prostitution and deviant practices flourished. Women were second class citizens whose Sexual powers were repressed. How do you think that influenced us . . . ?

Nisha: In my culture, I'm East Indian; women's sexual expression is still repressed compared to men. I never really understood why women have to be so repressed?!

Joseph: This is a consistent pattern, throughout ourstory, repressing women's sexual powers. And the reason is that men are afraid of your power. As an old teacher of mine once explained, "Sex is a woman's domain of power, like violence is a man's." He suggested we consider what would happen if a woman went into a bar looking for sex versus a man. Who would get it first?

Group: A woman!

Joseph: Right, then he suggested the same but exchanged sex for violence. In other words, what would happen if a woman went into a bar looking for a fight versus a man? Who would get it first?

Group: A man!

Joseph: Right again. These are our separate domains of domination.

This is why men have repressed women throughout the centuries. You find it to an extreme in a lot of Eastern countries. Men's fear of women's Sexual powers has been the source of major atrocities done to women! They know that women have all this power! They birth life, they can sustain sex by far longer than men, and they can experience pleasure beyond what men are physically capable of experiencing. A woman can easily have a man fall powerless through Sex. That is why men do everything to repress them, to convince them of the contrary. They know that if they let them loose--even a little bit--they would lose complete control over them! And they know they "can't wear out a hole with a pole," so what happens when "I'm tired? Who's going to take over?" When a woman's Sexual energy has broken loose, when you get her past that point. When she gets to the point where she's finally expressed, a man gets scared because, suddenly, you're riding a wild bronco and she's full of Sexual power, which you cannot control. Men know this. They really do know this.

So, what to do? I'd rather unite with her, "I'll get you started and you take me the rest of the way! I'll take you to the door but you take me through the other side." Men need women in order to experience this expanded Sexual consciousness. If you're afraid of expanding, if you're afraid of surrendering to this power that has you lose yourself, that has your ego feel small and insignificant, then you're going to blame and shut down the pathway to this consciousness. And that is what women are. They're a pathway to another state of consciousness we can now call Sex; a timeless, egoless consciousness. We need women to get there. We need each other, like yin needs yang and yang needs yin.

Nathan: How about homosexuals?

Joseph: In the case of homosexuality, you have to consider that there is always interplay of yin & yang in their sex lives.

Let's take a break.

* * * * *

"I have this weird thing that if I sleep with someone, they're going to take my creativity from me through my vagina."
Lady Gaga

Lynn: Welcome back, remember the share about the woman who liked to be fucked hard, hair pulled, etcetera?

Joseph: Etcetera? Don't stop there, remind us of the details!

(Laughter)

Lynn: That's a great example of what Joseph is saying . . . of the male energy being the power of *violence* and the woman owning the power of *Sex*. That was a perfect example of the two powers.

We don't know how that turned out, but if they were both into it . . . and not afraid of the force and power, then it was probably very enjoyable for the both of them. That might have been exactly what they wanted to expand into. We can transcend into the realm of Sex by utilizing and combining both our powers!

Day Two: *The Sex Seminar*

Joseph: If you're exploring fetishes and dealing with somebody you trust and care about, that could be a very positive experience. It's chancy when you're attempting it with a stranger.

Lynn: Then it could go bad real fast. Not bad as in right and wrong, but harmful.

Joseph: So any final thoughts from anyone? What do you make of this day and a half so far? What did you think you were going to be getting out of this, versus what you are getting?

Tami: Based on what we just spoke about, I'm realizing that, in my relationship, I'm clearly the unhealthy one. He's actually very Sexually open and honest about his fantasies and what he wants. He knows his issues and the abandonment he felt from his mother. I've been judging him like, "Holy shit, he's really fucked up," but now I see that he's the healthier one because he's been expressing himself. I've been the really repressed one, going, "What the fuck is that about?" It was a safety thing for me and I was like, "Maybe you should go see Joseph and Lynn and then we'll talk about it."

(Laughter)

. . . So I'm seeing that it can be healthy if it's trusting and caring.

Joseph: Absolutely, as long as you keep the lines of communication open and allow yourself full expression, then you can keep the flow of Sexual energy going. Communication is the key to working with Sexual energy.

Lynn: And that can lead you to experience something that you might not know.

Kelly: It's definitely helping me . . . I have two sets of kids, my teenagers and my younger children. With my older ones, I feel guilty because I didn't teach them enough. Jeremy and I have taught our son that its "Cool to shag chicks." Jeremy thinks its okay for our son to bring girls to his room, but it's not okay for our daughters to bring boys. I really haven't taken a stand, one way or the other, on the matter, which is horrible of me, I know . . . um . . .

Lynn: I'll stop you there; it's not horrible of you. It was naive of you, at best, and ignorant of you at worst. From what I know of you, it was clearly the former. You just didn't have enough knowledge at the time.

Kelly: So here I am and I'm seeing how awesome this will be for my two younger girls so I can teach them in a much healthier way. Plus, of course, I'm learning for myself . . . but it's going to greatly benefit my children.

Joseph: I appreciate that but you want to know that it's going to benefit you more than your children; it needs to because you are their leader. The stronger you are, the more you'll have to give them.

Your participation this weekend is going to alter you, which will give all your kids an opportunity to change. The older ones will see how you've shifted by watching how differently you're treating the younger ones. This will inform them anew about you. They will know they can grow because you have. This is how a family can continue to grow.

Lynn: One of the things that Joseph and I did, was we went back to our kids, who were now older, and said to them, "Listen, this is what I didn't tell you and I forgot about this, and I actually said this to you . . . I can't believe I told you that, but that's what I believed then . . . and I apologize because that's way off, but this is what I found to be the truth." It was a very powerful experience for our family.

Jeremy: So, it's not too late to say something to my kids?

Joseph: No it's not too late, but make sure you give them room to absorb what you share with them. They may not accept what you have to say, immediately. If you say "Hey look, I screwed up," don't expect them to say "Great thanks for telling me." No they may still be angry. Give them time to process it. They may be angry for a while but they'll work it out with the room you've provided them. That's what parents do at their best; they support their children's changes. They become the stabilizing force that children need to grow upon.

Simon: Jeremy can I ask you if you, like your wife, are seeing this thing with your son differently now? Has this changed anything, or do you still feel the same as far as your daughter's are concerned?

Jeremy: Well, I mean, for a father having girls and boys it is very different.

Joseph: The difference is safety. Remember, parents want to protect.

Jeremy: Yeah, I would still be the same!

Simon: I was just wondering, I don't think there's any right or wrong in it . . .

Jeremy: Yeah. No I haven't changed yet.

Joseph: Jeremy, we start wherever we're at and with whatever we can understand, and we keep looking.

I kept prying around certain difficult sexual subjects until I was finally okay with it. There were times when I couldn't even imagine being okay with things that I'm okay with today; just couldn't even imagine it! But I stayed committed to traveling down the road of discovery, hoping that maybe, along the way, I'd uncover something that would expand my mind. I'm not committed to being right. I'm committed to being clear!

Jeremy: I have an older daughter whom I adopted, and she had this thing where she would shit in her crib and then paint the bars and the walls with it. It was really frustrating because I was constantly cleaning it up and, you know, I didn't realize what that was. What I got out of today was that she was creating and expressing . . . probably expressing the shit that was going on at home at the time.

Yeah, that's what I got out of today. . . . It's been kind of an ongoing joke that she was an artist at a young age, but now I see that I shouldn't joke about that. I almost feel like apologizing to her.

Joseph: You can. You say "I now understand what it was. It was your way of being creative and if I squelched it in any way, I apologize."

Jeremy: I don't even know if it was her way in being creative . . . it was her way of getting acknowledgment, maybe?

Lynn: Well, she was creative in doing it.

Joseph: It was her way of communicating!

Kelly: Believe me, it hasn't changed! She still gets her shit all over the place.

(Laughs)

Just kidding!

Lynn: No. You're not kidding!

(More laughter)

Joseph: As we get older we exchange literal shit for symbolic shit. But we still throw our "shit" around.

So, congratulations to the parents who are here enduring these painful insights and truths. We understand your feelings of guilt and shame; and we hope that today has provided a wider context to help you better understand what created this mess in the first place. We hope you appreciate that without this context, without this additional knowledge, there was no way you could have done better. And, young parents continue to educate yourselves. Those who aren't parents yet, know that you are now way ahead of the game.

Jeremy: It really comes down to breaking the cycle of our parents because as time has gone on, it's changed, I don't parent my kids at all in any similar way to the way I was parented.

Lynn: As we expand our understanding of Sex and gender roles, we will expand our capacity to parent.

Joseph: **SO . . .** do your homework tonight and we'll see you tomorrow.

Simon: Same homework as last night?

Joseph: Same homework . . . give yourselves another chance. . . . By the way, do not allow yourselves to *live and die* with your experiences today! Keep breathing.

"Sex can give you the answer to what the reality of life is because sex is the most alive thing in you."

OSHO

DAY THREE

Joseph: Welcome back everyone! We're now more than half way through this journey; so tell us, share with us . . . *what thoughts and reflections have you had since Friday?*

Riley: *(Riley is an 18 year old male student who is a snowboarding fanatic)* I had a reflection about something we talked about yesterday or just before the video started. Uh . . . I am extremely uncomfortable sharing in these groups. I get a lot of anxiety with anything; even if I think about talking, I stop myself. It blocks me from actually coming up with anything, and yesterday, when we were going through our first memory with our shit, mine was when I was camping and I had shit myself. I remember being put on a rock and sprayed off for everyone to see. I was embarrassed. Essentially, I experienced it as if I was on a pedestal and everyone got to see my "shit." . . . I realized that the main reason I don't like putting myself out there for this, or anything like this, is because I'm afraid of being put up on a pedestal and embarrassed. That story has been told many, many times to me; anytime I see anyone family-related. So, yeah, that just came up and that's why I feel this way. I'm embarrassed just talking right now. I can feel it. Yeah, it totally rules my life.

Joseph: Well, it's nice to find out the why's; but, then, you're left with the same thing. You have to keep expressing and communicating.

Riley: Yeah and I'm very afraid of doing that; so, I'm trying to do that right now.

Joseph: Well, you're doing it. You're not trying, *you're doing it*! It's scary, and we do it. It's painful, and we do it. It's shameful, and we do it. We feel angry and we do it. It's just feelings. It's just a feeling . . . it's a sensation of anxiety. What do you make "anxiety" to mean?

Riley: Nothing good . . .

Joseph: Yeah; but, what do you make it mean?

Riley: I'm not sure. I make it wrong.

Joseph: Yeah, something's wrong, right? No, nothing's wrong. It's just a feeling! It's not about who you are.

What if anxiety has nothing to do with you, and it's just a feeling that you're supposed to feel, and then let it go?

Riley: Well, that would be a lot easier.

Joseph: Yeah, we do it all the time when we go to the movies. We watch a movie, we feel a feeling and when the scene shifts, we shift. But we don't practice that in our lives. If we live our lives the way we view movies, we'd be a lot better off. But no, we cling to these feelings and we add extra meaning. So, it's like living the extra extended director's cut DVD release of our own life. We extend it. But, if you just feel it, it passes. If you feel it, it passes, if you feel it, it passes! If you don't feel it, it chases your ass down until it drives you crazy. If you feel it, it passes. If you feel it, it passes . . .

You've gotta get that! If you feel it, it passes, and the deeper you feel it, the faster it passes. The fuller you feel it, the more authentically it passes and, then, maybe it doesn't come back. Maybe, because you've finally accepted the gift it was offering you all along, it moves on. These feelings are like little spirits looking to free us from pain. They offer us these feelings as gifts that are trying to heal us; trying to get us to let go, resolve and complete.

When we avoid these feelings, its like avoiding something that is rotted. Ignoring it is not going to stop it from rotting further. Rather than throwing it out, we hold on to it thinking that, "If I just leave it there I'll get used to the smell." But we never do. *Avoidance* is the way we hold on, Riley, not the way we let go. No, it doesn't work that way. We have to confront and then express it.

This reminds me of a quote from Meister Eckhart, a 13th-14th century German mystic who once said, and I paraphrase:

> *"When you're afraid of dying it occurs like there are thousands of demons trying to rip your life from you; but, when you've made peace with it you realize that they were nothing more than angels helping you to the other side."*

So, it's great that you have seen what happened and what caused this "condition." But, it's not enough; you NEED to express and share yourself and your pain. It's a necessity, what you all are not getting is that it's a necessity to self express. It's like breathing--you need to do it. It will set you free. . . . You think it's optional. I don't know where you were taught that self expression is optional. Where were you taught that?

Angie: School?

Joseph: How?

Angie: Like, in things, like art class, you know, having creativity graded and things like that.

Joseph: Yes, the system does restrict and suppress children, but we have to do that to them in order to create sufficient and proper boundaries in order for them to *fit in*. Then, when these children find their voices and self expression as adults, they'll have to uproot these teachings and boundaries--of course, keeping the parts that work--and replace them with their own. It's only through this process that true freedom can be found. This might sound like an oxymoron, but we need a strong ego to help us find spiritual freedom. We explain this in more detail in our Ego seminar. . . . How's that for self promotion?

(Laughter)

That's why we need to teach children self expression and communication. As a matter of fact, you could make it a LAW in your family, rather than a rule, since "rules are made to be broken." The law can be that you will support and teach your kids, to the best of your ability, to communicate their needs, pains, and concerns and you'll assist them in doing it in an efficient and effective manner. Laws work better.

I have a LAW that I will never break. I'll never shit in the middle of the street. That's a law for me! I'll never shit in the middle of the street--even if I have the urge.

(Mixture of laughter and disgust)

You don't shit in the middle of the street, do you? Of course not, because there are laws against it. But if it were a rule, we might because when it's only a rule we give ourselves permission to dramatize the feelings associated with the action, which then gives us an excuse to break it. "Oh, I can't help what I'm feeling . . . oh, I feel this overwhelming urge to take a shit in the middle of the street. I can't help myself." That's what we effectively tell ourselves when it's a rule, or less. A law, on the other hand, forces us to discharge the energy around the initializing event. In other words, laws cause us to confront our feelings, because we don't want to pay the consequence for breaking the law. It forces us to confront and process the event that caused these feelings to be bottled up in the first place.

Self-made laws are useful tools to help us dissipate the charges out of feelings. Then the feeling becomes just that, a feeling which makes it easier for it to pass.

Angie: What do you mean by "charges?"

Joseph: A charge is an accumulation of energy that has us lean one way or the other. It is generally created genetically, or through repetition of behavior or traumatic events.

Day Three: *The Sex Seminar*

Let's take alcohol. An alcoholic has a charge towards drinking alcohol. The charge increases the urge to drink and the stronger the charge the stronger the urge. In the case of alcoholics, the charge is genetically based. It's caused by a deficiency in the CREB gene. If the gene were fully charged, then there would be no overwhelming urge to drink. Of course in Riley's case the charge was created by the event.

At the end of the day, is one feeling really any different than another? It isn't, but if you repress it, it will build up energy and get even stronger. Of all the feelings we experience, it is the sexual ones that we tend to repress the most.

That's why sexual feelings are so difficult to manage. We have become *leaves in the wind* after so many generations of deviated expression and repression. Sex is a powerful force, as it is, so imagine what we create within ourselves when we try to repress it? Don't think that those who try to use it for power and control are any better off. No, they're just wasting their energy and it will eventually dry up. Selfish egocentric misuse of Sexual energy is as dangerous as the repression of it.

A sexually repressed society is a sexually obsessed society; it's as simple as that. So, it will take the practices of self awareness, authentic communication, and self expression to balance it; to discharge the unnatural charges that we have imposed on it. Believe us when we tell you that Sex has enough of its own natural charges to last you lifetimes. It can supply us with all the experiences we'd ever need from it, if we only surrendered to it. But, of course, that would require that we understand it is larger than us and that it cares for us.

So we have to express, Riley, even if it's painful; even if it makes us feel silly or inadequate. . . . That's the only way.

Simon: I used to have a similar thing as Riley. I used to have this overwhelming anxiety when I spoke in public, and it was unbearable. Then I found something that helped me, something Homer Simpson said. It made the anxiety drop and it freed me, and that was, *"Ladies and gentlemen, if I could have your attention for a moment . . . I would become a better public speaker."* So, I would start all my

speeches with that, at school, and it just made everyone laugh and my anxiety would go away. So if you can just think of something like that to help relieve the anxiety, then you can get more comfortable talking. It's worked for me because as you can tell I talk a lot . . .

(Laughter)

Yeah it's a useful technique and then, even further, to just get the importance of self expression! You have to get the importance of self expression!

Riley: Thanks for that, Simon.

Lynn: Thank you, Simon.

Joseph: Okay, since we're talking about self expression under limited circumstances, I think it's appropriate to stop here to show you a short film about meditation in prison.

(Group watches an edited version of the documentary "Dhamma Brothers," where prisoners are taught Vipassana meditation; which is a ten day guided meditation. Simon proceeds to approach and question Joseph about something immediately after the viewing. Joseph sends Simon back to his seat.)

Joseph: *(Addressing Simon)* Okay, you have a question?

Simon: Me?

Joseph: Yeah.

Simon: Yeah, I was hiding and I'm not ready; so that was my point because I was hiding from the group . . .

Joseph: Okay, so how were you cheating when you came over to me?

Simon: Because I didn't share my experience with everyone else, and I didn't ask for their feedback

Joseph: Very good.

You can speak with me during breaks, but when it's Show Time, its Show Time. If the "cameras" are rolling and you try to sneak something by us, we're going to doubly focus the camera on you.

What do you make of all this?

Simon: I apologize to the group.

Joseph: Apology accepted. Let's get back to the video.

Day Three: *The Sex Seminar*

So, what did you make of the film? These were hardcore prisoners; some were death row inmates. The full version of the documentary gives a more detailed story of the inmates, in case you're curious.

Simon: It's fascinating how all of them wanted Vipassana, and needed it, but didn't know how to get it. I wouldn't have found out about these seminars if it weren't for my girlfriend, Alexia. I always wanted to work on myself, but I didn't know how to do it, so I feel that this movie portrayed how much everyone really needs it. I think, deep down, everyone wants it but we have so much shit in the way that we're unaware of.

Joseph: Yeah, Joseph agrees with you.

Simon: I . . . I think that, I feel that . . . what did I even say, I don't remember!

(Laughter)

Lisa: I was so surprised that they did it. I thought after they told them all the rules and the schedule, I assumed a lot of them would have walked away, but they didn't.

Joseph: Why'd that surprise you?

Parisa: I was surprised because I did Vipassana twice. The first time I did it, by day three, I found myself angry at the person who told me to do it. I was angry for three days, but she told me, "If you leave, I will never ever speak to you again." She was my mentor. I started to feel the value by day six, but it was a nightmare. So, seeing this re-inspired me.

Joseph: That's because you've sat here feeling sorry for yourself thinking "There's no hope for me!" But when you look at these guys, you have to ask yourself, "Really, do I have it that bad?"

Kelly: I want to go do it now, Vipassana. Seeing that film makes me feel lucky that I haven't done something that horrible to have to go and fix myself; I've done things that I'm not proud of but not to that degree.

Joseph: I get it.

Nathan: I heard of Vipassana through a few different people. This is my fourth seminar with you guys and I've done a lot of work with the two of you and people in this room; and I've heard about it, and heard about it but I was like, "Yeah I don't know . . . ten days . . . that's a long time to take off work." I don't know if I could sit still, my back would hurt; I'd probably feel the same way as Parisa by day three. . . .

But, it's been a huge weekend for me, just that one discovery that I hate men--essentially hating myself--has me thinking about doing it. Lisa pointed out that I'm always apologizing, that's because I'm apologizing for being a **fucking man**. But as the minutes go by I realize that this is something I could do for *my man*; I'm way more open to it now.

Joseph: And, what do you think of the men in the film?

Nathan: I didn't hate them.

Joseph: I didn't ask you what you didn't think; I said what you **do** think of them.

Nathan: I admired them for putting themselves through it, and doing that for themselves given their circumstances. They're in prison, and some might never get out, but they are still looking to better themselves; that's amazing given their situation.

Joseph: This film definitely speaks to the power of self examination. It's going to be a lot harder for some of you to continue your lack of self care and self pity after this! On the surface, these prisoners don't have much to live for, yet, as you saw, they're excited about life.

Jeremy: When I did the course I was in a very, very dark place. I kept trying to talk myself out of it as I drove there. But I knew I had nothing to lose by going. And it helped tremendously.

I know I haven't said much in this seminar, which is unusual for me. I usually talk a lot, but I'm scared . . . really; that's the reason I'm not saying a lot. I had several things happen to me when I was younger that I've carried with me through my life, and watching that movie just brought me back to the feelings.

Lynn: You mean *sexual* things happened to you?

Jeremy: Yes. . . . In Vipassana, there's no talking for ten days, which is what they call "Noble silence." Now, like I said, I talk a lot, but when noble silence ended I wept for over an hour which I have never been able to do before. It's hard to express what it's like to be in silence for so long. It had me experience things inside me that I didn't even know were there. . . . I can, for sure, admit it is the hardest thing I ever did. I tried to leave after the first day, and then when my excuse to leave left, I had to stay, and I promised myself I would do a course once a year for the rest of my life. Like Parisa, I was cursing you guys the first few days . . .

Joseph: That's why we disconnect our phone.

(Laughter)

Jeremy: Yeah, and I understood at the end why it's silent. When I finally spoke to other people at the end, I was surprised to find out that they were going through the same thing; having the same thoughts. I think if we did know what we were all thinking, we would have probably left.

If anybody here has the opportunity to do it, it's life changing. There's no question. I came out of that course to a situation that I would have reacted to incredibly differently; if I hadn't done it before hand. But, it's hard.

Simon: I'm shittin' myself, I just signed up . . .

Jeremy: No, it's the best thing you'll ever do. I haven't known you that long, Simon, but I can guarantee it's the best thing you'll ever do for yourself.

Parisa: The outcome is very, very rewarding.

Simon: Everyone says that . . .

Jeremy: And you're all equal. I didn't feel higher or lower than anyone in the room. . . . But when you're silent in yourself, it's crazy, your head, you're mental; I can't explain how crazy it gets. All I can say to anyone attending is, "Just go there and stay the whole time." . . . I have to say, this weekend's the same for me. I'm experiencing things here, even though we're not being silent, that I've either never felt before or haven't felt in a long time. And the different perspectives you're giving are really blowing my mind!

Joseph: Vipassana teaches the tool of meditation; this tool is essential and invaluable to you in your Self work. We recommend Vipassana because it simply focuses on teaching meditation without trying to indoctrinate you. As we've explained before, meditation, reflection, and contemplation are the three primary tools needed for any real self exploration; any authentic self work.

Simon: I can see that what you're saying, Jeremy. It makes sense. But my feeling about it is a whole other thing.

Joseph: Feelings take time and you have to stay with them. You'll need to allow yourself to go deeper and deeper into them instead of giving yourself permission to say, "I'm tired of feeling this," and quit. If you're getting tired, then it means that part of you is starting to let go and it's getting tired of holding on, and that part is your ego! That's what's actually happening: you're exhausting the ego.

Let's look at Simon's anxiety of going to Vipassana. If he kept still, the feeling of anxiety would initially increase, and as he went deeper and deeper into it, he'd eventually begin to panic. This is assuming his ego would be resisting and holding on to wanting control . . . and that is safe to assume.

(Smiling)

Now, if he were to endure this panic by breathing through it, he'd begin to exhaust the ego and, if he persisted, he'd eventually drop into calm. Herein lies the dilemma. Assuming he can get past the panic, falling into the calm requires letting go into the unknown; falling into something larger than his ego, and that's a challenge.

We are afraid of the unknown . . . we are afraid of the abyss. That unknown and abyss is inside you, isn't it? That's where you don't want to go. You don't want to go deeper and deeper inside you. But really, what better place to go than inside **you**; if you're not safe there, then you're really fucked, aren't you? And, if you're that fucked then what do you have to lose by, at least, trying?

A ten day meditation is laughable for a monk, wouldn't you think? Or how about to a Yogi who does it in extreme conditions for eight or more hours a day at times? Vipassana meditation is conducted in such a safe and caring environment, that I think even for you little pussies it shouldn't be such a big deal.

(Laughter)

Actually that's an insult to pussies, so I take it back.

(More laughter)

. . . Because it's conducted over ten days, it gives you the opportunity to go at your pace. With each passing day you'll be able to go little by little, deeper and deeper, until you relax and surrender.

Think of learning meditation as learning to swim. Meditation is a great way to navigate through your mind and consciousness. If you never learn to swim, and you go to a beach, the best you can hope to experience is a tan and some shallow water wading, and that's about it! It's no different in life. Most of you live it in shallow water; it's quite shallow how you live your lives. Meditation will help you with the depths of life and with navigating the depths of Sex.

Simon: Sneaky. I was wondering why you guys were showing us a documentary on meditation; so meditation helps us in the same way with sex as it would in life.

Day Three: *The Sex Seminar*

Joseph: Boy, we can't slip anything past you!

(Laughter)

Absolutely. As a matter of fact, I guarantee it would give you a better love life! Wow, look Lynn, now we have everyone's attention!

(Laughter)

Mercedes: When I did Vipassana it broke the levy, and my whole life just fell apart after, but in a good way. All of my sexual issues came up, but I didn't realize it until after the course was done. All I knew was that I felt frustrated and angry the whole time and it wasn't till about day six or seven that I started feeling better. That was October, 2011, and I'm still dealing with the wake of everything that was let loose from that.

Joseph: Are you still doing your sits?

Mercedes: Sometimes.

Joseph: Do more of them; that will help this process. Now tell me: What does this have to do with sex?

Mercedes: Meditation is just like sex.

Joseph: How so?

Mercedes: When you're not having egotistical sex . . .

Joseph: Yeah, Joseph agrees with that.

Mercedes: When I'M not having egotistical sex, it's meditative because it's like focusing on this little point that's constantly moving and all of my thoughts are out of my head. It was the same at Vipassana. You're focusing on this one little point, and whether it's moving all over your body or on the tip of your nose, you're focusing on this one little point. Then everything extraneous in your head, within this practice, just disappears.

Joseph: In *my* head?

Mercedes: In MY head.

Joseph: Right. Because there are different types of meditation, so in my head it might be different.

Day Three: *The Sex Seminar*

Alex: I go back to the OSHO quote. I was thinking that the word "sex" for me should have been meditate. This is because, throughout my adulthood, I have yet to experience that depth of oneness through sex that I have through my meditation. That's my experience.

Joseph: What did we mean when we said yesterday that *"meditation is born from sex?"*

Nathan: Sex is a form of meditation?

Joseph: No. ...Meditation is born from sex; what is meant by that?

Parisa: To me, it's quieting the brain and being in the body and the sensations. Allowing myself to be in the moment because, to me, every memory is here; everything I have ever been through is here.

Joseph: I can see why Sex might scare you, then.

If the word, "meditation," or the practice of meditation freaks you out, then so does Sex. You don't think you do the same thing with Sex as you do with meditation?

If you distract yourself with meditation or distract yourself from it, if you run away from it or desperately consume yourself in it, if you have trouble focusing during it or you get fixated with it, or if you try to dominate it or are dominated by it, then know that's what you are doing with Sex. You approach both the same way; you practice your sex the way you practice your meditation. Like a child who looks and behaves similar to their parent, your meditation will *look* like your Sex.

(Fire alarms sound in the distance)

Joseph: It is alarming!

(Laughter)

Mercedes: I've just wanted to be out of my body lately, (holds back tears) that's why I couldn't do the homework because as soon as I do the homework I have to face the fact that I **have** a fucking body and I don't really want to deal with that. It's been completely overwhelming for me the past year. I flip flop from shame to anger-- whatever fits the circumstances in the moment; I'll flip: Shame or anger, shame or anger, back and forth.

Joseph: I understand how difficult it must be for you, but this is actually the best time for you to challenge yourself. Therefore, it's imperative you complete the homework because it will help you get past this. It will accelerate your progress with this challenge and . . . it will hurt! But it will help you see the next place you'll need to go. Besides, to avoid it would be as damaging as avoiding an infection; especially that it's already coming up. You want to know this is arising because it needs to be healed and you're old enough and strong enough to manage it; otherwise, it would still be sitting dormant.

So, as you read your responses, going body part by body part, feelings will come up; let yourself feel these feelings and emotions. After the feeling passes go to the next part and then the next part until you're done. This is the most efficient way to release this degree and depth of pain; part by part. Obviously, it's in the body that you're holding all the pain, so it's through the body that you can release it.

If you can experience your body as a separate entity--as a friend even--then you'll realize it helps you by holding on to your pain until you're ready!

Mercedes: Yeah and I'm so grateful for it . . .

Joseph: Some people just abandon the body. They see the body in pain and they say, "Okay, I'm out." So, you don't want to do that. You want to appreciate that the body is holding this for you. How long do you want to let your body endure this? You can work together on this with your body, but it also needs your intelligence. It can't take these steps by itself; it doesn't know where you need to go next. The body is not in charge of that, your intelligence is. The body, in this kind of work, has to keep still unless you're doing a different kind of meditation; a meditation of movement. Dance and yoga are good examples of this. Otherwise, its job is to hold the pain, and yours is to utilize the mind and access the emotions to relieve it from the pain.

Meditative movement is not most people's strong point, therefore, their bodies can't help them directly. I've practiced a lot of meditative movement in the past, so my body has helped me by continually informing me of any excess accumulation of energy long before it takes damaging foothold in it. Though the communication between my consciousness and body isn't as synchronized as it once was, it still gives me more than sufficient support. It knows what's blocking my clear movement and it helps me out by informing me.

Mercedes: What do I do if the pain gets to be too much?

Joseph: You take a break.

When I was in my deepest pain and grief, it seemed as if wherever I turned there was Pain; it was miserable and inescapable. So, I brought my problem to my Godmother, who was my mentor at the time. She simply said, "Ask for a break. Ask life, or whatever it is you believe in, for a break." And I did . . . I remember asking, "Please give me a break for a day and I promise I'll get back to it tomorrow," and it worked. It was an amazing relief because, prior to that, nothing else worked. Today, I have additional techniques to help me manage my life but this one is a good one. It works, even if it's your mind you're asking the break from.

So ask for a break, but then go do the work, 40-year-old Mercedes will really appreciate it. It's going to be much harder for older you than it is for 30-year-old Mercedes. If you put it off till she shows up, she might be able to manage it . . . but she won't have the same energy, the same youthfulness, the same excitement, and the same ability to handle it as you.

You can do this part of the work for her now. What if this is 30-year-old Mercedes' responsibility? That would be great, because you'll be helping yourself, loving yourself. It's easier when you know or choose, "This is the responsibility in my life right now. This is my part of this life's journey." See it like a job that requires you to complete it, let's say, between the ages of 30 and 33; that's what Jesus did. (Smiling) He stayed around for three years and did his job, and we still remember him for it. You can do this; you can get excited about it.

Mercedes: Thank you!

Joseph: You're welcome.

It's a tough job, but at least I have a purpose. (Smiling) This is my purpose; this is my mission. To reveal, to help you to begin to feel, to begin to heal. Then we'll go to the next level and heal that and then the next, until you come out on the other side. There are techniques like, meditation, correcting, and releasing, that help manage the stronger emotions; these techniques give us increased courage to invite the larger pains. But you have to call them up first, you have to be willing to feel; they'll drop, they'll pass, especially with your new *map*. But you need to use it, because this is about grief and healing. Now, what does this have to do with sex?

Tami: I realize I think a lot during sex. I think and I think, which doesn't allow me to physically experience as much pleasure as I think I can.

Lynn: "As I think I can?" (Smiling)

Day Three: *The Sex Seminar*

Tami: Yeah . . . I think too much. I push physical love away; I can't feel it as much for myself as I do for others. But when it comes to other people . . . when I was watching this video, I was amazed. I'm watching these men, who I don't know, and I'm sympathizing and I'm empathizing with them. I'm looking in their eyes and I see a child, and I feel their pain and I can see a change in them. I can feel emotion for everybody else, but when it comes to me, like physically, I literally push it away. And I'm sitting here like, "Wow, that's so fucked up."

Joseph: As my old, wise professor said, "The mind protects, the heart connects." You're protecting yourself with your mind. Your pain is from childhood. That's how you decided to protect yourself, sexually. I'm really sorry for your experience. (Tami begins to cry, Joseph goes over and comforts her, she cries in his arms)

Lynn: Let's take a break now.

* * * * *

There's sex and there's Sex! One, you consume and it consumes you while the other, you surrender to till it has found you.

Joseph: Welcome back! . . . Your meditation will change your Sex. It can help you clear yourself sexually. (Addressing Tami) When you were watching this film about meditation, it gave you some clarity, right? You realized, at least more clearly, "Hey, I do sex from the head!" Imagine what you'd get if you actually meditated?

Head Sex is the first of five different kinds of Sex we will be talking about. So what is Head Sex, sex from the head? What kind of sex is that, what does that look like?

Claudia: Control?

Joseph: Yes. It's controlled.

Kelly: Manipulative?

Joseph: Very manipulative.

Alexia: I feel like it would be mechanical.

Joseph: It's definitely going to be mechanical, because it's structured.

Nathan: Showy. You know like look how many positions I know! I'm fucking awesome.

Joseph: It could be showy, but that's back to the mechanical.

Kelly: Ego.

Joseph: Yeah, especially ego because the head is where the ego lives.

Tami: It's empty . . . for me it's empty. Like its fun and enjoyable somewhat, but it's empty.

Joseph: How far removed is your head from your genitals?

Tami: Oh, it's like super detached. I don't even know.

Joseph: Yeah, the head is very far removed . . . If you think your head is it for you sexually, then you've removed yourself extremely far from your Sex center. Its second or third person, isn't it? It's never first person, sex with the head; there's always an observer, always.

Simon: Is meditation first person energy then? You mentioned meditative movement . . .

Joseph: Yes, in a way. It's too complicated for the mind to grasp. It's only through experience that one can understand meditative movement, thus, Meditative Sex. It's the same with death, that's why we don't really think about death much because we can't truly grasp it. When you die, not necessarily in the physical sense, you'll grasp it; it's experiential. So, for now, let's call it first person.

Simon: How do I differentiate between movement and meditative movement? For me, I can't decide if surfing is meditative movement because all my worries and everything go away.

Joseph: For you, surfing is meditative.

Simon: But, it's fun and . . .

Joseph: Well, you're assuming mediation isn't fun.

Simon: It's work isn't it?

Joseph: No, it's neither. You need to go and do it so you can find out what it is. Its like asking me what Rome is like without ever going there yourself, "Please tell me what Rome is like . . ."

Simon: It's a shithole.

(Laughter)

Joseph: ". . . then tell me how it smells!" . . Again, I'm only going to get your perspective, and if I asked another, I'd get theirs; it will be different. Why do that? Have your experience. Why do you need to know so much about it beforehand?

Simon: My experience of meditation is that its work, it's just, like, hard.

Joseph: How many experiences have you had with it?

Simon: Every night I'm doing it.

Joseph: Using what method and learned where?

Simon: Just from what you told me in sessions, just to sit in my heart and observe it.

Joseph: Okay, but that's very specific and, though it's a type of meditation, it's not enough of a sample size for you to be able to draw any accurate conclusion about it. In your case, the meditation I gave you was particular for you; it was to help you to go and heal a specific area.

Simon: So that is meditation, or it's not?

Joseph: It's a form of meditation. Remember, I said there are different types of meditations for different purposes. Vipassana, for instance, focuses and utilizes breathing techniques to achieve its ends. While the Vijnana Bhairava Tantra, which is a sacred text, provides the seeker with 112 different sutras to choose from, these Tantric sutras (Tantric basically means technique) are all meditations. Meditations which cater to different needs and which are suited for different people. Not all meditations suit all people.

What I gave you is a specific meditation for you; it's for your heart center so you can see what's there and what needs to be cleared out. It was not going to be fun because its intension was to clear out pain.

Simon: Oh, I see. I understand.

Lynn: You've had no clue that when you're in *your zone* while surfing that you are in a meditative state. The minute that your ego or your thoughts pop in, you are no longer in a meditative zone and that's when you're more likely to wipe out. Riley, next to you, can understand that, through snowboarding, and at the level of snowboarder he is, he can only do it meditatively if he's going to do it well.

Simon: So my thinking messes me up.

Lynn: Your thinking fucks you. Always. Period. If you're thinking carries you away, you're off. Just notice what happens the next time you surf. Be observant to yourself and see what you do with your mind the next time you wipe out.

Joseph: How does *thinking* affect your Sex life? Do you get confused about what to do or say during Sex? Are you constantly monitoring your actions from the second or third person?

Lynn: Do you tell him how to touch you? How to touch your body, vagina, breasts, and clitoris? Do you talk to him or her? Do you talk to avoid or to dominate the experience?

Joseph: We need to talk and communicate with ourselves and our partners in order to synchronize. It's vital, especially at the beginning. Eventually, if done properly, a non verbal way of communicating takes over. But when we are having Sex from the head we may over or under communicate. We are not in synch with our bodies, so we have trouble feeling not just the other, but ourselves. So anything we say or not say gets in the way, because our head is in the way. That is really problematic when you're giving or getting head; no one wants to hear what going through someone's head . . . when they're giving you head!

(Laughter)

. . . Unless they're practicing their ABC's with their tongues, right ladies?

(More laughter)

Tami: My head blocks me from being able to feel and I'm, literally, thinking, like, "Stop" and "Shut the fuck up!" For a short time, I begin to feel again, but that works only for a little while. Then like a flashing light, it goes back on.

Joseph: I get your point, but I want you to take a look at the significance of "a flashing light;" you didn't use that analogy by accident. There something relevant there. (Tami nods)

Day Three: *The Sex Seminar*

Again the purpose of using your head during Sex is to protect; to protect the heart. Your head jumps into action when the heart feels vulnerable, when it is feeling more than it's accustomed to feeling. That's all that's happening! When you understand this, you'll be less inclined to need it to "shut up." What you want to do is allow it to spin so you can learn its mechanics. You want to just notice and say, "Oh look, I'm protecting myself." Just observe it without trying to change it or judge it.

We're like outlaws from the old, Wild West who carry a holster with two guns. The first gun is the *change* gun and the second one is the *judgment* gun. When we don't like what's happening or what we're feeling and we have limited comprehension or experience with it; we whip them out. "Bang, CHANGE THAT AND THAT, POW; we blast away! Or we take out the judgment gun and fire away judgments like: "You suck! . . . You're a loser . . . I'm a loser," and so on. Until we have a greater understanding of our actions, there is really no need to judge or change anything; we simply need to observe it first to see how it works. Everyone has experienced a degree of this. We are just talking about what head sex is and why we have it. It's protected sex, it's the sex taught by our parents. Parents teach us to have sex, protectively. But don't confuse that with *safe sex*.

You see, the only person who claims to have not been taught protective Sex is Angie. But what Angie's not seeing is that it's not what her mother told her about

Sex, but what she did with the men in her life--sexually and relationally--that taught her protective Sex.

How did she experience her mother's relationships? Were they loving . . . were they playful? Were they free and easy going or were they combative and abusive?

Angie: No . . . they were combative. Far from playful. I've only brought up what she's said and that's pretty different from what she did.

Joseph: Right! Kids don't listen to what the parents say! They *listen* to what they do!

Angie: Yeah.

Joseph: So NONE of us understands playful Sex enough. We're not taught that, parents don't teach playfulness and Sex; they teach sex for protection. And we're not saying they're wrong for doing that, we're just revealing what's going on.

Lynn: What we're doing this weekend is teaching ourselves more about Sex and, hopefully, we'll begin to experience the playful side of it!

Day Three: *The Sex Seminar*

Mercedes: I have a question. Is there a link between meditative sex and role play? Because when you role play during sex, you dump your ego, it's almost like you're not yourself anymore.

Joseph: You're not your Ego anymore.

What is the ultimate purpose of mediation?

Group: To expose? To observe? Inner peace? Heal? Drop your mind? To know yourself? To be quiet? To meditate?

Joseph: No, no, no, no, no, no, no . . . but the last is the closest so far. Go off of what Lisa just said . . . the ultimate purpose of meditation.

Group: To sit, to heal?

Joseph: Nope

Simon: To be meditative.

Joseph: Bingo!

Susan: To be meditative?

Joseph: To BE meditative, you meditate to BE meditative. You meditate to live a meditative life. When you become meditative you don't have to meditate anymore! Most people meditate for all the reasons you mentioned and more; but that's not the ultimate. Ultimately you can live a meditative life. So I ask you, Mercedes, "Is there a link between role playing and meditative Sex?"

Mercedes: Only if you're playing in both.

Joseph: EXCELLENT! Exactly! Playing is the key!

What's the difference between Head Sex and Heart Sex?

(Tami gives confused look)

Joseph: Of course you have no idea . . .

Tami: I have no fucking clue!

Joseph: She's like . . . where's my heart?

(Laughter)

Day Three: *The Sex Seminar*

Tami: I'm confused! (Tami begins to curl herself up into a ball)

Joseph: If I contort myself into the shape of a heart, would that help you?

(Loud laughter)

Joseph: Heart people, what is heart sex like?

Alexia: Connected; it's more affectionate.

Kelly: Heart sex can hurt.

Joseph: Yeah, heart sex can hurt; it often causes individuals to cry.

Parisa: And this is good, no?

Joseph: It's neither good nor bad; we're looking to describe it not value it. Heart Sex is just a small part of the full Sexual experience.

Parisa: I think for me it was 75% of my experience.

Joseph: Okay, so tell us about Heart Sex, what is it like to you?

Parisa: In my experience, it involves more cuddling and caring. Yes, the sex is there, but I value the cuddling and caring. I care for the person and, I don't know if it's healthy or not, but I'm expecting to be cared for. The hugs are more valuable than the actual sex.

Joseph: So for you, it's the expectation of being nurtured. It's the continuation of the nurturing process that wasn't completed in childhood.

Simon: So it's a feeling of safety.

Joseph: For some, yes. It provides a feeling of safety. Heart Sex is very *safe* sex. Many of you who are incomplete in this area prefer to engage in Heart Sex.

Heart Sex can also help those who are stuck in their heads. Through Heart Sex, one can drop out of the head and into the heart. By connecting through heart feelings or by simply sitting in the heart during Sex, you can expand yourself beyond head Sex. In other words you become too expansive for the head so you'll naturally drop into the heart, or Heart Center. The deeper you connect with Sex, the heavier it gets. The head can only handle light and airy Sex, anything else is too heavy for it.

Simon: You're saying the head can only handle the lighter feelings, but I go to some really dark places in my head?

Joseph: Thoughts are generally much lighter than feelings so that's what I mean when I say light; I'm talking about thoughts. Dark thoughts aren't necessarily heavy energetically, that's why we can be so detached and cold from the pain they can create. On the contrary, when we are in deep heart feelings, we cannot help but know the consequences of our actions. For you head extremists, the more you practice going into your heart, the easier it becomes to "drop into your heart."

Now, let us add a few more points about Heart Sex. Heart Sex is much slower Sex than Head Sex. It needs time to connect. The connecting can be accomplished through touch, eye contact, and mutual synchronized breathing to name a few. It also needs care, sensitivity, and gentleness; but understand, gentleness can be expressed through firmness. The risks of Heart Sex are 1) we can become attached and even addicted to this one type of Sex, and 2) because we're venturing into the heart, an area where a lot of our pain is hidden, we take the risk of exposing old dormant hurts. These hurts are heartbreaks that were previously locked in the heart.

They inevitably surface whenever we invite the *heart's* participation. This is why Heart Sex tends to unleash tears that often come up right before or after orgasm.

For a head person it could be very confusing to watch a heart person, especially when they appear to cry for no reason. But this is how Heart Sex heals; there's healing of the heart in Heart Sex. Could there be healing of the head with head sex?

What kind of healing can you have with Head Sex?

Simon: If I had sex with someone and had a bad experience, but then I repeat it with someone else and had a good experience. I'd then have two different ways of looking at it.

Joseph: Very good, so you get to reframe, you get to allow the mind to reframe the experience. This in turn, allows you to stay open to Sex. The head has the capacity to see the wide and the concise and everything in between. Through your left brain you get to see the detailed specifics; specifics that can help you see clearly and precisely. While the right brain gives you a greater overview of you, your partner, and Sex. There are definite benefits to Head sex.

Simon: I use it for safety!

Joseph: Yes, it **can** be used for safety.

Simon: It's interesting that both types are used for safety. I'll use head Sex to feel safe and others use Heart Sex for the same thing. So it is all just for safety.

Joseph: These types of Sex can be used for safety but it really has much more to offer than safety. The thing is we can project *safety* upon just about anything. . . . One last thing, even at its best, Head & Heart Sex is still Sex, at least, once removed. . . . Anything else on Heart sex?

Reese: I finally realized why I used to drink so much. I kind of have the feeling of almost being hung-over right now, and I just don't give a shit. It's the same feeling that I have after I drink and I finally just get to let loose and I don't care what anybody else thinks. I find that I always have the best sex when I'm hung-over.

Joseph: Nurturing oneself through alcohol never works. Ultimately, it will leave you feeling alone in a crowd.

The chains that you walk around life with are extremely encumbering and we blame everyone and everything for it, but the joke is that *you are your own prison warden*. There really isn't a large difference between you and the prisoners in the documentary. The only differences are you're the warden, and you're the prison guard, and you're the cook in the kitchen, and you're the one who spends time in the cell; it's a prison of your own making. You keep these chains intact that your parents once passed on. You maintain them. You keep them tight and strong. You have not seen that or accepted it, so you have to get obliterated to give yourself permission to step out of them for a little while. In reality, you could just step out of them at anytime; you're free to do so. You don't have to, from this point forward, give a shit about what anybody says or thinks of you; **you don't have to**! It's your decision. Unfortunately, we don't make that decision until it has become too distasteful or painful for us. . . . It's getting distasteful for you isn't it? (Reese nods) Then you have the capacity to change, now. . . Anything else on Heart Sex?

Nisha: What's coming up for me is I feel that, probably the only time I've ever allowed myself to feel vulnerable, is through sex.

Joseph: Through the heart? Or just sex in general? Or is most of your sex Heart sex?

Nisha: Predominantly heart sex. So that's the only time I've allowed myself to be fully vulnerable or present.

Joseph: This is helpful for you to know. What you do then is let the walls down, or maybe you open the door to the wall and let someone in for a little while, during sex. Heart Sex causes you to drop and be *vulnerable*. So, in your case it's healing; it provides you with much needed human contact and relief.

Heart Sex and Head Sex are types of Sex, and Sex is an infinite thing. We can do multiple things with it! It's a power, its energy, and its healing!

How about Body Sex; what's that like?

Reese: Awesome.

Joseph: It's awesome. What's awesome about it?

Claudia: Feeling.

Joseph: A lot of feeling. Where?

Claudia: Everywhere.

Joseph: Everywhere. The whole body right?

Heart sex is different, isn't it? With Heart Sex, when you really connect, you actually leave your body. You don't need your body much in Heart Sex. The body is just there to make the initial connection, the plugging in. Then you move a little bit until you can feel the heart connect, and once it's there, the body will keep doing what it's doing but you're no longer with the physical body, you're now looking to be outside of it; so you go into the *Emotional Body*. The Emotional Body is, literally, another one of our bodies.

In contrast, when we do Head Sex we look to leave the physical head/brain so we can go into our Mental Body. Head people, in general, tend to live in the Mental Body. It's a body! You have sex with different bodies, and you can have sex with different bodies with different people. I may have Head Sex with you and Heart Sex with you and Body Sex with you . . . I could change it up!

Simon: So Body Sex is like the least fulfilling though, it's like a one night stand . . . I'm just like "What was the point of that shit!"

Joseph: Well that's too bad for you; I've had some awesome Body Sex, boy . . . It's amazing the feelings the body can produce!

Simon: Maybe it's just me then.

(Laughter)

Day Three: *The Sex Seminar*

Joseph: Simon, what's probably happening is you're still having Head Sex and you *think* its Body Sex. You're head is so strong it keeps the body strong, just because you're dick stays hard doesn't mean you're connected. All you need is a little blood running through the fucker.

(Laughter)

Simon: Can you explain Body Sex, then, because I don't think I understand?

Joseph: We are exploring Body Sex right now, why would you want me to explain it. I'm asking the question, and now you're asking me the same question that I just asked! Are you that stupid! Are you choosing not to hear what's in front of your face?

Simon: I'm asking it as well to everyone!

Joseph: And so, that gives you what? A sense of importance?

Simon: I don't know . . .

Joseph: Why do you need so much importance? You have to look in front of the mirror and ask "Why do I have to be important!?"

Simon: Because I don't understand.

Joseph: I don't care if you don't understand. That's a different issue. I'm asking why do you have to be so important?

Simon: That's how I get my worth.

Joseph: Yeah, so you actually feel worthless then, and you work so fucking hard to convince   yourself you're not! Everyone else buys your self-deluding bullshit but I don't! **You're not worthless! Drop it, Simon.**

Body Sex. Tell me about Body Sex?

Parisa: I wish I knew . . .

Joseph: I appreciate that fully . . . I appreciate that fully! That's the cost for only doing Heart Sex.

Kelly: When you're really attracted to someone . . .

Joseph: Well what's it like?

Day Three: *The Sex Seminar*

Alexia: It's exploring? In my experience . . .

Joseph: Yeah. Body Sex has you want to explore every inch of that body; you just want to feel as many sensations as possible. Body Sex also has a will of its own. You might catch it in a moment of objectivity and go "Holy shit, it's doing its own thing; I can't believe what my body's doing!" The body moves through interconnected sensations; one movement leads to another, one sensation leads to another. It's sensual; it's all based on the sensations in the body, not the sensations in the mind or in the heart, but in the body.

Body Sex, like the other two, is healing. It releases pains locked in the body. A telltale sign of this is perspiration; a lot is released through sweat. A good round of Body Sex can leave you soaking wet after. It's detoxing, and when you're finished you feel like your body is breathing on its own.

You can actually feel the body breathing, not just out of your nose but through the whole body! The body does breathe and you can become conscious of it when you're connected to it through this type of Sex. When you're this connected with your body, when you're this fine tuned, you'll experience subtleties of feelings you didn't even know existed. Each movement brings *new* and *different* feelings with it.

Susan: So it's like Vipassana meditation.

Joseph: Again, all of these are parts or types of meditation; meditation was born from sex, so you'll see it in both. People who are head centered will see through the head and people who are heart will *see* through the heart during their meditation. . . . Body Sex?

Parisa: The moment I feel my body in sex, it freaks me out.

Joseph: Because you hide your pain in your body. This is why you only stayed aware of this (motions to heart) when I asked you about sex, you didn't realize that this (motion to whole body) is soooo sexy.

(Laughter)

Parisa: I suppress it because it is so scary!

Joseph: That's because of a hurt that you may not even remember is there. It's frightening to you like it would be for a child in the dark of night.

I remember when I was a child; being afraid of the things I saw or heard as I would try to sleep. Something as simple as a coat on a chair would become a person who might harm me or a rattling sound against a window would become the tapping of a ghost who was out to get me. Most of the time I tried to find out the source of it and that discovery would end the torment. But sometimes I was just too afraid and it would repeat itself. Then there were the times that I would look, but not find the cause, and I'd be forced to endure the pain and fear.

Parisa: Then I have to be with the right person. Sometimes, that's what we have to do, we have to sit in the fear and pain and allow it the time to be processed. It does eventually pass.

Joseph: You can do it alone. You don't need another. When you unlock the pain in your body and start to feel the hurt, pain, or fear the other person becomes irrelevant. The best they can be is someone for you to project on. . . . *You're the right person.* You're your own greatest lover.

So you're ignoring your body. If you want to be a better lover, start with your own body! Touch yourself. This is why you want children to know that masturbation is okay! So they begin to love themselves; especially for little girls!

Dr. Laura Berman made a great point about this. She essentially said that, in this society, most females think a man causes their pleasure, their orgasm. But if a little girl were to masturbate and have an orgasm, before she was ever with a male, she'd forever know that SHE could source her own pleasure. Then a man or woman would be a bonus. That's a big difference because, then, she'll never *need* a man in that way, or a woman for that matter. If this dysfunction is eliminated in childhood, then the woman will never really understand the need for a man. It would be like, "What? What do you mean I need a man, what's that? Why do you need a man?" They would be independent, we're not talking about an outraged or angry *independence* like "Fuck them! Why do you need a man? . . . not me!" We're talking about an independence that comes from a transcendent experience of uniting with men, not from lack but from fullness.

Mercedes: Men are taught the same thing, though, that a woman's orgasm comes from them.

Joseph: Yes, it's a mutual delusion. Like I can cause you your orgasm; right! It's an exhausting belief.

Mercedes: Yeah I can't count the number of times I've been pressed afterwards about "How was my performance, how did I do? Was that a real orgasm?"

Joseph: Yeah, "*Did you cum? Did you cum good?*"

(Laughter)

Claudia: "Why can't you come? What's wrong with you?"

Joseph: Yeah what's wrong with **you**, I don't want to take responsibility. . . . It's exhausting. I've exhausted myself in my life. I must have exhausted years out of my life; the sands in the hour glass went through a lot faster with me trying to create the orgasm, not knowing I don't have that power.

Most women don't realize that the only reason they have an orgasm with another is because they've surrendered to the other; not because the other has caused it. The best the other can do is create an environment that will enhance the surrender; an environment that increases trust and safety. And this trust and safety can come in some very unusual ways. For instance, a woman could feel safe with a partner who smacks her around because that's what she's accustomed to; that might mean, to her, the partner cares. She might orgasm more with an abuser than with someone who's gentler; it all depends on how she's wired.

The point is, women are in charge of their own orgasm. A man or woman doesn't cause it unless you want it, unless you allow it.

Nathan: That's why guys are like "I gave her the best orgasm." When it's a good one they'll take credit for it, "Yeah that was all me," but really it has nothing to do with us.

Joseph: Not as much as we think. To understand this is to be able to imagine what Sex would be like without the preoccupation of orgasm. That's another fantasy for some of you; to have sex without the preoccupation of orgasm. That would be like dancing completely free.

Dancing is a kind of Body Sex; that's why it is so sexual and sensual. You'll usually find that people who have trouble with Body Sex have trouble dancing.

Nathan: I find yoga is a lot like Body Sex.

Joseph: Yoga definitely includes Body Sex because it gets you back into your body. It forces you to feel every part of your body and prepares you for better Body Sex. Yoga is great for those of you who have trouble with Body Sex.

Simon: So, if I'm in my head, then why does a female orgasm excite me so much physically? I can orgasm instantly after she orgasms. Is it because I feel that the woman is actually surrendering to me?

Day Three: *The Sex Seminar*

Joseph: No, it's because it provides you worth. It's just another area in your life you get worth. You're like an entrepreneur who collects dividends from different investments. You get it from women, money, sports, or when you try to be the smartest one in the room. You can actually get off whenever the opposite occurs, too. Worth and worthlessness makes you orgasm. This needs to be confronted because it's running your life, not just your sex life. It's a vicious cycle. The problem with using sex for confirmation is that you're only as good as the next time.

Simon: I can see that. So Body Sex can get me out of my head?

Joseph: Yes, as could Heart Sex. But what you first need to realize, before you practice Body Sex again Simon, is that *your body loves you*. (Simon's face quickly saddens) . . . Be with the sadness, we're all here for you.

Parisa: In Vipassana, we are not supposed to think of sex or have sex or anything while we're doing it. But on the eighth day while I was doing the breathing, I began to feel sexual sensations in the body and I started to have an orgasm, without a man. Afterwards I felt guilty because I was not supposed to do this when I was doing Vipassana.

Joseph: Firstly, I think you misheard or misinterpreted them around not having sexual thoughts. They're not going to tell you you're not supposed to think sexual thoughts but rather, you're not to engage in masturbation or sexual activity. The thoughts are fine; they probably suggested you don't overindulge in any one thought or set of thoughts.

In meditation, it's best to *watch* your thoughts as you would watch boats or fishes passing by as you sit on a river bank, objectively and with no judgment. What I believe they we're saying is not to jump into the water after the fish; especially the sexual fish, since it's such a powerful one. When you keep still, while observing your thoughts, what will happen by day ten is you'll become more focused and stronger minded to the point that even sexual thoughts will have trouble luring you in.

They don't teach how you're SUPPOSED to do meditation; they show you a way you can meditate. It's easy to misinterpret under such settings because we go into *should and shouldn't* mode. We take a small example and we make it an absolute. Like poor Christ, they asked him "Hey Jesus, tell us how to pray?" So, he goes "Okay I got a good one. For example . . . Our father who art in heaven, hollowed be thy name . . ." and he gives them this prayer. And they take it and run with it; and they haven't stopped running since. But it was only meant to be an example!

Now, let's get to your orgasm, Parisa. This experience was more than you indulging in sexual thoughts. As you said, it started from sensations and increased from there. This was a very healthy experience. The guilt that you felt afterwards was nothing more than past programming from childhood; that, to can be felt and allowed to pass.

Mercedes: An older friend of mine, she must be over 50, said that the style of meditation where she just sits and tries to ignore her thoughts never really worked for her. So instead, she would count on every in breath or out breath up to 108 and then back down again. She did this for a few years, and much to her surprise she started having multiple orgasms during these meditation sessions. For people who are really afraid, I found it really easy when I'm doing my Vipassana technique to just count up to 108 each in breath and out breath and then back down again. It's so much easier to stay focused; I haven't had the multiple orgasms yet, but maybe one day!

Joseph: It all depends on where you're at and what's being unlocked. Yes, you most certainly can orgasm, and multi-orgasm through meditation. But it can also come in different forms. For some it happens in the form of bliss, that's a differently experienced orgasm. This can be further explored in Tantric Sex. I don't know if we are going to get to Tantric Sex in this seminar, we did in the last one, but if not, then it's definitely worth you looking into.

Now, the next kind of sex is Animal Sex. What is Animal Sex? It's not head, not heart, and it's not body. . . . us human beings, we also have Animal Sex.

Kelly: Is it rougher?

Joseph: It has a rougher component. But not any rougher than what Head Sex can create.

Riley: Is it instinct?

Joseph: Yes, it's from instinct. Exactly. It's from your animal self, not from your body . . . not from your mind or heart, but from the animal that you are, that I am. The animal that has you do shit you have no control over. Suddenly you're biting and scratching and pinching and squeezing; the animal in you comes forth. Animal Sex is a quite unique and different experience. . . . What's Animal Sex like for you?

Reese: It's surprising! It's fun . . .

Joseph: It's always surprising and it's always fun. There is a fun aspect to Animal Sex, absolutely. Why is it fun?

Day Three: *The Sex Seminar*

Parisa: You don't follow any rules; you just allow your instinct to guide everything.

Joseph: Joseph has had that experience too . . .

Parisa: **I don't** follow rules and I let my instinct guide me. I have this vision of people doing it for a long time with lots of sounds and movements.

Joseph: Well, tell me how you would do it.

Parisa: Me . . . No!

(Laughter)

Joseph: Well, how do you do it in your head? Be one of the people in your head and then tell us what it's like.

Parisa: It's like two people together . . .

Joseph: No. You're telling me about people again.

Parisa: Oh, me. Okay me and someone else in the bed and the body is. . . .

Joseph: Your body?

Parisa: The instinct, my instinct is in control of everything, the body, the mind, the soul and everything it's like you lose space and time.

Joseph: I do?

Parisa: Well I haven't done it! I wish I have.

Joseph: Well, that's why we're asking you to picture it. It's an opportunity to open yourself to the experience; open you to the possibility.

Parisa: I just pictured losing all sense of space and time, and yeah, I'm afraid to fall out of the bed . . .

(Laughter)

Joseph: Yeah! Animal Sex!

Mercedes: I don't have to worry about the other person as a person! I don't have to worry about caretaking for their emotions . . . or stroking their hair after; "Are you okay, honey?" It's like, "Let's get our fuck on" and that's it! It's very simple and uncomplicated.

Joseph: Yes. It's simplistic, it's animal, and if you're both sharing the experience, it can be wonderful. What kind of Sex doesn't this work well with?

Mercedes: Heart.

Joseph: Right, it doesn't work well with Heart Sex.

Mercedes: Yeah, someone's going to leave crying . . .

(Laughter)

Simon: So it's fucking.

Joseph: No, you can fuck using the head or heart.

Mercedes: It's unemotional.

Joseph: No, there are plenty of emotions.

Parisa: Can Animal Sex involve peeing during Sex?

Joseph: If I understand you correctly, then yes . . . anything goes with Animal Sex. Bodily functions can be a part of it. It could birth urinating and defecating fetishes. Animal Sex can provoke all kinds of fetishes because the monitoring head and heart are out of the way. Animal Sex often exposes hidden fetishes. Everyone here has a fetish in one form or another, because we live repressed! No matter how unrepressed *you* try to live, if we're repressed, you're still going to be affected by it.

Mercedes: I've heard that fetishes are more common in men?

Joseph: No . . .

Mercedes: I read a pop psychology article . . .

Joseph: Yeah, *pop* it right out of your mind. . . . Repression creates deviances and this energy doesn't select according to gender. Maybe women's fetishes are less obvious, like Valentine's Day. You understand? What else?

Kelly: My husband has a steak and blow-job day fetish.

Jeremy: Hey, wait a minute!?

(Laughter)

Mercedes: I'm not telling my boyfriend about that one!

Day Three: *The Sex Seminar*

Joseph: Just put them together and have a tube steak. Make it easy!

(Laughter)

Mercedes: You're bad!

Joseph: You made it too easy! I couldn't pass up on that one.

Lynn: I realized how warped I was when I got with him!

(Laughter)

Lynn: If he's a freak, I must be a freak!

Joseph: So Animal Sex! That hungry, craving, biting, feeling every part, trying to tear each other apart . . . It leaves us with a sense of body, mind, and heart satisfaction; they are all interconnected. Animal sex comes from your instinctual self. That's why after this type of Sex you're often left asking "Where the fuck did that come from?"

All of these types of Sex can be done separately and together. The more we understand Sex and Sexual energy, the more versatile we become with it.

Okay, so let's look at the fifth and final type of Sex; Man-made sex. What is Man-made sex?

Mercedes: Faking orgasms.

Tami: What we think sex should be . . . our interpretation of it. For me, thinking about it, as opposed to just letting it be.

Joseph: Man-made sex is the kind of sex we have the most in this society. Head, Heart, Body, and Animal Sex is often tainted by Man-made sex. So, what is Man-made sex?

Lynn: It involves thinking but it's more than just thinking.

Lisa: Porn?

Joseph: Close. It's boxed sex. We take Sex, this infinite power, and we try to box it. We delude ourselves that it can be boxed like, as we said before, children do in the ocean with a bucket. We box it and then we turn it into a business. We try to control it and make money out of it. We take it and create advertisements and pornography which are, unfortunately, usually formulistic. Just like movies and television where dramas, melodramas, soap operas, and sitcoms follow formulas, we have taken Sex and have done the same. Mainstream porn is very predictable: blow job, cunnilingus, doggy . . . turn left, turn right, cum shot; we all know what's coming next.

I've heard from men that watch a lot of porn, that they know exactly when to fast-forward to get to their favorite part. I don't know anything about that . . . but men have told me so.

(Laughter)

. . . It's formulistic. It has its precisions and angles and it's formatted . . . not creative. It's very boxed. I can package it and sell it! I used to sell them in a big box called VHS, now we sell it in a smaller box called DVD's, and an even smaller box called data files.

Man-made sex portrays Sex as something that can be controlled, possessed, and owned. It's giving a whole generation of kids a completely distorted view of Sex. Presently, it is quickly becoming the primary way in which the young are gleaning their sexual education. The youth of today believe that pornography and the TV sex has a lot to teach them, largely because of how it's packaged and boxed. They're accustomed to and expect to have everything, including Sexual knowledge, come in an easily consumable form. This high gloss *Mad Men* style of sexual advertising easily persuades the impressionable into believing that "They know what they're doing and I'm going to buy what they're selling!" They, of course, being the ones who are cashing in on Sex. Unfortunately, sexual knowledge is quite limited in these forms. We're not saying these mediums cannot provide Sexual education; we're just saying it hasn't, so far. Instead it's being sold as an intoxicant, thus, potentially creating a future generation of addicts. Man-made sex is the kind of sex you get high on; it's a drug. We use Sex as a drug.

Man-made sex is the new *pill*. The original pill was a female contraceptive that changed the world, not just sex. It's effects were so powerful that it became known as 'The Pill!' There were a lot of pills out there at the time but no pill had the effect that THE Pill had. It changed the entire landscape of the women's movement, marriage, and Sex, to name a few. Everything changed in society when the pill was introduced. There were some very influential and courageous individuals, like Margaret Sanger, who held the fort until The Pill came along. *Pornography*--which needs to be redefined to include areas and individuals of Sexual influence such as advertisers and advertising, Sexual creators and creative Sexual art, and museums--has also had its heroes, like Ms. Sanger, who have fought and sacrificed so we could have the Sexual liberties we enjoy today.

Day Three: *The Sex Seminar*

Lynn: I'd like to add that there are organizations today that have picked up where Margaret Sanger left off. Let me read to you some interesting findings from an advocacy group dedicated to Sex education called Advocates for Youth:

"Research has found that teens, aged 15-19 were 50 percent less likely to experience pregnancy with comprehensive sex education than those who received abstinence-only education and 60 percent reduced unprotected sex!" They also stated that, "No abstinence-only program has yet been proven, through rigorous evaluation, to help youth delay sex for a significant period of time, help youth decrease their number of sex partners, or reduce STI or pregnancy rates among teens." Lastly, "Public opinion polls consistently show that more than 80 percent of Americans support teaching comprehensive sex education in high schools and in middle or junior high schools."

We need more open-ended Sex education programs in our schools.

Mercedes: So what do we do, in the interim, since kids are still turning to porn for their education?

Joseph: Obviously, we need to get our school systems up to par. They have responded, more often than not, to the repressive pressures rather than to the needs of our children. But as importantly, it's time that we begin to hold the porn industry equally responsible to Sex education.

It's become quite apparent that pornography is more influential than ever and is here to stay. Therefore, it is abundantly clear that the providers, many of whom are in it strictly for profit (money and/or power), need to begin to understand that, like it or not, they have been thrust into the forefront of Sex education; which comes with great social responsibility. A new Sexual social consciousness needs to arise so that pornography can begin to become a healthy and functional instrument to Sexual advancement. How can this contribution play out? Maybe, at the minimum, pornographers can set aside a percentage of their profits for Sex education. . . . But I digress; let's get back to the pill . . .

So, what new pill has Man-made sex created?

Mercedes: Viagra!

Joseph: Right! Viagra was born from all the energy put into Man-made sex. In addition, Man-made sex has created a new phenomenon! It's called "manity." What's that?

Mercedes: Vanity for men.

Joseph: Right again. Men are, once again, challenged with the same thing women have always been challenged with: a demon called vanity. Men are exhibiting more vanity. They groom, they crop and prop, they shave, wax, pluck, pump and flex, they live with the mirror! Men are now suffering from manity.

Simon: Is that a problem, though? Obviously, there's an extreme you can get to. I feel like I look after myself and a lot of my friends judge it as borderline Gay. So is it a bad thing?

Joseph: I'm not saying it's bad or good; neither is being Gay, by the way. Of course any extreme is a problem, but what we are saying is manity is a product of Man-made sex.

Brennan: What is Man-made sex causing women?

Joseph: The effects of Man-made sex upon women have a long, old, barbaric history. Traditionally, it can be argued that Man-made sex was the cause of prostitution. In addition, it can be further argued that it had an equivalent effect upon creating women as property. This is not to say that women have forever been victims to Man-made sex. No. Historically, there have been many periods where women were in charge, and when they were not in charge, directly, they wielded tremendous power indirectly, behind the scenes.

Today, because of Man-made sex, women are battling challenges such as lower pay for equal work, sexual enslavement, and, as we looked at earlier, self mutilation. In contrast, they are also finding increasing power in pornography and politics.

Women are fast becoming power brokers in politics and they are *the* power brokers in porn. Women are starting to change the game a little at a time; a game that men began.

It was "Man" who originated and cultivated Man-made sex. He set up sex to suit his needs, wants, and fantasies. That's why it's easier to call it **Man**-made sex… but don't forget, "Man" is also in wo-Man.

More is expected of a woman, sexually, today because of Man-made sex. In pornography, and in advertising, women model behavior, which is photographed and filmed, that is imitated by most, if not all, young women. Younger women are watching and taking notes! They're asking themselves daily "Is that how I'm supposed to act?" Or are being told by men "Look, this is how you're supposed to behave."

Day Three: *The Sex Seminar*

Mercedes: Is it because of Man-made sex that we perceive it's only women that are harmed, or taken advantage of, and not men? There's all this anti-porn action because of the women being harmed by it, but there is no discussion of how the men are being harmed within the industry. The men and women are being harmed in an equal way.

Joseph: Man-made sex has a lot to do with it. People today, unlike in the 70's, are now wondering if there are any victims in porn.

Kelly: I feel like the girls are having a great time!

(Laughter)

Simon: There's a documentary I watched called *After Porn Ends* . . . women are not having fun.

(Joseph goes over to the AV technician and says something to him in his ear)

Joseph: This is impromptu. We're going to take a quick look at a short interview of a porn star named Nina Hartley.

Nina Hartley is a pioneering porn star from the 80's who utilizes pornography for the purpose of Sexual education. She has a series of instructional videos for individuals and couples that not only answers questions on Sex but also demonstrates it with great care and intelligence.

For about 15 years, if I remember correctly, she was "married" to two people at the same time; a man and a woman. Now, it's hard enough to be married to one person for that long but to have done it with two, well, at least on the surface, it is quite an accomplishment. Personally, I would love to sit and speak with her to understand how that was managed. It's not part of my experience or comprehension to be able to pull off a successful relationship between three individuals. She is an interesting woman, to say the least.

(Group views Nina Hartley Video)

Joseph: So, what did you think?

Kelly: Wow, she wasn't a victim!

Mercedes: Yeah, and she's really clear.

Reese: I found her pretty intelligent.

Joseph: Be careful, you're starting to sound like the people who say "That black guy is so articulate and well spoken."

(Laughter)

Nina is very straightforward and, as you heard, she takes exception to people who project that she's a victim or that all porn workers are victims. We're not saying that there aren't people being victimized within the industry because anything that is Man-made is going to have corruption and victimization. Look at Government. It's Man-made and look at all the corruption and victimization that exists there! Anything Man-made eventually victimizes to some extent and eventually corrupts. That's because it's not natural; it's not from nature. Nature decays-man corrupts-nature balances-man victimizes. It's that simple.

So, Man-made sex is unique from the other types of sex because it depends on mimicking what someone else has produced. We have sex according to how someone else says it should be and look. So what are some of the pluses and minuses of Man-made sex?

Simon: It gives false information to the public about what's real and what's not real in Sex.

Joseph: How about this? It creates its own reality.

Simon: It creates a farce.

Joseph: Well, for some people it's a farce, but it's just a different reality. For some people it gives them a sense of safety, a sense of consistency in their sex. How do we find safety in Man-made sex?

Riley: It's predictable.

Joseph: Exactly, predictability creates the safety; the illusion of safety, that is. This illusion has made some uncommon Sex practices from the past, common today. A perfect example of this is anal sex.

The sex industry has packaged anal sex in such a way that it has become a norm. Young guys today, who are growing up on porn, believe that anal sex is part of the Sex act because it is *predictably* performed in most sex videos. They have come to expect it from young girls who often comply strictly from the pressure they experience from the boys or their peers. Now, there's nothing wrong with anal Sex . . . and if you didn't hear me the first time, **there's nothing wrong with anal Sex**,

Day Three: *The Sex Seminar*

(Laughter)

. . . but if it's engaged in because of pressure or lack of knowledge, it can have some very damaging results. A lot of these young teens, who are following what they've seen in porn, are having it the wrong way so they are getting damaged. Pornography doesn't remotely prepare the novice on how to properly approach anal Sex. Fortunately again, Nina Hartley does an excellent intro-instructional anal Sex video that both educates and demonstrates a healthy way for partners to participate in the act. And of course there are others; there are individuals who perform seminars on how to properly have anal Sex. The education is out there; we just need more of it.

Lisa: These videos and courses must relieve a lot of the tension and ignorance around Sex.

Joseph: Great frustration gets to be released in these ways. Tension will naturally build when we feel inadequate in anything we do; especially in Sex.

Before the advent of the VCR, men's only, non-coital, outlet for sexual frustration were porn shops and strip bars. As I may have mentioned before, the porn shop I worked at was in Times Square, which was an area flooded with large corporate companies. Lunch time was our busiest time and we would get bombarded with all these corporate types. It was amazing how many men came in during their lunch breaks, and immediately after work. When I first started working there I couldn't figure out for the life of me, why they would waste their lunch hours there. I never "needed" to go to a porn shop, so I just thought they were losers. But that quickly changed as I witnessed how these men, and sometimes women, would walk in tense and walk out relieved. I then understood that this service was an important source of relief and that I had clearly underestimated the value provided by these types of establishments. . . . As a matter of fact, there were times when a man would walk in and I'd think "Holy shit, that's one dangerous mother fucker!" But a short time later I'd see him pass by my counter, as he was leaving, and I would be amazed at how light and easy going he suddenly was. All I could think was, "Thank God, that's one more day a woman doesn't get raped by this guy!"

There are unintended benefits from this industry. So, imagine what would happen if intention was applied?! . . . We need to figure out how to work with this pornographic industrial complex.

Let's take a short break

* * * * *

Day Three: *The Sex Seminar*

Our inability to encounter this infinite energy called Sex has caused us to box it in and create it into a business. The product it produces is Man-made sex and we consume it daily. We consume it through the radio and every other billboard we pass while driving. We consume it through newspapers, magazines, and TV. And we especially consume it on weekends and holidays through entertainment and advertising. There seems to be no end to when and where we get to consume Man-made sex.

Joseph: Welcome back. So what's coming up for you?

Reese: What's the difference between Man-made sex and Head Sex?

Joseph: Man-made sex was spawned from Head Sex. And since the head is the physical home of the ego, then Man-made sex can also be called *Ego sex*. Give that some thought. . . . Anyone else?

Claudia: I've seen porn a few times, and I always thought that the women in it had major issues and that's why they did it. But listening to Nina Hartley has me rethinking the whole thing.

Alexia: Yeah, me too. Do we really know what it's like for these porn stars?

Alex: I'm kinda wondering about the guys in it. Don't tell me they're not lucky.

(Laughter)

Joseph: We'll you're in *luck*. We have a short clip of a series of interviews with male porn stars. Let's see what it's like for them.

(Video is played)

Joseph: Okay, so what do you make of that? Man-made sex, what do you think it causes men?

Angie: I think it destroys the *real sex*; it makes me really sad. It's funny because it relates back to my work.

I work in fashion and I work on a lot of male models; I've worked with at least 30 male models in this year alone. And I do body make-up on these guys who are known as some of the most stunning and gorgeous men out there. People are like "You get to shade in their abs and rub oil all over their bodies?"

Kelly: And what's the problem?

Day Three: *The Sex Seminar*

(Laughter)

Angie: Well it's changed my appreciation of the male body. You . . . I have to turn off a little bit, and they're just a canvas for me. I think I can relate to the porn stars, I can empathize with what they are going through because that is just work to them. My sex is different since I started doing this job.

Joseph: Different in what way?

Angie: Don't get me wrong, I love Sex, but its different . . . it's not as close. You know these guys; (*porn stars*) as we saw in the video, are lonely. I mean, they have no intimacy in their personal love life. . . . It takes a little more for me to get into it.

Joseph: Man-made sex operates on a lower wave length than Sex; it is extremely limited. These types of jobs are born from this type of sex so constant use of this energy does take a toll on its user. This is what's happened to the male porn stars and what's happening to Angie, to a lesser degree.

Solar power. What can it power?

Mercedes: Everything . . .

Joseph: Like?

Mercedes: Life.

Joseph: Be specific.

Simon: Photosynthesis.

Joseph: No, *what* can it power in our lives? What are the different things we can use solar power for?

Group: Lights, heat, vitamin D . . .

Joseph: What does man use solar power for?

Mercedes: Energy?

Joseph: What does he use that energy for?

Group: Cars, appliances, signs, clothing, house . . .

Reese: It goes back to the consumer, whatever the consumer wants.

Day Three: *The Sex Seminar*

Joseph: Yes. We take this amazing thing called *solar power* and we use it mostly on consumables. Then, after a while, we begin to believe that the things we are consuming are providing us with the greatest source of power. We begin to think that they *are* the source of power. We do the same with Sex.

The *way* you have sex is not Sex, it's just how you use that power. There are infinite ways in which we can use Sex energy! We've created a whole new area of sex called Man-made sex with it. But it's no more Sex than a solar-powered car is the sun! Do you get that distinction? Now you're beginning to understand what Sex is or, at least, what it isn't. We've mistakenly believed Sex is Man-made sex. We're deluded and arrogant in this belief and we are consuming ourselves with our own creation. . . . Like some of you do with your children. . . . Sex is like the sun!

There are different ways to have sex. For instance, you can have sex as a *parent*, as a *child*, or as an *adult*. You can have sex seriously, playfully, or as a consumer.

Reese: Can you talk more about the consumer part?

Joseph: That will require we look at sexual consumerism. So let's start with the question "What is a sexual consumer?"

Kelly: Someone who purchases sex?

Joseph: Yes, someone who purchases and does what with it?

Alexia: Uses it.

Joseph: Yes, they consume it and they use it. And sexual consumerism, what's that?

Simon: It's the whole *business* of sex, isn't it?

Joseph: Yes, it's the *idea* that Sex can be sold, bought, and consumed as a commodity. It's not the reality of Sex. But if you believe in this notion, then you can be a seller, buyer or consumer; or you, personally, can be sold, bought, and consumed.

Claudia: Wow! I've worked in the restaurant-bar business and a lot of what we market is sex based. I can really see what you're saying.

Joseph: In the *Sexual Consumer* game, like in any game, there are spectators and players, owners and referees. The owners produce and oversee the game while *always* trying to expand the game. Their goal is *to amass* sexual currency. The refs have a dual role; they ensure that the rules and laws are enforced, while continually trying to control and repress the parameters of the game. These referees can be played by anyone from a church official to a court judge. The players, who can be any of us, attempt to follow the rules, regulations, and laws that are given while employing tactics to accomplish their ends: *to attain* sexual currency.

The owners, or *sellers* of sex, usually take on an authoritarian, parental or, on occasion, an "expert" adult role. They tell you what is sexy, what to buy, and what to consume. The players are either *buyers or consumers,* who operate from parent and child modes and child mode respectively. It's a very calculated game.

Brennan: Who's the spectator in this game?

Joseph: Any of the three roles--seller, buyer, and consumer--can be experienced from either a participant or spectator position. For instance, let's take consumers:

1) They become *participants* by simply being involved in a sex act or wearing something sexy or

2) They can become *spectators* by watching the sex act or observing the sexy clothing.

Who's the spectator in this game? Who isn't? Man-made sex is the largest spectator game in the world!

In the 1970's a movie came out, which some of you may have heard of, called *Deep Throat*. It was a spectator's wet dream. This silly little porno, hit a chord throughout society that had just about everyone wanting to see it, and most did. It was quite apropos that a movie about a woman who could fully *consume* the length of a large penis, became one of the most *consumed* pornographic movies of its time. Sexual consumption of the fringe nature was now above ground; within 10 years, with the arrival of the VCR, Sexual Consumerism became a way of life.

Today, Sexual Consumerism is in high gear. Individuals are becoming *owners,* producing their own materials at an ever expanding rate. Because of the internet, we can sell, buy, and consume just about any form of Man-made sex.

Susan: It's easy to see why we think we control Sex.

Joseph: Yeah, we have contained sex like we've contained water in a bottle. The only difference is we know we don't control water. Can I control water? Can I delude myself that I can control water? Only a child can delude themselves of that. But, somehow, we've deluded ourselves that we can control Sex. Sexual

Consumerism has given us the illusion of control. I mean "I can even play creator! I can create sex, for yours and my viewing pleasure!"

Lynn: Now, how did this all come about? How did this happen? Can we pinpoint when Sexual Consumerism started? Probably not, because advertising, for one, has a long history which dates back to ancient times and there must have been some form of Public Relations with our earliest governments. But we can identify which technologies and individuals caused the acceleration of Sexual Consumerism in the 20th century. We've covered some of the technologies such as the internet and the VCR, so let's look at an individual who we believe is responsible for much of what goes on in PR (public relations) and advertising today.

Edward Bernays, one of the fathers of Public Relations, was the nephew of Sigmund Freud. His approach to PR work was strongly influenced by his famous uncle who mentored him for a period of time. Like his uncle, he applied his knowledge of the subconscious to his work. But, unlike his uncle, he used this knowledge in a completely different way. Where Freud looked to uncover our demons and free our thinking, Bernays' sought the opposite. He held quite conflicting beliefs on human nature than Freud. He believed that we, as a species, needed to be controlled because we were "irrational and dangerous." He further held we *wanted* to be manipulated and needed to be manipulated because we were more like children who didn't want to have the power of running and controlling things. Bernays believed that power belonged to the intelligent few and that these few should be running things. Throughout his career he assisted politicians and commercial companies on the art of manipulation. The knowledge he gathered from his uncle on how humans respond to their primal needs (safety, security, and sex) was instrumental in forming his approach. An approach, we believe, that the advertising industry's business model is built on.

Angie: I see that going on all the time in my industry. It's all about selling at the end of the day and we do it as covertly as possible.

Lynn: Bernays approach was covert. He insisted that the consumer was not to know that he was being influenced, on a subconscious level, by "invisible forces."

Joseph: Isn't it amazing how creative some of today's commercials are? That's because we have some of our most brilliant minds working for PR and advertising firms. They are, literally, using their vast intellectual and creative abilities to con us into consuming more.

Day Three: *The Sex Seminar*

At this stage, we're perfecting sexual consumerism. Pornography is produced, packaged, and sold with greater efficiency than ever before. The porn product is more stylized and specialized.

By the early 80's, porn producers began to look to produce quality films with better actors. Believing that the viewership was changing to include a wider female audience, they began to develop elaborate and extensive storylines to accompany the sex. That continued for a while, until they got wind that men generally preferred to "cut" right to the sex. The market was dictating; since men were still the main consumers of porn, they decided to return, in large part, to producing "old school" reel to reel type video porn. It became a waste of production money to include a story that men were going to fast forward past anyway. That's why porn in the 90's and into the early 2000's was more formulistic and why we had movies like "New Wave Hooker Part 7," and "Taboo Part 23." They were giving people what they wanted; short, quick, and right to the point porn. They were splicing it and dicing it and feeding it to us just like mom once did. In the meantime they were reducing their budgets and were packaging it in the most palatable way possible. Today, because of technology, pornography has become more diverse than ever. It has expanded to include, again, storylines; there's now homemade porn, Gonzo porn, self produced porn, and computer generated porn to mention a very few.

Pornography is following the lessons of Bernays. They are supplying us with a highly consumable product that speaks to one of our most basic of primal needs: sex.

Lynn: Bernays is responsible for why women smoke so much, and he used sex to make it happen. When the cigarette companies hired him, women didn't really smoke all that much. It was about one in five. But, after he created a connection with sex and cigarettes, through poses that made women look sexy with a cigarette, it went up to three in five within a couple months! Just from one ad.

Simon: So where is the line drawn between art and consumerism?

Lynn: That's a great question because he was also responsible for bringing ballet to North America.

Prior to him, ballet was out of the question for most men because they didn't want to be perceived as homosexuals. So he created an entire campaign which reframed dancing for men. It became so successful that seeing a man at a ballet became commonplace.

Joseph: As we mentioned earlier, there are some great artistic minds in PR and Advertising. Therefore, it's not so cut and dry; art will overlap into consumerism. Any man-made invention comes as a double edged sword. Whether it's an atomic bomb or atomic energy, it all depends on how we use it. The only issue we're taking up here is we need to become aware that humans are causing and producing these experiences, not Sex itself. We are producing products that manipulate and control our desires. Without this awareness we are just what Bernays thinks we are: primitive children who need to be told what to eat, drink, and screw.

Lynn: He said, in essence, and I'm paraphrasing, "As a culture you are hypnotised, so all we have to do is plug in to what they will think they want and need."

Very few of us know anything about Edward Bernays, yet his ideas affect every day of your life. That's why Life magazine voted him one of the 100 most influential people of the 20th century.

*****

Man produces and creates in order to know God; not to be God.

Joseph: When we place something in a container, what we're attempting to do is to know it better. In a container we can study it, examine it, and put it under a microscope. We can create smaller variations of it.

What do you think a front lawn is? It's nothing more than us experiencing being in nature. What do you think a carpet in your home is? It's the same thing . . . recreating nature within your home. Carpeting allows you to feel the softness of *grass* under your feet. Nature is where we got the idea from; everything we've ever created is born from nature. We are always taking ideas from nature and recreating them by incorporating them within our lives. But when you don't give credit to the source of these *re-creations* you begin to think you ARE the source and that's when we go astray.

Imagine having sex and knowing you're *not* the source of it. What would your approach be? Would you be more honourable with it? Would you seek instruction from it? Would you give it greater care? Would you want to know more? As long as we think we've created it, and invented it, and we believe that now more than ever, we've become our own gods. Clearly we're heading in that direction; we've become so important that we video record everything we do!

Day Three: *The Sex Seminar*

How we grow is by holding, containing, and studying the things of life. But you cannot forget, in the process, that this thing--life--is larger than all of us. We have also forgotten this when it comes to Sex. You started to get clued in to that on Friday when you looked at the why's and what's you have sex for. You came up with more why's and what's than there were people in the room! We are looking at Sex in the wrong way. You cannot know what Sex is by looking at what we create and produce with it, but by what it creates and produces in us and in nature. It's important to know what Sex is to you, where we're at as a society around Sex, and from where our children are learning and experiencing it. Most of us experience Sex linearly, single-dimensionally. There's the seduction, the surrender, the sex, the pleasure, release or orgasm, then the escape

Sexual Consumerism produces meaningless sex--empty sex--and, for some people, that's great because that's better than nothing; thank God it exists! Again, there is no judgment here; we just want to put it all on the table so we know what's what and stop lying to ourselves. We can do it asleep. Consumer sex dies easily, and quickly. It can even continue after death. There are people still masturbating to Marilyn Monroe pictures; that's a form of necrophilia. Man-made sex kills life, though, because life is ever growing and expanding, so it has a tendency to kill the life of a relationship, the sex life out of you, and the life out of you.

How about these male porn stars, what life do they have? They have fucked the life right out of themselves. It's so sad! The empty lives they live with.

Lynn: How about the scene of the long haired guy pathetically walking away, after telling the truth of his deep loneliness, and then joking quickly so he didn't have to be with the pain of the emptiness that is his life.

Joseph: It produces emptiness. It limits the fuel in your life. You'd know this if you got in touch with real Sex, because then you'd understand endless energy. When you tap in to Man-made sex, you eventually run out of gas, and the *sellers* want that. They want you to run out of gas quickly so you'll buy another one of their sex products. *Playboy* mastered that back when I was younger.

We were a little more content sexually than young people of today. Our *drug fix* lasted at least a month with Miss June; or longer for women with their Harlequin romance novels. We could masturbate to Miss June while patiently waiting for Miss July to *cum*.

(Laughter)

Day Three: *The Sex Seminar*

Today, I can not only see old Miss July again on my computer but I can see every playmate from every month of every year of Playboy's history. Click, click, click I can see thousands of pictures, movies, and clips from all over the world. I can take fix after fix after fix. Click, fix, click fix clit,

(Laughter)

. . . fix . . . .It's endless, really. My drug supply is endless!

We've accelerated the distribution of sexual information, and that's great because we are more exposed to each other and each other's feelings and thoughts. But, *you knew that was coming*,

(Some laughter)

it's not the essence of Sex, it's about how we consume it and how we feel and think about our consumption. We are some consuming motherfucker's! We just consume, consume, consume, consume . . . And now we're self consumed: us with our *selfies*!

It's okay to consume if you're, as I mentioned earlier to Simon, observing yourself; then consume away. If you're meditative and aware as you are consuming, then this predicament can begin to shift. But if you are consuming asleep, then nothing will change. Take accountability and consciously consume; it's better than repressing. This kind of awareness will make you more tolerant with yourself and others. I don't care if you are using 167 dildos in a session, have fun, but do it consciously. Afterwards, you can sleep on them, like a bed of nails, give it multiple purposes. . . What do you make of this?

Mercedes: I'm wondering if there is a connection between necrophilia and Man-made sex, because it's a dead object.

Joseph: Absolutely there is. There's a thin line between Man-made sex and death. Sex and death are so closely tied, because we experience a *little death* upon each orgasm. It's the closest we get to experiencing death because we get to leave our bodies for a moment.

Mercedes: What about the guy who Roofies' the girl in the club and rapes a lifeless body. Is that a form of necrophilia too?

Joseph: Yes, but more precisely its Man-made sex; man created the drug. The sex is short, quick and largely lifeless and it allows the man to go into his head and create whatever fantasy he'd like with his sleeping victim.

Day Three: *The Sex Seminar*

Mercedes: I bring that up because it's a widespread problem that didn't exist before. Rape has existed from the beginning of life but this new ability to cause a person to go unconscious against their will . . . is that a result of man-made sex or widespread pornography?

Joseph: The problem is not in pornography, it's in the man or the woman who uses this *drug* against another. It's in Man-made sex. The need to consume comes from the need to avoid our deepest pains. The larger the pain, the deeper the insecurity . . . the larger the appetite becomes to consume. Again, it's in the consuming that we find relief from this hurt. But, the deeper the pain the easier it is to lose our humanity. We'll do almost anything if the pain gets too much. . . . Believe me, this pain we're talking about is excruciating. I have great compassion for those in this type of pain; though we all suffer from it in varying degrees. What would it be like if you had to sit in this pain without seeking relief? Well you would feel like a junkie who is in a constant state of withdrawal; it would be hell!

We turned away from Sex and the energy it provides. Sexual energy. It's like turning away from the sun and relying on body heat alone to warm up. It's limited, and there's only so much of it to go around. Sex, like love, is life affirming. It fills you and will satisfy you beyond this lifetime. You can live twenty lifetimes and there would still be plenty of Sexual energy to fulfill you. Meanwhile Man-made sex cannot even fill one lifetime! We're too busy sucking our own dicks! We're too busy consuming our own products and playing God . . . so that's where the problem lies. The problem is not in the forms we've created . . . it's not even in the art we've created. It's in how we're busy consuming everything, more than in any other time in OUR history. Not in all histories but in our Victorian-Puritan history. We're just consuming like mad and we have to because our whole economic system is tied up in it! We've trapped ourselves in a maze; in a Matrix.

Mercedes: Is that an indication that male sexuality is somehow in crisis?

Joseph: Oh it is . . . all our sexuality is in crisis, man and woman. I mean, you have these poor girls and women cutting their labia. Geez, what am I supposed to do now? I used to play with Labia; I'd do origami with them! It was just awesome . . .

(Laughter)

. . . and now you're cutting it off?? What am I supposed to do now? . . . Those beautiful rose petals!

Angie: I used to work in a sex shop when I was younger, as well. I read about this experiment a few years ago, when iPhones and iPods first came out, where they gave a group of people all the same color phone, free of charge, and asked them, six months later, how they felt about it. They were all still stoked about it. Then, they gave the group the option to switch to a white one and some of them did and some didn't. Six months later the ones that did switch were asked how they felt about it and everybody was like, "Uh . . . I dunno if I made the right choice!" and they weren't super happy about it.

I think this relates to porn. Our porn shop had such a wide selection! Latinas, cougars, barely legal, that kind of stuff . . . and I just wonder, in our sex lives, if there are too many options? I don't really know how to express this, but do we have too many options? What is that doing to us as a society?

Joseph: It's not complicated . . . you're just a bunch of eaters. You will eat whether it's a single meal or a buffet and you will eat a lot of each. You're self consumed consumers who will continue to consume until there's nothing left . . . or until you find something larger than you. The problem is it's not truly prevalent to you that there is something truly larger than you; not the way this generation has been raised. You're blind to it like you're blind to the stars in the sky. You have become the stars that you once saw in the sky.

When you ask a bunch of kids what they want to do for a living they'll usually say they want to be a singer, a musician, or an actor. So, if that worked out for them we'd be fucked with no doctors, no lawyers, no nothing in the future because everybody wants to be a star! So, Angie, when you ask "What is that doing to us as a society" you need to rephrase it and ask "What is our consumption doing to us as a society?"

We need to own where we're at; but that's, of course, after we know where we're at. (He said smiling)

Our consuming is turning us into zombies. Why do you think there is such a big fascination with zombies today? It's reflecting how we're living. We're insatiably hungry and we're consuming everything, including each other. We are consuming ourselves until there is nothing left but the mouth that consumed it. It always shows up in our art; if you want to know where a culture or society is at, look at their art. Art will always tell you where we're at.

Unless we return to the sources that have always been there for us, which have created us and have sustained us all along like the sun, the stars, or anything transcendent; we're in trouble! These powers are like parents watching over their kids at playgrounds. They just hang around and let us play our game. They feed us, clothe us, provide us with things like vitamin D hoping, one day, we'll grow up.

Day Three: *The Sex Seminar*

Like a child, we become aware of these *powers* only after something's gone wrong. Then you run to it like a little kid who runs to mommy and daddy screaming, "I hurt myself, I hurt myself!" We're the same! "Oh God, look what happened to me!" . . . You're kindergarteners! Embrace it, accept it! We are fucking little children! We're not that smart; if I could somehow take you to other worlds, which are way beyond us, you would have a clearer understanding, that this is just a lower grade of existence. We're kids and we do what kids do. Kids play and consume . . . little consumers. They'll eat you out of house and home, if you let them.

Angie: Thanks, that really clears it up for me! I'm seeing how much I tend to look to the outside and blame other things and people for my problems.

Lynn: The sex toys, the variety of pornography, how many or how few lovers you have, how much or how little money, your clothes, your social status, your Facebook status--none of it is causing your pain. Your search for your identity, your individuality, and your inability to find it within is what causes it. Remember, we consume to avoid this pain.

Joseph: What we're looking to accomplish in this seminar is to assist you in experiencing a power larger than you--even if it's just for a moment! This will allow you to get away from your own little mellow dramas and maybe see that there are authentic sources of nutrition to feed from. At this point, you're consuming from a man-made tit for all your satisfaction and nutritional needs. Yeah, I prefer tit over teat.

(Some laughter)

. . . What you don't realize is that these tits might as well be filled with sand; they're big giant sandbags you're suckling from! . . . You're sucking sand. There's no more milk left in those tits. That's where we're at, there's no more milk left in the tit, keep sucking, though you'll get some good sand down your throat. Then, after a while you'll get sore and full of warts. Genital warts, warts on the mouth and the throat; all kinds of damage will come from this *sand*. This is what we do to ourselves when we consume something that was never meant for human consumption. We get filled, bloated, and stagnant; and, like water, when stagnant we become diseased or sources of disease.

We have to know that there are larger powers in this world than us, I don't care whether you believe in a God or not, there are larger powers than us that we can tap into; powers like Sex and Love. So let's take a closer look . . . Lynn.

Day Three: *The Sex Seminar*

Lynn: *Okay everyone, place your feet flat on the floor. Everything off your laps, hands apart and eyes closed. . . . and just let yourself breathe easily and effortlessly. Breath in and out . . . in and out . . . there's nowhere to go, nowhere to be. . . . We've been seeing a lot this weekend and we've been in a lot, but now we're going to leave it for a while. We're going to leave all this consumerism, all the consumption; we're going to leave all the stuff that we do as humans. . . . Just for a while we're stepping aside. So, can you allow yourself to breathe easily and effortlessly while you breathe in and out? . . . In and out . . . keeping your hands apart and feet flat on the floor allow all the tension you feel in the room, and in you, to just be there while you continue to breathe in and out in and out. With every breath you take in, allow yourself to be filled with relaxation, and as you exhale feel the tension leaving your body. Continue to do this for a little while, breathing in and out . . . in and out . . .*

Now, feel the tension in the room; feel the accumulation of all our pain, fears, worries, hurts. Feel the pains of all those we know and love as you continue to breathe in and out in and out . . . and as you breathe in know you will be converting this tension into relaxation and as you blow it out, all the tension disappears. Breathe in all the tension, blow out the relaxation. We've taken a lot from the world, we've consumed from the world. You're now giving back to the world. As you continue to breathe in and out in and out . . .

Can it be okay that you give to the world? Take in the tension, and give to the world, give back on your exhale, relaxation. Keep doing this until the whole room is filled with relaxation. Until you are fully relaxed . . . and everyone around you is relaxed . . . and we are all sharing in this relaxation. Breathe in the tension, and give back relaxation, until there is nothing else to breathe in but relaxation. Eventually, everything you breathe will be nothing but relaxation, because of all the giving you've done.

Stay conscious, stay breathing, and feel how the room is filled with more and more relaxation; that all you can consume now is relaxation. That which you've supplied and have shared and given to the world, not recreated, but given anew. You are able to create relaxation! New, not recycled, new, from the breath you take in, you give back relaxation.

Now can you allow yourself to feel your need or desire for Love? Could you allow yourself to feel how in your life you need and desire Love? Let it be okay that it's there, as you continue to breathe in and out in and out. . . . If this desire and need is not there or unreachable, can you let that be okay, just for now? Let it all be okay, let the emptiness be okay.

Day Three: *The Sex Seminar*

As you be with the emptiness, as you be with the want, know that all it needs is love; it wants to receive the love . . . Just notice how you're feeling now, just notice what's happening, just take what comes up.

. . . Notice the emptiness you might feel; it has no love and that might make some of you feel worthless, or alone. Can it be okay that you let yourself feel the worthlessness . . . the aloneness . . . the lack of Love?

Now, know that we avoid Sex to avoid these feelings, yet we wish to belong so we're conflicted, we need it.

Just be with how many bodies you have used and been used by in your lifetime. Allow yourself to be with how many bodies you have used and been used by. Take your time . . . go through them all. Your lovers . . . strangers . . . one by one, and be with what the sex was like with them.

*Now imagine you're in a pool and be with all your lovers in this pool; feel this pool of sex you have created. Every lover and every stranger that has touched you and that you have touched. Quickly, slowly, whatever way it comes. Be with the lover you are with **you**, whether it is a considerate one, an oblivious one, or everything in between. Include you in that . . .*

Now I want you to feel what it's like to be in this pool you have created, this sexual pool of yours that you live in. Try not to run from it, just be with it . . . just take notice, and just take what comes up. Can you accept what you have created, can it be okay that this is what you created from the little that you knew, and can that be okay? Just for now . . .

Now if you want to know Sex, as you stand in this pool, allow yourself to ask it to come for you, to lift you from this pool. . . . Now you begin to feel some sort of force coming, swirling around you, and as it swirls and swirls and swirls, it starts lifting you, like Dorothy in The Wizard of Oz, *but it lifts you ever so gently and carries you over and out of your pool and places you into a calm, beautiful ocean.*

It illuminates you, bathes you, invigorates you, feeds you, holds you, and cares for and about you. Feel yourself in the center of this infinite incredible ocean; it goes further than your eyes can see. Feel its energy, its strength and calm, and ever so slow movement radiating into you as you breathe in . . . and radiating out of you as you breathe out. . . . . Radiating into you, inhale, and now out of you, exhale.

From this place, look back over your past and say to yourself, "This is what has been. This is what has been . . . ." Now leave it there. As you return to the present in *this magnificent ocean of life, can you accept the energy it is giving you? This vibrant force that keeps everything in it alive. Can you accept this Sex energy; this creative force that truly has no form? Can you now allow yourself to feel it all around you, all around each other; all around all your past lovers and strangers . . . ? Can you invite them into this same place into this infinite energy for them to find their way and **their** healing?*

Can you invite all your friends and family into this energy to heal, to be fed, and to be held? Can you let yourself feel this sharing right from your center and out . . . and then right back in to your core? Can you connect with this Sexual energy that's located in no particular part of your being, but can be found everywhere you feel and look? From here you can begin to ask a question about what this energy is, this energy that creates life, that pulls us to do, that allows us pleasure, exploration. It is vast, it is encompassing, and it is never ending. There is enough for everyone; enough to go around for everyone; it can be shared. Just allow yourself to fall into it. Let it hold you. It is stronger than any mother or father you will ever know, stronger than any lover you will ever have. It's a place where you and your lover can share time. It will hold you both. For some of you it offers the opportunity for many other lovers, if you choose to explore in that direction. It's not limited like an apple pie; there are more than enough pieces to go around. It's infinite . . . and it is loving.

Slowly begin to feel the floor underneath you, the ceiling above you, and the walls around you. Feel the chair you're sitting on. Feel those to the right and to the left of

you, and slowly . . . at your leisure . . . when you are back in the room you can open your eyes.

(Group readjusts and several members can be seen crying)

 So, what was it like for you when you started to first go into this pool?

Kelly: Something really weird just happened to me . . . it was a jolt and I saw a really white light! That's never happened to me and I wanted that feeling again but I couldn't get it back, I tried to get it back but couldn't.

Joseph: That's Sexual energy; you have just connected with Sexual energy.

Kelly: I'm going to try that again!

Joseph: Just don't bottle it. . . . What was this like for you? We can talk about any part of this Lab.

Day Three: *The Sex Seminar*

Mercedes: The water was really murky in the beginning, it was boring . . . it wasn't colourful, it was more like a beige sludge than a pool, it was like, whatever, who cares. The actual Sexual energy was this beautiful clear ocean. It was daytime in the pool with the icky sludge and it was night-time in the ocean, all the stars were out, it was nice at first but then I couldn't wait for it to end.

Joseph: Then you need to explore. Explore the Sexual energy, now; you stopped giving, you were just taking at that point. What would have happened if you had given, in that moment that you got bored, what would have happened if you started giving? Would you have still been bored?

Mercedes: I imagine it would have been moving instead of stagnant.

Joseph: You became stagnant, the ocean is never stagnant. You follow? So you got to see what you quickly do with this power. So you need to give.

Mercedes: I'm starting to see that some expressions of it were so beautiful and others felt ugly.

Joseph: Well, that's all you because water reflects us. So it's in the giving. You need to give!

Nathan: My pool wasn't very big but as soon as I started feeling the Sexual energy around us, I'm still feeling it, I just got a shiver. When my eyes were closed I could feel it. I could feel it moving out my left hand the whole time; it was surreal because I can still feel it. But it looked like the vastest sky, without an end and no horizon; it just kept on. There was no seam between land, sky, and the universe . . . it was all just there.

Joseph: This energy is always there. Good. Anyone else?

Angie: I needed to be reminded that it was infinite. I was in this ocean and I could see the horizon and I knew that it went past the horizon, but some part of me had it end there. I was fighting through the whole thing. . . . I have a pretty vivid imagination so I could see all of these things but I wasn't quite connected, I was struggling to keep my eyes closed. Then when you said this isn't apple pie, this is infinite, all of a sudden my eyelids disappeared and it was like DING! And all I heard was, "Oh, there it is!" Then you started to bring us back to the room and I didn't want to come back, I was like, "No! I want to stay here, right now!"

Joseph: You like to wait till the last minute before you surrender. . . . Remember, this is meant to give you a *glimpse* so that you know where to go, where to find it and that it exists.

Day Three: *The Sex Seminar*

Tami: I was almost unconscious and I felt myself coming in and out. I came back when you talked about the pool and it was hard for me to imagine it. But as soon as you referred to the ocean, it was clear as day. There was a clear line of the past and the future. It was super clear and felt good; but afterwards I shut it off. Now I feel ill, kind of sleepy, and physically ill.

Joseph: Up to now, your relationship with Sexual energy has been what you experienced in the pool; basically unconscious. The good news is that you do have an opportunity to create a relationship with it based on your experience with the ocean. It is showing you what can be.

So these are things that are in the way of this being a continual relationship with Sexual energy. You're beginning to see what your relationship to it is. We are plugging you back in so you can begin to create a new relationship with Sex and its energy. . . . Anyone else?

Susan: I didn't want to invite my past partners right away because I was loving it by myself. Eventually I did, but initially I didn't want to.

Joseph: Okay. What do you make of that?

Susan: I think I was enough by myself at first.

Joseph: No, try again.

Susan: I didn't want to share.

Joseph: No. Why would you need to stay in it longer without them yet.

Susan: Because I didn't want them to experience it?

Joseph: No, you're being stupid. I gave you the answer. . . . Because you needed to stay in there longer without them. You needed to stay longer to finish filling yourself.

Susan: Well, isn't that like I was enough on my own?

Joseph: Not initially. You resisted the instruction to *imagine yourself with your lovers;* instead you stayed in the present.

Susan: Why am I doing that?

Joseph: To finish filling past emptiness' and loneliness'. This happens when we marry too young; which I'm sure you did. That's why you wouldn't let your lovers

Day Three: *The Sex Seminar*

join you. When you're full, happy, loving, and full of life, don't you want to immediately invite others to join in! So you're going to lie to yourself and think, "I'm okay alone?" No, no, no, this is the infinite energy of Love and Sexuality, which we can't help ourselves to share. You get it now?

Susan: Yes.

Joseph: We're just isolating Sex, so you can experience the difference.

Tami: When you said that (*to invite your lovers*) I got, immediately, tense and it felt like a weight and I was like, "No. Hell no, that's not going to happen." I didn't even question, I just completely left it behind.

Joseph: Susan is feeding herself. You need to do the same. It's time to drink, feed, live, and allow yourself to be taken by this energy. Once you've done this, it will be easier to invite others. You won't be able to help it. You'll want to share! You see lovers are generous, they want to share, and they get excited, and they'll speak to perfect strangers when they're in Love . . . or in *Sex*.

The problem for all of you is that you're consumers! You take and take and take and take and take . . . what the FUCK do you give to this world and the people in it? What do you give, really? You don't give. When we give we change. When you watched Nathan give yesterday, he became Sexier and brighter! We get Sexy when we give, dumbasses! It's in the giving that causes Sexual energy to come forth!

You're too busy fucking taking, sexually! What are you giving? You think when you're flashing your tits, asses, and muscles, you're giving? NO, YOU'RE TAKING! You want attention; you want everyone's attention. "Oh, look at me! No look at me!" It's in GIVING that you start a communion with Sexual energy, it's in GIVING that we become Sexy and excited. It's in the giving! You're a bunch of takers! Sucking your thumbs and consuming your own shit. What are you giving to the world?! And I'm not talking about giving to someone less fortunate! You're all fucking less fortunate, every one of you in this room. Don't waste your time giving to only someone less fortunate, ***give*** . . . give your time, your attention, your eyes, your touch, your care, your thoughts, your compassion, your heart. Whatever you have, just give . . . your smile, your enthusiasm . . . just give. You sit here, like a bump on a log and you don't give. You hide, and you protect yourself, and you wonder why you're deprived sexually. . . . Can you give of yourself? I get that it can be scary or even petrifying, to expose yourself . . . to expose yourself to the experience of rejection or inadequacy. But there is an answer and that is to give! True giving will fill you, it will increase your energy and Sex naturally becomes a part of it. People will want to be around you. They'll want to share in the love making you're *creating* through your giving; whether you're giving physically, mentally, or emotionally. This giving *invites* Sex! This is how to invite Sex, creative energy. . . . But you have to give! You are programmed to take first; we normally give conditionally . . .

Parisa: I give a lot. But I was stabbed in the back . . . I do not want to give anymore.

Joseph: Then you gave conditionally.

Parisa: NO! I gave unconditionally for many years!

Joseph: No, because you wouldn't be so hurt if you gave unconditionally.

Parisa: I gave a lot . . . I loved my family, I served I gave . . . I lost my life, I didn't get anything. So there's a balance between giving and receiving and I learned that too late in life.

Joseph: I agree there has to be a balance, but what did you give? . . . You gave your life?

Parisa: I gave love. I raised my nephews. I loved my brothers, my sisters . . .

Joseph: What did you want in return?

Parisa: Nothing!

Joseph: No, you're LYING! NOTHING? What did you want in return!?

Parisa: I lost my life!

Joseph: WHAT DID YOU WANT IN RETURN! Answer my question, not yours!

Parisa: I wanted to have a life!

Joseph: What did you want from them!!?

Parisa: Nothing from them! I loved them!

Joseph: Then why are you hurt?

Parisa: I'm hurt because I lost my life!

Joseph: What happened to your life!? Where did it go??

Parisa: It's lost! I lost my youth, I lost everything!

Day Three: *The Sex Seminar*

Joseph: Who did you give it to?

Parisa: I gave!

Joseph: Why did you give your life?

Parisa: Because I was stupid; this is what I see now!

Joseph: You didn't give anything!

Parisa: I gave! You don't know what you're talking about! I know what I'm talking about because I loved everybody . . . unconcitionally. But I lived a war! I lived a war and I loved. But you know what? The people were shit because I was raped! I was sexually abused so don't tell me about not giving! I matter and I deserve to receive when I give! It should be balanced! Giving without balance is stupid!

Joseph: You didn't give. I'm sorry, but that is bartering you're describing.

Parisa: I gave. It's your assumption that I thought I gave, but I know that I gave and I loved, and I know what's inside my heart.

Joseph: You gave conditionally.

Parisa: No, I didn't. For a very long time in my life I did not give conditionally, and I was stabbed!

Joseph: You were stabbed . . . I get that.

Parisa: Yeah, then I was hurt.

Lynn: Parisa . . . What he's pointing to is that we all give. We all give because we are learning about this thing called Love. But initially, we give to receive. I understand you worked really hard to try and be loving to your family . . .

Parisa: I gave unconditionally and there was no expectation from it! . . . I know what I'm talking about!

Joseph: Okay, then we will stop *giving* to you. Because if you already know then there is nothing we can give you. Is it possible--just possible--that you could be wrong? If it's not possible, then we will leave you alone. I will accept that you know. Is it possible that you might be wrong, though?

Parisa: No, it's not possible because I know I give unconditionally and without any expectations.

Day Three: *The Sex Seminar*

Joseph: Okay. You do not have to explain any further, I respect that it's not possible for you... Anybody else? What do you make of this ... to give! What does that mean to you, to give?

Kelly: What I think you mean is to give without expecting anything back.

Joseph: That's part of it but what do I mean by give ... what are you giving?

Kelly: Time, heart, emotions ...

Joseph: What can *you* give? Let's make it personal. What can you give to the person on the other side of the room? Just check yourself?

Kelly: I *can* make them feel good about themselves.

Joseph: Yes, the key here is what CAN you give, not what you SHOULD give. It's in the CAN that a balance will be struck. Then we never over-give and leave ourselves depleted. What CAN you give is the question.

Simon: What I've got to give ...

Joseph: Pardon?

Simon: I can give what I have to give.

Joseph: Yeah, how much of it?

Simon: As much as I have to give, not everything I have but just what I have to give.

Joseph: RIGHT. What do you do with the rest?

Simon: Keep it for myself.

Joseph: Absolutely, *my love for you is the excess of fondness and affection, AFTER all MY needs and desires have been met!* After I have filled my life! Then and only then can I love you! To give till you're depleted, is not giving.

Lynn: To give depleted, leaves you, then, feeling like a victim of love. It leaves you feeling like you loved and didn't get back.

Joseph: So when I yelled and screamed for all of you to start giving who am I asking you to give too?

Kelly: Ourselves.

Joseph: Ah, yes. I'm fighting on your behalf. Because you don't *give* to yourselves, you take. You deplete, but you don't give yourselves. You don't fill yourselves.

Susan: Was I giving to myself in the pool?

Joseph: Yes. You were finally giving to yourself rather than to everyone else. You chose to put yourself first instead of playing martyr. That's the usual role you've taken in order to secure a safe life. You've honoured the traditional woman's role of your family and culture; and its depleted you. . . . No. Give to you and when--and only when--you are overflowing, you can give. You're heading in the right direction.

Nathan: I got a question. So, if, for example right now, maybe not right now, but next week when I'm not quite so full, because I'm going to be overflowing by nine tonight.

(Laughter)

SO, next week, once all this has settled for me because I'm still figuring this shit out . . . Since my cup is not full, can I go out and give compassion or a smile, or my time. Do those things fill me?

Joseph: When we give from our core to others we give to ourselves in equal measure. That's how you know if you're giving properly. When you finish giving them you will feel, and be, full.

Nathan: I feel good when I walk down the street and I smile at somebody, because I never used to be able to do this, and they smile back.

Lynn: These are great steps. Give wherever you're at; give what you can. Where do you start? Anywhere: friends, family community . . . anywhere.

Mercedes: The only time I ever feel ripped off is when I give something because society expects me too.

Joseph: Right, it's those obligations again . . .

Mercedes: It's only been in the last year where I've even bothered to ask myself what *I* want. I've done the Communication Seminar and understood the bottle conversation, but I never fully got it until this year. Just to even ask myself, that's a big step. I don't negotiate my needs anymore. I will my wants, but not my needs.

Lynn: You're becoming more sensitive to you. I remember when you first started with us; you had a strong wall of ice surrounding you. The ice has mostly melted now. We cannot know what to give, or if we even have something to give, with a wall of this type blocking our view.

Joseph: You need to be able to see in order to give properly. These walls, like walls of pain or anger, make it very difficult to gauge when we've given too much. Most people deplete themselves because they give the *little* they have, until there is nothing left. And they are giving to consumers who are not going to give anything in return because they, too, are depleted. We need to learn to give after we've filled and not before!

Susan: But what if I'm low on energy and an emergency comes up, are you telling me I shouldn't give?

Joseph: No, of course not. I'm saying if we commit to steadily filling ourselves, we'll always have reserve for difficult times.

Mercedes: My bottle was always mostly empty. I was taught that if I gave attention or sex to a man, that he would owe me love. So I've attracted men who thought that if he bought me dinner and flowers on Valentine's Day, that he was owed sex.

Joseph: When we run on empty we create these rather distasteful types of bartering. Because we need to feel we *exist and matter,* we are 'forced' to enter into relationships that are degrading to our self esteem. They give us disproportionate return on our efforts.

Nisha: I have a question. I know I've always given to my siblings, conditionally, and since the Communication Seminar I've been more cognizant about what I'm giving because I see I don't have much in my bottle these days. So, I've had more boundaries with my five siblings, but all of them come to me when they need something; so it's been a challenge. I wonder why they're coming to me when they're in need. Am I creating an energy that has them being dependent on me?

Joseph: The well is a central part of all ancient cultures. Before we figured out irrigation systems, we relied on the well to source water, even life, for the community. You've made yourself that *well* for the family so you could feel a sense of value. Maybe today you're finding value elsewhere and no longer need your siblings suckling from your teat. But they haven't received the memo yet. You've changed the game and it's going to take some time before they realize it. But, if you want to be *The Well* for your family or community, and this goes for all of you, you'll have to understand that it takes time and specific efforts to accomplish it.

Day Three: *The Sex Seminar*

To create a physical well you have to first carve out a space for it. Then you need to line it with stones and seal it. Finally, after the seal has taken, you'll need to fill it with water or wait for rain to fill it. This is how it's done physically and spiritually. If you've followed these steps, then others can come and drink from it, without it bothering The Well one way or the other. If you want to be The Well and you're bothered when your siblings come to drink, then all that means is you haven't finished building it yet. SO put up a sign saying 'under construction, come back in 2017!'

Most people don't aspire to be The Well, they're content showing up with their buckets, bottles and cups when needed, and that's fine! That's a particular life experience. Apparently, whatever created us wanted us to have that experience so it's provided us with wells. Therefore, how could I say anyone's wrong for showing up with a bottle or cup? Who am I to call the expression of life a moocher? . . . Nisha, the only question you need to answer for yourself is whether or not you want to be a well. And if you don't want to be a well and you just prefer a smaller life again, that's fine!

Nathan: I find that I have a hard time, especially with women, to say no. I just can't do it; my sister takes advantage of that.

Joseph: Your situation is the same as Nisha's, you find worth and significance through others; in your case you find it through women. You need to, first, figure out if you even have *it* to give. . . saying no becomes easier when you've learned to fill yourself. Lighten up, this is elementary school. If you want to be a well, then be a well, if you want to be an astronaut or an actor, or if you want to run a bookstore, it's all okay. Life is easier when we reduce our significance.

Nathan: Well, through my job I've become the *person,* for a lot of guys, that they come to with their issues and I have gained some trust from them.

Joseph: So, life's trying to balance you.

Nathan: . . . but they come to me regularly.

Joseph: Yeah, that's what happens; life uses others to balance us. You've over taken care of women and now you're being balanced. Life can use whatever it wants!

To illustrate this, there's a scene in the *Dharma Brother's* documentary where one of the prisoners' talks about how heavy a fly felt on him while he was meditating. Since he was supposed to be keeping still during it he was unable to swat it away. Then the fly flew up to the ceiling and drew *everyone's* attention in the room creating even more tension and heaviness. He later commented on how he couldn't believe how powerful a fly could be to torment a room full of hardened prisoners. This mere fly created a balance of power by overpowering an extreme group of powerful men. By the way, don't confuse power with strength.

Nathan: So, embrace these men that are coming to me?

Joseph: Yes. They are coming to balance the weight, to level the imbalance between your yin and yang. When they're done you'll know where you're at! And when you know where you're at you'll know when it's appropriate to give. It will be easy to say yes or no because you'll be able to see when you're helping vs. when you're enabling.

Lynn: I had to be very still in my giving as I grew older because I came from a system of barter. My mother and sisters taught and practiced barter love. "I give you, you give me." Even when I gave more, I was alright as long as I received approval in return; but it was still barter love. If you come from such a system you're never going to know balance and what real giving is because you're waiting for something to return as you give. Now I give through stillness. I sit and meditate . . . and give.

Joseph: We are not talking about the giving "that it's better to give than it is to receive" type. That's an elitist religious minded, "I'm here to help you . . . you less fortunate one" idea of giving. We're talking about the giving that starts with the self; again, only from there can you give properly.

Emotions need to flow, but when we are giving more than we are receiving or vice versa, our emotional piping and sewage system gets backed up. In turn, Sexual energy cannot flow, thus, leaving us with an insufficient amount of life force. Consequentially, we are compelled to substitute this energy with the aforementioned artificial energies. It's only by creating a balance between giving and receiving that we facilitate the flow of Sexual energy to us and through us.

Nathan: I was taught that "It's better to give than it is to receive." So I think that has something to do with why I think I have to help women.

Joseph: Well, you were half taught because the saying is meant to be practiced with women *and* men. . . . This idea of giving is a manufactured idea that goes against nature. It goes against the ebb and flow of the ocean. It goes against the equal inhalation and exhalation of our breaths. This type of giving will exhaust you.

Day Three: *The Sex Seminar*

Giving doesn't have to be a sacrifice. It serves us best to only sacrifice under dire circumstances. When we say you need to give we're not talking about this artificial giving but, rather, the giving that loops from you to the other and then back to you.

When you begin to practice this kind of giving, just like when you practice deep breathing, you invite additional energies; energies that are needed to help you clear your pipes. Most of you are clogged to some extent--whether it's your hearts and minds because of unresolved grief or your bodies because of self mistreatment; so you need this energy.

Alexia: Are you saying that Sexual energy heals?

Joseph: I didn't. Marvin Gaye did.

(Some laughter)

... For our intents and purposes, yes, Sex energy heals! It WILL clear the pipes. It seems that subconsciously we are aware of this analogy because we often refer to our Sex as *clearing or cleaning the pipes*. . . . You want to give and if you're clogged then give to yourself. You can only really give to you if you're unclogged.

Take in Sexual energy with your breath, with your giving, in your Sex and from heaven and earth.

Simon: Where does Sexual energy come from?

Joseph: I can't tell you where it comes from, but I can describe to you how we gain access to it.

We are connected to the earth through our feet and the heavens through our heads. Now, I want you to imagine these powerful energies existing in both Heaven and Earth. The Earth energy circulates from its core up through our own core just above our genitals, keeping us grounded. Similarly, Heaven will circulate in the same fashion from celestial heights to come just below our genitals. The intercourse of these two energies, which encompass our groin area, is what makes sexual energy so intense; this communion between both energies from Heaven above and Earth below creates a type of vortex for Sex energy. Illustrations of this can be found in several works of ancient African art.

Mercedes: I see now why the Sex center is so powerful. Why life begins from that area of the body.

Joseph: And you can further understand why it's so important to keep that area flowing. When the Sex center is blocked, then you not only have Sex problems . . . you have *life problems!*

The majority of us connect primarily to the Earth making our interactions and Sex more animalistic and less human. It's from this limited area that Man-made sex is created. If we made the conscious effort to access more energy from the Heavens, or what some would half correctly call spirituality, this energy would provide us with the ability to balance our earthbound nature and create a synchronicity between these powerful forces. This, in turn, brings us to full humanness. And it's from this full human position that we experience the ultimate flow of give and take.

When we are unobstructedly receiving the Earth's energy, it fills us with a needed life force that is immediately shared with all that is from this Earth, including other humans. In addition, as we, simultaneously, do the same with the energy of Heaven, we also immediately share this with all that is above the Earth. So it follows that when both energies are synchronized, the flow from you to the world is powerful, centered, and correct.

When we rely predominantly on one of these energies over the other our actions are quite different. For example, if I'm receiving and accepting energy from the Heavens more than from the Earth I will appear as high minded and what I say is not going to help anybody much. I might appear to be very intelligent and, maybe, a bit spiritual, but what I say will not be able to be applied on a practical level. In reverse, if I'm too grounded, what I say will be experienced as too heavy and definitely not uplifting.

Parisa's in the process of balancing these energies. She alternates between one and the other, avoiding getting centered where the pain sits, in her Sex center. That is why she reacted so strongly . . . Know you're processing it; you're beginning to heal it.

When you store your *junk* in the Sex center you eventually cause yourself to cut off from the waist down. You then take up residence in your heart or head, thus, explaining Heart and Head sex.

Lisa: I was struggling with this last night, I had made plans to go out with some friends and when I got home I just really didn't want to. I wanted to just be on my own and be in my feelings, and I struggled so much about whether I should cancel or not and I did end up cancelling but I felt SO guilty about it.

Day Three: *The Sex Seminar*

Joseph: That's your enculturation. You're supposed to, you're obliged to, and it's expected. You're to take care of friends and family; just like your mother does (Susan). There are people who are enculturated to *not* take care of friends and family; so they don't have this issue. A Paris Hilton or Kim Kardashian would be good examples of this. It depends on how you've been enculturated, how you're conditioned.

Your culture says "If you're a good girl and obedient wife life will *take care* of you; men will take care of you;" so you come to expect it. But it usually doesn't work out that way, thus, leading to the complaint "Oh I do so much good, why am I going through this?" I've heard myself say this and I have to tell myself to "Cut that shit out!" . . . Really, I'm going to try and take it from mere mortals!? We're all in this together. We're here to support one another, not carry one another. We're not each other's food, we're not the source. I don't make my wife the SOURCE of my happiness, of my feeling of love, of my worth and value. I don't use her to source that. That's a burden on another human. I utilize all these other infinite, amazing energies out here, instead; and it's these energies that fill me and allow me to be a Well. They allow me to give unconditionally.

You are stumbling over your conditioning; not your conscience. The guilt you feel is manufactured by your belief system; it's not authentic guilt. The good news is you're starting to see the effects your culture is having on your life! You can see the conditions that are causing you to live this way and doubt your instincts and intuition. You don't have to live like this! The problem is, when we begin to notice these restrictions, we often respond by pulling back rather than challenging them. We wind up backing ourselves into a corner, causing us to live a very tight little life; a dead life. That's when we need to start giving so we can receive life's force: Sexual energy. This energy pushes and expands the walls until we are alive again.

Mercedes: Can I get you to clarify something? Parisa was saying . . . um, sorry so many things were coming out of your mouth at once . . . but I heard you say rape and molestation. So in terms of giving and taking . . . I've experience both of those things and I did not give those freely, at least in my opinion.

Joseph: No, those were taken.

Mercedes: But I felt obviously very angry about that.

Joseph: Because it was taken.

Mercedes: SO how come in her case . . . I just didn't feel that she was acknowledged . . .

Joseph: That it was taken?

Mercedes: Well she said she gave unconditionally but, obviously, that wasn't freely given.

Parisa: No. I gave love to people in my family, unconditionally, but one member later sexually abused me. So that's where the disappointment came in. But the point Joseph, to clear it up, is since I was a child I was taught that I was worth nothing; that I owed everything to my family.

Joseph: Right! Do you understand that?

Parisa: Yeah, that's why I had that problem. I'm 34 now and I'm just learning to give myself.

Joseph: So you have to give worth to YOU before you can give again. You gave without worth of self. Your system set you up for that. If you were taught that your family, basically, owned you and you owned none of you, then it would be easy for someone to think they could help themselves to your body. When you buy into this, which you couldn't help do because you were born into it, you cannot possibly give unconditionally; you own nothing to give. You don't own you, so how can you give you to anyone? Therefore, any giving you do is self sacrifice. That's not giving. Giving should not be a sacrifice. You sacrificed your energy and your very life force when you continued to give. This would have, eventually, led you to death's doorstep. . . . That's why you felt like you were taken advantage of by not just your sexual abuser, but your entire family. I understand that.

Parisa: I have been working on myself now since 1999, since I decided I had enough. . . . I've been doing self work for a long time and sometimes it feels like I'm going nowhere.

Joseph: Yeah, I've been working since 1973, so I understand . . . You're getting close. Let yourself be with the hurt more than the anger, for now.

There's always work to do! Always room for growth because I want to grow old, I don't want to get old; I want to keep growing! So, I have to keep feeding me and keep growing. I resist sacrificing; it's not giving. Religion will tell you sacrifice is good. That's part of their business plan. Churches, Synagogues, and Temples might have ceased to exist a long time ago, as a business, if we weren't willing to sacrifice for them. They're going to tell you that sacrificing is the work of God! That's a hard one to resist. No it's not. Sacrifice always weakens you; even when it's needed.

If I am full of worth and my wife cheats on me, yes it would hurt and I would feel the human pain of betrayal, but it wouldn't destroy me! I would have enough reserve to continue on. I might even understand, especially if she did it from pain or deep unhappiness.

Lynn: He would have compassion for me at this point. Like Rick from *The Dhamma Brothers* who had compassion, and ultimately love, for the man who brutally mutilated and murdered his daughter; he would have compassion.

Joseph: Rick could only have done that from a full state of worth. He didn't do it from a place of sacrifice. The mistake we all make, because we don't know better, is that we sacrifice ourselves in the name of giving. Giving true forgiveness, for instance, cannot be done from a place of sacrifice.

Sacrificial giving leaves us vulnerable to being taken advantage of. That's when it gets confusing because we think were being good by sacrificing. Parisa and

Mercedes, you both have to understand your mistake was not in giving but in from *where* you gave. You gave, the way you were taught--sacrificially. If you knew better you wouldn't have done it . . . and you no longer have to.

These childhood set ups are intended to be gifts to us. We are challenged, throughout life, and as we find our way through the challenges, we acquire skills and lessons that strengthen us for our larger life purposes. When we fail to overcome these initial challenges, often because our souls are over ambitious, we wind up falling far short of what our souls have determined for us.

Simon: And these gifts come from different areas?

Joseph: Yeah, any area we are challenged in life holds gifts for us. There are so many wonderful areas to get gifts from.

Simon: I can understand this from the fact that I was working for free and I started charging money, but I find it hard to figure out how to get worth for myself.

Joseph: So, the challenge is in finding worth in your work.

What you need to learn is you can feed off the creative part of your work. If your work is creative, then you can feed from that very same creative energy that sourced your work in the first place. You're looking for money to feed your sense of worth; it can't. Money is only something that sustains you and helps you live.

Simon: So, it's the work that I can get worth from.

Joseph: Yes, you can find self-worth through the work. Not by how much you sell it for, that's what another is willing to make it worth, but by what has sourced it. You can feed while you're producing the work. Drink and eat more of that! That will be what excites you! Money flows as a by-product because at the end of the day money is a manifestation of the creative, but not a source of self-worth.

Simon: So, I've been doing the same thing, when I try to get worth from other people, when they've given me work.

Joseph: Yes, you're trying to get worth from money and other people. What you're usually going to get from others is approval or disapproval. At most, they can share creative energy . . . but they cannot source it for you. You need to feed from the source and you can source it yourself through your creative work.

You come to sit and ask me questions to resolve or help with issues and I sit and source. I source creative energy and creative intelligence and all that is creative in me. I become so full that I have to take a moment to remember you're in the room with me; and by you, I mean your ego. Then I think, "Oh, you're here" and I give!

After which, I'm left with more energy than when I started. So it's not what you give me that feeds me, or in the money you might pay, but rather the source that is supplying you the answers.

Simon: So, I can take from the creative experience I'm in.

Joseph: Good, but even better; you can *fill* yourself from the creative experience.

Lynn: And that's really what Joseph and I have been saying to you, it's not in the knowing, sweetie; it's really in the experience for you. That's where you're going to fill you.

Simon: It's taken a while to get it, but I think I've got it.

Joseph: You think!?

(Some Laughter)

 . . . All we can do is to continue repeating it until you get it.

Lynn: Man-made sex is very sacrificing. You're either sacrificing yourself or the other.

Mercedes: What do we sacrifice?

Day Three: *The Sex Seminar*

Lynn: Your dignity, your worth, integrity, and other things.

The young girl who you saw mutilate her labia was her sacrifice for your validation. For you to tell me I'm sexy, for you to tell me I have a beautiful vagina, for you to want to fuck me, I may have to sacrifice parts of me. It would be my sacrifice for all of your approval. That's what we do, and we think we're giving by cutting off parts of ourselves; we think that's giving. We especially think we're giving if the other is happy or approves of our actions. "Come on show me your tits and I'll give you some beads!" Are you happy now? Do I get your approval? ...Do you approve of me now since my labia doesn't hang anymore?

Joseph: Her sister actually called it a ham!

Lynn: Yeah . . . "I don't have that ham anymore!" . . . SO she sacrificed. That's how we sacrifice with Man-made sex. There is no supposed to be; we make that up! With real Sex we experience. It doesn't ask us to sacrifice anything except for what we know; what is safe.

Joseph: Yeah, we can give ourselves *Sexual* experiences; new experiences. We can give ourselves the opportunity to experience things anew by resisting our insistence on knowing. . . . Each sunset is divine because it's new; each and every day is new. We can give ourselves permission to receive each moment anew. We just need to stop projecting and that is much easier when we surrender to something larger than ourselves.

Tami: So, it's really about rooting myself in something. . . . I think you told me that, years ago. To root myself in something that's deeper or bigger than me. There was this one time that I'm really in my head, so I decided to just look at the moon. I literally stared at it for I don't know how long, and I found this peace. It was amazing. I feel the same when I'm in water. Nature is the most amazing thing to me, it's like my thing.

Joseph: These tangible elements that are larger than us can really help; it's a good place to start. Then it becomes easier to invite and experience the intangible ones, like Sexual energy and Love. Surrendering to the tangible will make it easier to surrender to the abstract. So start with the tangibles, start with the moon, and the sun, and the ocean. Things larger than us!

The fact of the matter is that the moon is really just a representation of an energy that can't be seen so it shows itself through the physical moon. It gives you a feeling. How do I know that to be true? If I could, somehow, put a fake moon up there, you wouldn't get the same feeling from it. It would be dead energy. It just wouldn't feel the same to you.

So, understand the things we *look* at, the things that are in form are there to help us experience the form-less. What we're *looking* at is a representation of the abstract; just the tip of the iceberg. When I look at Susan, I'm looking at the form that is Susan. But if I'm fully present to her I will experience so much more. I will experience more of her than she can even access of herself. I will experience the formless part of Susan. Putting it simply, I will *see* her spirit, not just the body.

Even in a criminal, I could see the spirit, yet I don't underestimate what he can do wrong. I'm not going to be a fool, but I still see the spirit; a spirit that can be *unlocked* with something like Vipassana.

Tami: So I don't know if it's me being selfish, but I can always see other people's problems really clearly. But when it comes to myself I can't see anything. Is that selfishness?

Joseph: No you're just cut off! You have cut your body in half; the lower half of you is barely hanging in there. On top of that, you avoid this problem by focusing on others. Eventually, what's going to happen is that you'll energetically break apart because this unused part is going to get weak. You may become physically ill because of it.

Why do some of you let yourselves be used and abused sexually? Is it because you're so disconnected from Sex, from yourselves, that you figure "Go ahead, fuck away" I don't feel it anyway! . . . It's time to reconnect.

Our doors will re-open at six o'clock. Have a good dinner.

* * * * *

"This is your last chance. After this, there is no turning back. You take the blue pill -- the story ends, you wake up in your bed and believe whatever you want to believe. You take the red pill -- you stay in Wonderland and I show you how deep the rabbit-hole goes."

Morpheus (The Matrix)

Joseph: Welcome back. I hope you had an enjoyable dinner. . . . So, what thoughts or reflections have you had; what's come up for you?

Day Three: *The Sex Seminar*

Mercedes: I was thinking about the idea that most of what we see is just a front for something bigger.

Joseph: True, but only if you're not projecting.

Mercedes: What do you mean projecting?

Joseph: Projecting, like they do at a movie theatre. That's when we take a projector, turn it on and project preconceived, pre-produced images on a blank screen. In your case, you're the projector, the preset images are your ideas, experiences, and pre-judgments and the screen is anything or anyone that you're blank to. That's what you do when you're *looking* at someone rather than *seeing* them.

Simon: What's the difference?

Joseph: When you're *looking* at someone you're projecting; even if you're projecting a hazy image upon them. When you're *seeing,* your projector's off and you're actually in touch with the person. In other words; as Don Juan told young Carlos Castaneda, "*Seeing is the capacity to perceive the essence of a person or thing."* When you're seeing you have the opportunity to see the rest of the iceberg beyond its tip. So Mercedes, if you're *looking* at the front, as you put it, you're only looking at the front of what you're projecting. Anything behind it is of your own imaginings; it's not real, although you may experience it as real. But, if you're *seeing* the front, then you're seeing the front of the person or thing and that gives you the opportunity to see more of the real person or thing.

You're all constantly projecting when it comes to Sex. You rarely see the real!

Susan: My best friend was married for many years and she thought she saw her husband, clearly. Meanwhile, he was carrying on an affair, for years, right under her nose. So I get what you're saying.

Joseph: Unfortunately, that is not unusual. Think back to the elements necessary for an affair and what remains common throughout is the inability for one to *see* another.

Let's take a look at this more deeply and *see* where we're at.

(Joseph and Lynn divide the room up with women on one side of the room and the men on the other)

Joseph: Okay guys, follow me.

Day Three: *The Sex Seminar*

(Joseph leads the men to another room where he proceeds to guide the men through a seated meditation; this lasts for 25 minutes. Lynn has the women take a seat and proceeds to put on a film for their viewing; it's an excerpt from a pornographic movie that Joseph and Lynn have edited and added music to. After the women finish viewing the 20 minute clip, the men and women switch places and Joseph leads the men through a showing of the same clip. Lynn, like Joseph guides the women through a 25 minute meditation. After the film has been shown they take a break then return to the room)

Joseph: Welcome back one and all! So what was that experience like for you?

Mercedes: It looked like fun. I don't know if anybody else found it disturbing. I didn't find it disturbing at all . . .

Joseph: I want to know more about what it was like, than not like. So it was fun for you. Good.

Simon: I felt really angry, I wanted to punch the guy, and even though they were doing it together it was just pissing me off that he was doing that to someone else. I found it really hard to feel sympathy for the guy.

Nathan: I felt the same way, it seemed so one-sided. There were moments where it seemed very sweet and then he would just fuck it right up again and just go all haywire. It's just like, I never wanted something to end so badly, I was just like okay, turn it off, I get the point . . . that's what I got.

Lisa: The first two thirds I felt nauseous and I felt angry and I thought I was going to throw up. I felt angry. I thought "why the hell are you guys making us watch this." I wanted it to be over; and then, the last third of it, I realized that she really wanted it, too, and it was really both of them. Then I thought it looked funny, just the way they were, I don't know. It wasn't as serious to me.

Joseph: Anything else?

Parisa: I wasn't able to watch more than two minutes, my eyes were closed. My ears were closed, and I was still hearing it and I kept thinking, "why am I here?" I did not sign up for this. And I don't know what feeling because I wasn't even able to have a feeling because I was so scared of it. It was more than scared, if there's a word worse than scared . . . Yeah, it was too much for me.

Joseph: Okay.

Day Three: *The Sex Seminar*

Angie: There were little elements of it in the beginning that I found to be upsetting, like the writing on the bathroom wall. It made me a little sad, but the rest of it, I agree with Mercedes, it kind of looked like fun. It didn't feel to me that it was non-consensual. It didn't feel like anybody was actually being hurt, any more than they wanted to be. It kind of felt like an exploration. It didn't feel evil; it didn't feel like rape or anything like that.

Nathan: I was okay with the opening of her in the tub writing; *give me strength* on the wall. But the folded up priest attire with the cross . . . that really put a wrench in the whole thing for me. Like Lisa said, I mean there was a point for me where I was obviously like "Okay, she's enjoying this." In the beginning when she was gagged, that kinda seemed beautiful to me because it would take a lot of work to force somebody into something like that. So, clearly, she wanted that. Where the majority of the scene, like I said; there were so many elements that were hard to avoid. My first impression was she was not happy because of what she had written. I wasn't sure if she had written it in blood and she had been cutting herself or maybe she was using lipstick. And then, like I said, the priest thing; that guy was pissing me off! After that it was too late because I was already pushed over the border; probably because I hate fucking men.

(Loud laughter)

. . . I can agree with everybody, like obviously she wants to be there. And then it was like, what Angie and Mercedes pointed out, there are some fucked up people in this world man, you know, and good for them. But as long as they keep it to their hotel room and they pay the fuckin' cleaning lady . . . .

(Laughter)

Angie: I'm not saying that I'm into the idea of a bag over my head . . .

Joseph: Wait, wait, wait . . . no, no, no. Forget about what you want and don't want; just feel what you feel. *You feel what you ought to feel, I feel what I ought to feel.* So allow yourselves to feel what you feel.

Tami: I felt an array of confusion, and I was angry and kind of sad. Then I was like, "Okay, what happened to you as a child?" I don't know it was up and down.

Alexia: I was kind of in the same place. I was thinking about how, in our childhood, when we feel really shameful and that it's just like two children acting out. One's feeling shame so she's getting what she wants . . .

Joseph: That's too impersonal. What was the experience like for you, personally?

Day Three: *The Sex Seminar*

Alexia: Well it brought up a lot of shame for me. It brought up the carelessness, and I know not to that extent, but I've done that. So it just brought up a lot of shame.

Mercedes: I don't know if it was careless, so much as it was perfectly orchestrated. We don't know the conversation they had before that scene occurred.

Joseph: This is wonderful! The film might as well be a blank canvas that brings up what's there. All you're expressing is what's there. What if it's your inner film that you're playing back to yourself on a blank screen and you're just sharing what's there for you? What's there in your sexual connection, or lack of connection, with Sexual energy. This clip illustrates the entire spectrum of sex types; from Head sex, to Heart sex, to Animal sex, to Body sex to Man-made sex--it covers it all.

Simon: It's damaging, though.

Brennan: I thought it was absolutely beautiful! The trust that these people could have with each other . . . to know their limitations and experiences together. Just a whole range of emotions that they're going through together on this journey and to allow each other to feel the way they wanted to feel. And that's HUGE trust, absolutely HUGE trust.

Mercedes: It might look like rape, but that scene was the opposite of rape. How would you guys feel if that were two women acting that scene out?

Simon: There's no way that you can do that scene without hurting someone. There's a high possibility that you could end up really damaging someone. It doesn't matter how much they prepared beforehand. It could still happen, and that's what freaks me out about it; that could fucking kill someone!

Brennan: But what if you want to be hurt in that way, and that pain excites you?

Simon: But that's what's freaking me out!

Brennan: . . . and what if it's an outlet for not beating myself up? If I can feel pain in the bedroom, and not live in my own pain.

Joseph: You see, again we live in a repressive society. So, Simon, the other day you were saying, "I don't understand, everybody here can't say the word shit." Now the shoe is on the other foot, now you sound like them and they sound like you. So, we've just done a complete 180 with you and the group. It's more important what it brings out in you so you can see what's there.

Day Three: *The Sex Seminar*

This lab brings out what's blocking, or assisting, your connection with Sexual energy. This brings to the surface something in everyone! These feelings you're expressing are *your* feelings. They are not caused by the clip; your feelings are a *reaction* to the clip. The original action is inside you. You're approaching this as if the cause of your feelings lies outside of you. No, they are from *inside* of you. All you need to do is be with the feelings. Don't go reaching for the judgment or change gun; just be still.

Many of you have done this very thing all weekend: thinking something else is causing your pain. No, you're the cause of your lives, and this lab allows it to show up so you can begin to have choice in your life. Revealing what's affecting you and causing you to make the choices and decisions you are making. It's showing you your relationship to Sex. We can't control this energy; we can only find a harmony with it. People are going to do what people do. Our power is in how we respond to it. And we can't respond if we're all inundated and scared and shut down from past injuries. . . . This lab is pushing the limit for most of you--we understand that. But this is the *Sex* seminar, not the, "let's court and get to know each other, seminar."

Parisa: So, I hated it. What does that mean? I wasn't able to watch.

Joseph: It's not that you can't, it's that you won't. It's very difficult for you to find Sexual meaning if you're not experiencing Sex; the same goes for life. You looked away thinking it was bad or harmful, in some way, without really fully seeing it. That's akin to watching the beginning of a movie and then writing a movie review. We can't accept your review; you can't accept your review. In other words, because you didn't stay open to the experience, you are not able to conclude anything worth a damn about it . . . and you also want to know, *what you don't complete, you're doomed to repeat.*

Parisa: I want to be able to function Sexually and be happy, but in saying that, this is not what I choose to experience. I don't want this to be part of my life. Are you saying it will affect my sexual life?

Joseph: Yes, because this hate you speak of--you said you hated it--is still in you long after the movie finishes playing. . . . Long after this seminar is done.

Parisa: I choose not to see.

Joseph: That's absolutely fine; these are just opportunities. Sometimes we're ready for them and sometimes we're not. We can choose whatever we want, but what came up for you had nothing to do with the clip. You need to understand that.

Day Three: *The Sex Seminar*

This *Sex Lab* is designed to bring up deeper Sexual issues and insights. If you are strong enough to endure it, you can see quite a bit about yourself. These types of painful and challenging situations are intended to help us grow! You see, what a soul mate really is, is someone who brings up all your shit and helps you see it so you can heal it. That's what a soul mate is. That's the real spiritual definition of a soul mate; one who brings up all your shit! And if you help each other heal, it creates a bond and connection that's there forever. A soul mate is not someone you have sweet times with alone . . . that you project romantic love on; it's someone who helps you find freedom. That requires a great deal of endurance and patience, though. . . that is, if there is such a thing as a soul mate.

Kelly: And you only have one?

Joseph: You can have different soul mates at different times of your life. It can be any mate that has helped you grow and move forward . . . or transcend even. It's usually not accomplished in a pretty fashion. What if these two in the video were soul mates? What would you say to that? . . . All that most of you did was project your experiences on them. You don't know what happened before and after their Sex, it's all your projections. Maybe now you can see how much you project.

This is good. See what's coming out, so you can see what's there. I'm not agreeing or disagreeing with anything that anyone said, I just want to hear it. These are your experiences; they're fascinating to me. What did it bring up for you?

Nisha: When I saw that, it brought up a lot of pain. I was going back and forth whether it was consensual or not. But even if it was, I felt so sorry for her that she has to go through this. What you're saying really makes sense, because those are my big blocks and pains.

Lynn: That's great! You're seeing you on that screen; it provoked the hidden. Every person here has had a different reaction so far, which tells more about where you're at than where they're at.

Joseph: If the clip was, objectively, showing a truth about something horrible, like a Nazi atrocity, or something great, like a disease curing discovery, then everyone's reaction would be similar. But in this case, the clip says neither; that's why your reactions are so diverse. It's a perfect scramble of things that creates a blank screen.

You can project whatever you want on it; you can get hooked by whatever you want. Look at what hooks you. Look at what provokes you; take advantage if you can. This can be freeing. That's all that matters at the end of the day. That you get free of whatever is blocking your relationship to Sex.

Day Three: *The Sex Seminar*

Mercedes: So what if you weren't bothered by it at all?

Joseph: Then you weren't bothered by it at all. But it's not about whether you were bothered or not, it's about what was your experience. Even Parisa had an experience even though she avoided it. Avoidance was part of her experience.

Lynn: Just check and make sure you weren't disconnected. There's a big difference between not being bothered and not being bothered because you're disconnected.

Mercedes: No, I thought it looked like fun. I thought, "good for them!"

Tami: What if it was like a wave of emotions? I was scared in some parts and interested in others. At the end I was like, "Wow, it's actually quite beautiful," the passion at the end when they kissed each other was beautiful . . ,"

Lynn: It sounds like what you've been saying all weekend. You go in and out of your head, all of a sudden you experience it and then you're in your head again. "Whoa now I'm scared!" "Oh, this seems crazy!" It sounds like you in your relationships.

Joseph: Just recognize and see what it brought up, because we brought the energy to you! People do different things with Sexual energy.

Nathan: There was so much going on. Did it bring up my different experiences?

Lynn: Yes. Your experiences or your beliefs.

Joseph: If you have strong religious beliefs, what do you think it would have brought up for you? You know, the cross or crucifix. If you had strong beliefs about power and domination, what would that have brought up for you during the domination and submission section? You understand? It brought up *your* beliefs and experiences.

You see these are the things you do in your relationships, but you just hide it from yourself. You stretch it out over a year or two or three or ten. Now, if we took all those scenes and stretched them out over ten years: on Tuesday he gags her, on Wednesday she runs away from him, on Thursday she jumps on top of him. Five months later he's having anal sex with her; on Christmas he's having a huge fight with her and calling her a bunch of names. On Valentine's Day she's doing the same, in reverse, because he didn't buy her a bracelet. Come on, this is what you do! You just extend it over a period of time. We just crunched it all together for you. Again, you got fixated on the acts, and not the energy. What was the energy? What was going on, energetically, between them? You needed to feel the energy between these two people, not just go by what you were seeing, to really understand what was going on between them. But what happened was that your personal energies got in the way.

For some of you, the energy brought up shame, because that's what's there within you waiting to be felt. For Nathan and Simon it was anger. Now, you can see what's blocking your intimacy with Sexual energy and what you need to work on. It's neither good nor bad, it just is. We're all here to reveal and see where we're at; now you know, much better, where you're at. . . . Main and Vine.

(Giggles)

Joseph: Where are you at?

Parisa: So if I have nightmares after this does it means I have to check my energy?

...I know I am going to have nightmares from this!

Joseph: You don't have to worry because you didn't watch it, so don't worry about the nightmares. Whatever comes up will be the nightmares you already live with. If you do have a nightmare, write it down and meditate on it, contemplate it. That will help you in a way you can accept.

Parisa: I won't be able to meditate because the vision will come into my head.

Joseph: What vision? The vision will not be from the video because you never watched it. It will be the visions from your past pains. Parisa, you want to know you are strong enough to handle it. It will be challenging and I have compassion for your pain and . . . you are strong enough to manage it!

Parisa: I think there's something that I don't want to remember. The body remembers but the brain doesn't.

Lynn: The thing is Parisa; you keep having a dilemma with yourself because you keep wanting to be free. You've been working really hard to become free and get expanded, but the wall keeps coming up.

Parisa: There are many walls . . .

Lynn: Yeah, exactly. Those walls have you in prison; it's your prison. It's not Reese's prison and it's not Mercedes'. This is personal to you, and all of us have

Day Three: *The Sex Seminar*

huge compassion for you; yet, we see you suffering within those walls, still. Parisa, what's going to be greater, the fucking suffering and pain behind those walls or the pain you'll feel going after it?

Parisa: For me, I don't want to bring up the pain. But it's not just the sex it's 17 years of war, of seeing the violence of war; so it's not going to be overnight!

Joseph: Everyone in here is battling an internal war; everyone. None are easy. Of course it's not going to happen overnight but we have to *begin*. Stagnation is not the answer; stagnation is not the same as harmony. You're expressing the pain we're all in to one extent or another. You all have this war going on and it's time to see what it is, what's caused it and how we got into it in the first place. You are born into **this** particular time period that offers its own challenges; that has its own war and war environment. It's important to take that into consideration.

You can keep away from these questions and challenges or we can face them. It's our choice; we finally have a choice. So you don't have to go after it one way or the other but it looks like *Par* wants to go after it and *Isa* doesn't!' Right? It's like you're split, and that's okay because that's where the war is going on, between the split.

Parisa: It's like opening a can of worms, suddenly. This is what's happening right now. You opened a can of worms and it's not going to be okay with a few words. I'm in a state of shock.

Angie: I have a quick question for Parisa. (Faces Parisa) While we were sitting in the room watching this, I saw you and wondered if it was **that** disturbing to you, why didn't you leave the room? I felt like half of the experience of watching the movie was watching you. You chose to sit in the front of all of us with your head in your lap and your hands on your ears and it just felt like I was watching a little kid throwing a temper tantrum. You could have gotten up and walked out, right?

Parisa: I couldn't. I didn't want to disturb anybody . . .

Angie: Maybe you didn't want to disturb us, but what you did was disturbing!

Joseph: Let's make this really clear: nobody put a gun to your head and told you to come to this seminar. You chose it. You've worked with us before; you knew what you were getting yourself into. . . . Obviously, you want attention, from what Angie is saying. You are asking for help. The sooner you get this, the sooner you can get help.

Parisa: There's a lot I could say but I'm not, for a reason!

Joseph: There are no secrets. You may not be saying exactly what's going on for you but nonverbally, you're screaming it! I don't need your verbal communication. Remember, 93% of all our communication is nonverbal. You haven't stopped communicating since Friday.

Why is it so easy for you to feel attacked and victimized. Why is it so easy for you to feel overwhelmed and angry? Do you think that I or anyone here is causing that? No, you are these feelings waiting to happen. The feelings you're having are from your past and the conversations and exercises you have been put through this weekend are designed to assist you in bringing them up so they can be released.

Parisa: I think, maybe I blew a chance.

Joseph: I agree, you missed this opportunity but you can invite another. You can ask for it to arise again. Maybe this *was* your first step in releasing this, obviously, deep pain. But you're going to need more assistance, preferably one-on-one assistance. I can give you all sorts of remedies that would work for the average person, but it won't work for you. You've already said *"no."* You'll need to feel safe and guided before you say "yes" to re-experiencing the pain. Please don't feel like you're broken or disadvantaged. Quite the contrary, resolution of this degree of pain will expand you beyond anything you've imagined. These are the kinds of growth that create wells.

Parisa: Thank you! (Joseph's smiles and nods)

Joseph: These Labs are possibilities and opportunities. They allow you to uncover, in a safe, guided manner and place, things that you wouldn't normally access. Yet they aren't *soft*. We're not going to give you soft and easy little tosses. We're going to give you the harder ones so that when you're back in your life you'll be able to handle the easier ones.

It's like going to the gym. We load heavy weights on you and we spot you. You lift what you can and you get stronger, so that when you're back on your own you'll be able to lift more than you used to. Let's say you used to lift ten pounds of weight, prior to this weekend, and we've had you lift 80 pounds during it; after, you'll be able to easily lift 40 pounds without us. This is how you become emotionally stronger. This is *emotional bodybuilding.*

Now getting back to the Lab, I found it rather interesting that it was the women of our group that were more open to it than the men, even though men watch porn more than women do. What do you make of that?

Day Three: *The Sex Seminar*

Alexia: Yeah, Nathan and Simon were looking to protect us while Mercedes and Angie were like, "It looks like fun."

Tami: Yeah, when I was watching it I was like, "I wonder how the guys are going to react to this." . . . it was harder for me to meditate than it was to watch that.

Joseph: It wasn't as much about gender, as it was about our personal stuff.

Lynn: Now, let's look more specifically at Sexual energy. Take out your copies titled *Sexual Energy*.

(Group takes out worksheet, and Lynn reads it out loud)

This is how we use Sexual energy in our unawares. We use it . . .

- To manipulate others
- To control others
- To abuse others
- To manipulate control and abuse ourselves
- To get relief
- For power and gain
- To degrade and harm self and others
- To communicate past hurts and pains
- To trap others
- We use it as a drug

What's this energy's purpose?

- Spiritual
- To inform
- To uplift
- To express
- To give space
- To connect
- To experience oneness
- To procreate

How could we treat it?

- As a gift
- As a loving force
- As a power of the divine
- With respect
- With reverence
- With honour
- With awe and gratitude

And when we miss the point of Sex verses sex it . . .

- Seduces us
- Enslaves us

As you can see, some of you have missed the point.

Joseph: I'd like you to open your minds for a second and imagine that Sex was actively leading this seminar and it was S*ex* who actually had us put on this, now controversial, clip. What would you make of the Lab then? What would be Sex's purpose in having us watch this--not Joseph and Lynn's purpose--but Sex's? What would you think if this large creative, caring, expansive force that knows what's good for us better than we do wanted this? Sex, which has been supplying this world its energy since the beginning of time . . . Sex, which has been here long before us and will continue to be around long after we're gone; what if it wanted us to have this experience? What would its purpose be?

Reese: To make progress! To bring up whatever's there that's hindering us from experiencing it

Claudia: To provide us with the opportunity to do more with our lives.

Joseph: Good . . . anybody else?

Simon: Provide us with the opportunity for growth. To change my opinion of what men and women's relationships are all about.

Joseph: Yeah, yeah . . . progress, opportunity, clarity, and balance. What else? What did it want to accomplish by showing you this video?

Lisa: To make peace with ourselves.

Joseph: Yes!

Parisa: To remind us that we are animals?

Joseph: If we experience adult Sex as a child, as you did, it will most certainly be perceived as animalistic . . . but, it is true we are animals and we're human. Unfortunately, we tend to cut off or repress our animal natures because we see it as the source of our problems. If we link it to Sex, as many do, we inevitably make Sex wrong. Our animal nature isn't our lower nature, but part of our nature--a part we need to make peace with. We are going to have to find some peace with the animal

Day Three: *The Sex Seminar*

part of ourselves and the animal part of others. . . . that's if we want peace. Who do you make peace with?

Nisha: Yourself . . .

Reese: An enemy?

Joseph: Yeah! You make peace with an enemy. You're not going to make peace with a friend. We make peace with enemies. So, if we need to make peace with ourselves what is that telling you?

Nathan: We're our own enemies.

Joseph: Aaahhhhh, yes! So, what if this thing called Sex, is loving? Very, very loving? And what if it was trying to love us through the video; trying to have you make some peace with your parts and your Sexual past? We've seen all kinds of 'demons' and battles come up this weekend. These battles, as we're seeing, have nothing to do with others as much as we thought they did. At least, most of you are starting to see that. They are inside each of us and it's our mate, our parent, our world that provokes these inner feelings at every turn. You work so hard, so exhaustingly hard to avoid them or keep them at bay. You waste priceless energy that would be better spent on confronting these inner feelings.

Lynn: In the first day and a half we explored what others have started and cultivated in us and why we have give up so much of our power and authority. We've seen how its weakened us to the point of apathy. Today we've looked at what's blocked us from it and what it will take to regain it. . . . and we've done it with the help of Sex. . . . So, let me ask--instead of Joseph--what if Sex is a loving spirit that has a purpose for you? How would you like to treat it now? . . . And yourself in the process?

Mercedes: I know I am blocked, but that doesn't bother me.

Joseph: What does it do?

Mercedes: It inspires me. I don't feel so alone right now.

Joseph: Good. You're not. . . . So, continue to reflect on your experiences, on your reactions and those of your seminar mates. Keep your hands off your *guns* and breathe, and then ask Sexual energy for help. Remember what it was like to be in that ocean.

Simon: I'm still angry. And I want to kick that guy's ass!

Joseph: You're filled with much self judgment, and it's spilling out onto these two performers. Put your judgment gun down and be with the feelings, with the sensations, as you do in your meditation. Just observe; observe yourself objectively. You need objectivity.

These two people in the video are doing what they're doing, and it's none of your fucking business! None of your fucking business, but boy, did you make it your business. You projected your righteousness and your judgment! These are two consenting adults. . . . Imagine someone knocking on your bedroom door saying, "I don't like what you're doing to him or her!" Now you get to see--you're all inside their business. What are you doing in their business? Your only business is to see, "How did it affect me? What is this divine energy trying to show me about me? What is it revealing to me?" . . . You can also help each other with feedback. We need it. Share what you've observed about each other. Can you be courageous and generous enough to share what you've seen?

Kelly: For me, I didn't know if she was consenting because I thought she might be paid.

Joseph: Well if she's paid, she's consenting.

Kelly: Well, sometimes I thought, "Oh poor girl, she's going through pain, because that's her job." But then I saw that she liked it . . .

Joseph: You're too caught up in judging rather than observing and being open to the process. Therefore, you want to know that, when confronted with something unusual or disturbing, at least Sexually, you go to judgment; and judgment blocks your experience. It would be a better alternative for you to ask questions next time such as, "What is it doing to me? What is it making me feel? What does this divine energy, Sex, want me to understand or experience?" These questions will, at the minimum, keep you from judging and might provide you with the room to see . . . more clearly.

Mercedes: What I kept wondering, while watching it, was what was blocking her, sexually, that they had to play out so many power dynamic games? She is given the freedom to actually let go and be free in the Sexual process with him.

Joseph: I didn't quite see it that way but it's a good question for you to answer. Why do **you** need to play out so many power dynamic games?

Mercedes: . . . Um . . . yeah, I guess I do that. Well . . . I like the intensity it creates.

Day Three: *The Sex Seminar*

Joseph: That's great. Yet, I get you don't want to surrender to your lover. What would it take to surrender? It's the same question you can start asking yourself, not just with your lover, but with Sex--with all creative energy. Maybe it would be easier to consider surrendering to Sex and play out intensity games with your lover. That's a win-win! That's what I think the woman in the clip was doing. I get that you saw the fun in it, but what would surrendering look like? When we surrender to Sex it doesn't mean we become limp rags. No! We can still be in intense movement, except its Sex that's moving us. So, good, you're starting to see what the Lab's message was for you. This is where you're at, no judgment; you just want to see where you're at.

Simon: What's the difference between, say, if I were to inject myself with heroin because I had a trauma that couldn't heal, versus them acting that out?

Joseph: Firstly, you're clearly implying they are acting out their pain. Secondly, this gives a hint that you have a pain that the clip provoked. But I must ask, how do you know they're in pain? You are presuming to KNOW exactly why they are doing what they're doing.

Simon: Well, I'm just looking at the harm they're causing themselves.

Joseph: What if you're projecting that they're causing harm on themselves; or in your instance, he's causing her harm?

Lynn: If Joseph and I go, after we leave you, and act that out tonight, is he doing harm to me; or am I doing harm to him?

(Loud laughter)

Lynn: I missed it . . . !?

Joseph: Not sure they needed to visualize that.

(More laughter)

Lynn: . . . Let's say it's our thing. Let's just say it is and we enjoy it. Simon, can you imagine it being done for fun, as a fetish?

Simon: I don't see any harm in it; I'm just saying that physically it MUST be harmful!

Joseph: Physical harm can come from anything!

Lynn: I take a hike and get physically harmed. My feet hurt, I scrape my knee.

Day Three: *The Sex Seminar*

Joseph: How much physical harm can playing sports cause?

Simon: It can cause all kinds of pain.

Joseph: So, we shouldn't play sports?

Simon: Like boxing, I don't think you should box. I did boxing for four years and I don't think it's a good sport to do.

Joseph: So you think you have the right to decide what other human beings *should* or *shouldn't* do in sports?

Simon: I'm just saying, I wouldn't ever do it again.

Joseph: That's different; now you're applying it to you! Like with the Lab, you've projected on the entire sport of boxing because of your personal, yet limited, experiences. Why do you think you're projecting on these things that appear violentto you? What violent Sex is to you may be nothing more than enjoyable Animal Sex to another. That's just your moral universe you are describing. How you believe things *ought to be*.

As taught to me by my old, wise professor, there are four primary Moral universes: *Competition, Chance, Pretence, and Sensual.* These are the avenues through which we *play* out the game of life. The first one, Competition, is played by people who believe everything is a competition. It can be played with a team, like the corporate game, or person-to-person, like boxing or chess. The second one is Chance. This is played by individuals who believe everything is up to chance. They are the gamblers and lottery players who are perpetually waiting for lady luck to show up.

The third one is Pretence, and this is played by people who enjoy pretending. They play it out at playhouses, movies, theatres, and in their personal lives through melodramatic and soap opera like relationships. Lastly, there are those that live in the moral universe of the Sensual: the surfer, the snowboarder, the dancer, etc. They love flirting with balance and they believe that life is about balance. . . . These are the four different moral universes and each person who lives in them really believes that *this is how the world ought to be!*

You can experience each of these moral universes as a participant or a spectator; you can be active or inactive. You can even switch back and forth, if you choose. Spectators will watch people compete, take risks and chances, act, or dance and swim instead of doing it themselves. So, Simon, which is your moral universe?

Simon: Sensual!

Day Three: *The Sex Seminar*

Joseph: Good. Now you don't have to be so righteous against the other moral universes. As Shakespeare said in Hamlet: *"There is nothing either good or bad, but thinking makes it so."* This will make it easier to make room for yourself and others. Then you can look at the violence and pain you have stored up in your sex; you can ask Sex for assistance. This misdirected anger you and Nathan have, if properly channelled, can help you uncover and endure the pain that's hidden behind Sex. Anger can provide you the necessary energy needed to overcome your pain. Take the energy that anger has to offer you and use it to confront, and, if necessary, destroy this monster.

What you've missed all along is Sex has been there the entire time holding your pain and taking the hits on your behalf. After you've made peace with this fact, you will forever know you have a friend in Sex. Like the loving parent that it is, Sex has provided you and the world, with all things you've ever needed to grow! Lastly, but most importantly, it wants nothing in return. Unlike Man-made sex, there's no bartering with Sex in either direction.

Lynn: As you may be seeing, by now, we have blamed Sex for most of our pain. In reality, we're in pain because of our misuse of Sex. You've seen the evidence. We've explored the cost of Sexual repression and manipulation for personal protection and gain. We've shared the pain it has caused us, individually, and we now, hopefully, understand that our lack of education in the matter continues to perpetuate the problem.

Joseph: Before you judge something, you need to see the thing you're judging as a whole. Only then can you decide how to adjust it. Judging is not going to change anything! It hasn't, believe me. You have nothing on religion; they've been judging forever. Religion's deviated purpose is very clear. They want control and money. What is your purpose? I guarantee you, most of the time, it's selfish.

Lisa: It's been really hard, confronting these feelings, this weekend. Don't get me wrong, I'm seeing a lot. But, I wish it were easier.

Joseph: I get it. But, if it were any easier, any more comfortable, you'd be sound asleep; not just asleep. The nature of growing, learning, and expanding is always uncomfortable. Without awareness you live in a *Blue Pill* world. That's why it's no coincidence that in the world of Man-made sex we take Viagra--a blue pill!

We're looking to move in a different direction and create a different relationship to Sex. It will be uncomfortable because it will require us to change several habits. Prior to this weekend you didn't even know what Sex was, so how were you going

Day Three: *The Sex Seminar*

to have any real relationship with it? Now, you have a chance to develop one. Don't get distracted by the video; re-focus on you!

Lynn: The porn performers would probably laugh at all your reactions. The actress, from everything I've read about her, seems to *really* like her job. Maybe this is her surfing. I don't know if she was molested as a child or not! But remember what Nina Hartley said, "Ask us what we need! Don't assume we're all victims who have been molested."

Joseph: At least for some porn performers, they know what they're doing it for and they understand the difference between what they do on screen versus what they do in their personal relationships. At this stage, I believe we're doing as much, if not more, degrading things to ourselves and each other than what is seen on porn . . . but it's great that it brought up so much! And that's great, because you get to see another part of you, another facet of you.

We're all works of art. There are multiple layers of you that you've yet to discover. When you look in the mirror all you see is height and width; not much more! So, basically, you see yourself two dimensionally. That's crazy because you live in, at least, a three dimensional world and you are multi-dimensional! If you were able to see yourselves fully, you would realize you were more like some incredible hologram than the two dimensional person you're used to perceiving yourself as!

Cubist painters like Picasso and Braque tried to reveal that to us through their paintings. The paintings you see of people painted from different angles is closer to what we really look like than we think.

You're beginning to see Sex from different angles because of the work you've done this weekend. You are starting to understand that Sex is, in fact, multi-dimensional! That's fantastic! . . . Get angry--good! Get angry at the *Blue Pill Matrix* life you've been living! This Man-made and ego inspired sex life.

As you notice, I've enjoyed your anger; it shows us you're still alive. The anger, which has lead to sadness, which has lead to a slew of other emotions, has begun to loosen up your stagnant grief and is allowing you to release the pain; it's allowing you to begin the healing process. For those who have already healed some, you can now expand into a new world called Sex.

It's taken great bravery and courage, on your part, to be here, even if you stumbled into it. In a short time you will leave here changed. You have taken the *Red Pill*; it's too late to go back. You'll never see Sex the same! When you think of us, and

Day Three: *The Sex Seminar*

we'll be long gone from Vancouver by then, you're going to think 'These two fucking people have fucked me up!'

(Laughter)

What do you make of this . . . what's coming up for you? Take a moment before you speak, as you take in what this weekend has been like for you. Start from Friday, when you walked in, and slowly travel forward to this moment.

Simon: Friday when I walked in, I thought there was going to be loads of talking. You know, smashing pictures and focusing on the physical act. . . . It's wicked to see that Sex actually affects every single part of the world. That was a huge contrasting change in just a couple days. I was able to change my view of what Sex is.

Joseph: Yeah. This wouldn't have worked in half a day, or one day, or a day and a half. Any shorter than three days, and we would have lost you. You would have fallen back to sleep. We had to push, gradually, to gain your trust and to build your trust with yourselves and each other. Breakthroughs, breakdowns, and breakdowns that cause breakthroughs. You experienced, you shared, and you gave insight. That's how you did it. So what else . . . what's this been like for you?

Nathan: I had no idea what to expect. I had some of the most profound breakthroughs for myself and, as I think about the sessions I've had with Joseph, it's always the same thing; I'm like "Fuck, I keep on hearing the same thing!"

Joseph: Yeah, we need to hear things repeatedly to get it. Especially the hard stuff.

Nathan: Constantly! I was like this is fucking bullshit, what a waste of my money!

Joseph: I don't have to be a psychic to know every client of mine thinks that!

(Laughter)

Nathan: And I know I hate men because I've heard it from Joseph before . . . But, for whatever reason, I didn't want to hear it; unlike this weekend where I can see it. . . . This has been a HUGE breakthrough for me, just . . . EVERYTHING. It's crazy, and it's just beyond me, right now. I'm just so grateful that I came and that you guys are all here, and you let me share. Sex is so amazing to me now; it's far beyond anything I could comprehend. Trying to put it in a box was the biggest limiting factor for me. Just knowing that I don't know it all brings me enormous relief. The growth will never stop; the work is never going to, either. I'm never going to stop doing this. I lived a life of drugs and this is my new drug: me, inside, right here.

Joseph: Yeah, better to switch it to a healthy addiction.

Nathan: Totally. The feeling's way better.

Joseph: Thank you for sharing.

Parisa: I would say these three days is not where it stops for me. I thought I knew a lot about my life especially after Vipassana, but there are a whole new set of thoughts and feelings visiting me now. And the exercises you gave us, it's like, "Holy shit!" I wasn't able to do more than two minutes. It's like this is maybe a yearlong practice for me. . . . So this doesn't end at 9 o'clock.

Joseph: We're happy to hear that.

Lynn: Thank you for your full out expression! You stayed in your seat, no matter what you felt and just shared everything! You could have left!

Parisa: Thank you for being patient with me! You pushed my buttons . . .

Joseph: You were impatient and upset? When?

(Laughter)

Parisa: No. Not at all!

(Laughter)

Tami: What I take away from this weekend is not to be so judgmental. In the last lab I had to keep reminding myself to stop judging. Ultimately, I have to stop judging myself so much and just fucking relax and play a little!

Joseph: What if all Sex wanted from you was that--to be able to encounter it playfully? What if we approached our whole lives like that. Encountering it gratefully and playfully! We don't mean irresponsibly or selfishly, but playfully. We mean play-FULL; full of play.

This is what this weekend has been all about. It has been an opportunity to see Sex from a larger perspective: historically, culturally, politically, and personally. When you understand Sex in the way we have been exploring it, you will be able to confidently say "I have choice; I have Sexual choice!" Sex will be one more thing you can trust in life. We all need to find trust in something. It would be especially helpful if it were something transcendent like God, Love, Freedom . . . and Sex. These powers are the solid pillars of our lives. You came here this weekend to explore Sex and you're leaving with the additional opportunity to have it as one of the pillars of your life. Sex is not just a necessity of life but a pillar of life. . . . Sex is an infinite and timeless source of life and creativity. Though it's larger than us and can destroy us effortlessly, it's patient, kind, compassionate, and loving. This is all ancient information that just needed to be re-spoken.

We want to thank you, very much; we want to thank you for your trust in us, once again. Thank you for your support and your participation; for risking and challenging yourselves. We can't say enough about the courage that we've witnessed this weekend.

Lynn: Yes, thank you again for your trust and the honor and the privilege of leading you down this amazing beautiful tunnel of Sex. I feel like we've had Sex with all of you!

(Laughter)

Joseph: . . . and you think I'm a creep!

Group: Thank you guys!

(Applause)

Joseph: Okay, now go out there and have a good fuckin' time. (Laughter)

Occasionally, Joseph & Lynn decide to extend a seminar based on how far the group has taken it. Two weeks after The Sex Seminar ended they decide this was one of those occasions . . .

Hello Everyone,

We hope you are all feeling well after the seminar and we congratulate you on your hard work and courage. Please feel free to email or phone us with anything that you may need to discuss.

We would also like to invite you to "The Follow Up." This will be an open forum where you can complete and tie together any loose ends you may have. It will be conducted on *Saturday May 25th from 4:30-7:30pm* (will extend if necessary) at our location.

Please RSVP your attendance no later than Friday, May 17th.

Also, feel free to bring any food or drink you may require or would like to share.

Thank you again for your participation,

Joseph & Lynn

" . . . *if Sex could sit here and talk, it would be laughing right now, it would be saying 'Are you kidding me? You can't control me; you can't possess me! . . . You can't closet me! . . . You can't contain me! . . . You better just allow me to flow through you, or you'll be left with nothing' . . . But we don't have the privilege to speak to Sex directly so we have to look at it ourselves.*"

The Sex Seminar Follow-up

Joseph: Okay, welcome everyone to *The Sex Seminar Follow-up*!

We decided to offer you the opportunity to reflect back at our experience together last month. We figured there were some questions, ideas, or comments you may still have or want to address and share.

So let's complete *The Sex Seminar*; who'd like to start?

Parisa: Okay, I'll go!

Jeremy: (Laughs)

I was waiting . . .

(Laughter)

Parisa: You want to go . . .

Jeremy: No. I can't wait to hear what you have to say!

(Laughter)

Parisa: I'm not going to say much!

(More laughter)

The seminar was a lot to absorb; too much maybe. I thought I was absorbing it all, but then I realized I needed another seminar to actually digest what I learned. So, I'm glad we're doing this.

There was a huge shift for me after the seminar. I understand that my beliefs about how sex should be or what sex is, was totally wrong and now I'm open to a new one; and how to get there . . . well, that's where my struggle is.

Joseph: Well, the good news is that there is no need to struggle. You can't ask for anything more than to realize, *"The box I have contained myself in, doesn't contain everything that is Sex."* Therefore, you can stretch the box, to let more in, or you can flatten it. You can let the walls down and rebuild them further out.

It's fine if you decide to make it a little bigger, because then there will be room to absorb more. Sex is an ever-expanding thing that we can absorb-expand, absorb-expand, absorb-expand with. So, it's just a matter of pushing your box a little

Follow-up: *The Sex Seminar*

further; that's the effort but it doesn't have to be a struggle. Then you can set up boundaries; that part happens naturally.

You're going to set up boundaries around sexuality, after you've expanded. Like you do after a relationship ends, or expands for that matter; you set up new boundaries. You don't even realize you're doing this when you start setting them up. You may say "I'm not doing *this* anymore, I want to do *this* some more, I want to see what *THIS or THAT* is like now," but you'll still do it, naturally. So don't worry about that part, that's the natural part of the process.

What happened to Parisa was her walls came down and, because of that, she can now view sexuality, and her relationship to it, from a completely different light. She has created an expanded relationship to it.

It's very unlikely anybody in this room is going to leave here with a full understanding of what Sex is all about, just like you are not going to leave this world knowing everything about it. They're both too vast! It's simply a matter of understanding more and pursuing what matters most in life.

When it is said that Christ or Buddha was all-knowing, it's not meant literally. They didn't know how many gallons of water there were in all of the oceans or how many grains of sand there were on earth, but rather they knew what mattered. They knew all that mattered. They knew everything about all **that mattered**. Last month we started expanding and learning about something that really matters in life, and that is Sex.

I was watching an old Oprah episode, the other day, about these young girls who were becoming nuns. It was clear they had limited sexual intelligence and probably even less sexual experience. So, you would think that these young girls have chosen to know nothing about sex, right, since they're becoming nuns? But no, quite the opposite. Now they're going to have to be sex obsessed because they're going to have to practice celibacy, with a limited understanding of Sex.

They're going to have to, at the least, find a place for it and, at the most, repress it before its power takes them over. They will have to limit it in order to keep it at bay. Their work with it will become very intense; their work will become *very sexual*. Ultimately, they'll have to disconnect from it if they fail to find full devotion.

They'll go in thinking "Okay, I'm done with Sex" but, in actuality, their work with it will only be beginning; that's because Sex is one of those things in life that matters.

Follow-up: *The Sex Seminar*

So, for some, if not all of you, your minds have expanded. We like saying "Wow! That blew my mind," but it's just an expansion of your consciousness. Sometimes we get our minds blown but, most of the time, it's just us being a little dramatic. So, don't worry, naturally new borders will form from what you've expanded into.

Parisa: I wish I would have watched the video! I'm angry at myself, like "Why did I not watch the video!" Because, now I can; my brain is open to it.

Joseph: Good for you! But remember the video was a lab; a lab called *The Sex Lab*, plain and simple. It was a lab intended for you to see how you react to certain stimuli, so you actually got something out of it! In your case, you got to see how you reacted to the *prospect* of certain stimuli. Now you have something to work with. You can decide whether you want to continue to respond the way you did. Presently, you at least know a territory that you may want to expand. We cannot expand our limits until we know where they are.

You got what you needed to get. Everyone had different experiences and received different insights from that particular lab. We left it for last because it's the most profoundly challenging one. It's always going to hit the hardest. So, whatever your reaction was, know that it was revealing more to you about you than it was about Sex. It was NOT about the two people in the video, but about you!

Parisa: I can see that now.

Joseph: So what else? About this or things that have come up for you, things that you feel incomplete about . . .

Nathan: I just want to thank you guys! This is my fourth seminar, and I think it took this fourth time for me to really hear it. This one really just sunk in, and like, there's such an ease about that bit about "not knowing everything," that just totally opened up everything for me. I could take a deep breath now because I realize "it's all good." I don't need to know everything.

Joseph: Yeah, absolutely. The need to know and to compartmentalize everything is a very painful process for us.

We put ourselves in small boxes so we can feel we have control, safety, and where we can somehow . . . know everything. What that creates, in turn, is a tightness of living; an oppressed way of living because we have to keep it small. To expand it would mean to lose the control you're working towards. This is a hefty price to pay for something truly insignificant. We're afraid to expand, but if we did we'd see that we can't control, that the safety we are so desperately pursuing is an illusion. That would, initially, freak you out but with time you'd find that since you can't control, then why even bother? And at that point you'd effectively be saying "screw it."

Then, you would relax and you would do whatever you'd do, from a sense of freedom; not a sense of safety. This is much easier and a lot less pressure full.

When you buy into the illusion that you can control and force safety, you become obsessed with it, and the more you want control, the tighter you'll make your life and the tighter you make your life, the less room there is for you, and others, to move around in. Eventually, the less room you have, the less you can rest because it gets so tight and narrow you can't even lay down; you can only go to sleep standing. It gets so tight that you'll even tighten everyone around you. They'll have to tighten in order to fit into your narrow space. They may have to adjust or change their personalities to fit in with you. When you're forced to extend your space to accommodate others you'll do the same. You will shape yourself according to the amount of safety you'll need *from* that person and it will change from person to person and, in the process, you wind up developing multiple personas. This is unnecessary when you live from freedom and balance rather than safety and control. Lynn was recently sharing with me about how she has to be this way with clients. She has to narrow herself in order to fit into their world; it's only then that she can expand them.

She explained how if a client saw her as, or needed her to be, a mothering type, then she'd take on that role so they could hear her, so they could receive her; and if her next client needed her to be something else, she'd accommodate them for the same reason. She has to be all these personas! It's a lot of work, when you're dealing with one individual at a time. When she's speaking to ten thousand people, then she can be just one persona. It's a lot easier to live a bigger life! It's really easy. You don't realize that, though. You think a small life is easier. NO! A small life has you in the illusion that you can control things, so you try and control everybody, "What have you been doing? "Where have you been?" "Who did you go out with?" "What did you do with that money?" "Did you take money from me?" "Did you take enough money?" "Are you okay?" "Do you have a coat?" We act like we can control everything and all this is because we are living a too small and too tight a life.

People think that a big life is something to panic over . . . no. It's when your life is too small that *real* panic is present. An expanded life actually creates the room for more help and less panic. It's when I'm underwater, with little air left in my lungs, that authentic panic is present not when I have multiple choices on the horizon and I am not sure which to pick. That kind of panic is *in*authentic panic; it is manufactured panic based on the illusions you hold about the infinite. It's the finite that you should be panicking about, not the infinite; you got it backwards.

When we had *The Sex Seminar* everybody had a pretty closed idea about what Sex was and since then, it has expanded. So in your case, Nathan, what you're feeling is the calmness that comes from the acceptance of the infinite. Therefore, as you would say, "It's like wow, I can actually breathe, it's not so tight anymore."

Nathan: It's so calm! This happened two days after the seminar; this never happens to me. That whole thing about me hating men . . . well it's changing. When I go out, now, men seem to be pulled to me. The other day I'm sitting there and some guy's sitting next to me and he just started talking to me. That never happens to me! It's been happening more and more and more and I don't know if it's by just having an awareness of it?

Joseph: *It* has expanded you, you're never going to recoil back to where you were, understand? So, now there's room for people to show up. When your box was smaller and only had room for women, men weren't going to show up. There are people who go around saying "Why can't I find a girlfriend?" "Why can't I find a boyfriend?" "Why can't I get any friends?" Well, there's no room! It's too tight-- their world, their box, is too tight. That's why. You've grown, so men can show up now.

Nisha: I had a different experience throughout the seminar. I felt more anxiety, more emotion, a bit of everything, and since then, it has been overwhelming. I don't know if it was the seminar or maybe it hit something within me that I still can't process exactly what it is. I don't feel calmness. I wouldn't say I got calmness from it.

Joseph: Well, for you, it brought up the anxiety that was already there. It magnified and exacerbated your uncertainty and fears about sexuality. The proverbial can of worms was opened through the seminar, and you're trying to stuff them back in. That's creating even more anxiety. What you need to do is keep breathing through the anxiety, and wait to see what else is there. Accept the anxiety, for now. Be, as if you're on a boat crossing a pond waiting to find out what's on the other side. Know

Follow-up: *The Sex Seminar*

that *you've* propelled yourself out onto that pond to search the unknown. You're searching! Understandably, it's frightening for you, which, in itself, proves you're in unchartered waters. You could, potentially, get to a point in your life where the new becomes exciting but, for now, the unseen Sex is scary, hence your anxiety.

So, breathe through it. That's all you can do for now. Breathe through it and it will pass. When the dust settles, it will all make more sense. That's what you need now because you left incomplete on the last day. You need to breathe within the space, within sexuality. You have a renewed view and experience of Sex under your belt, so feel it. It's new; newness is coming! . . . How do you normally respond to new emotional experiences?

Nisha: . . . I see . . . I'm usually apprehensive.

Joseph: If you normally respond fearfully, then know what you're presently experiencing is new! Sex or the seminar didn't cause anything it just brought you new stuff! And your reaction to the new is anxiety.

Most people are fine with new *physical* experiences because they can see, touch, smell, taste, and feel them. On the contrary, emotional experiences create the opposite because they can't really put their hands around it. Like water, you can't grab it; you can't hold it for long. How does that resonate for you?

Nisha: Pretty good. I think I'm trying to do something about it and, in fact, you're saying to just breathe through it.

Joseph: There's nothing to do.

Lynn: It's just to feel, it's just emotions, it's just feelings and they will come and they will go. It's automatic for some of you to just grip as soon as you're in the new. The harder you grip the more anxiety you'll feel. When I let go and just let it take me, anxiety disappears and is always replaced by a feeling of freedom. So you're doing the gripping before you let go.

Joseph: There's a cute little animation in the movies right now called "The Croods." It's about a cave family whose motto is "New is bad!" And as the film goes along you get to experience what a life lived in a tight small box looks like.

When you live in a tight small box, the new will always be experienced as bad. It can't be helped. You can only wonder "Where am I going to put it? I'm already full, where am I going to put the new?" The new is suffocating when you're full so you assume it's bad; but, if you had a lot of space then new would be good!

Follow-up: *The Sex Seminar*

If I have a big house, and I get new furniture, that's good! If I live in a small apartment and it's already filled with furniture and you bring me new furniture . . . if I win at "Let's Make A Deal" and they bring me new furniture . . . that would feel bad! Where am I going to put it all? When people come into each other's lives, they bring their own furniture, clothes, things--and their *baggage*! So if you have no room, then it will appear as if they are crowding you. You'll think "Hey you're fuckin' up my life; you're no good for me!" It all depends on what you live in. What kind of room do you live in? Is it a small box? If so, and you want to add another to it, then you'll have to look to see where you can widen it, stretch it, and expand it; again, larger box, larger life, an easier life.

We expend so much energy in a small life, protecting the little we have, worried that someone or something is going to come along and take it from us. We become hyper protective. Every window and door is monitored and locked, every person and item accounted for and scrutinized. It's a very tight and exhausting existence, and it requires the expenditure of more energy than a larger life; fractal geometry has proven that.

Lynn: We live in a 19 floor building in North Vancouver that is hyper protective and it often makes Joseph complain that it makes him feel like he lives in a prison. So, when we recently went to visit our daughter, who lives in a 40 something floor New York City building, we were surprised to find how lax their security was. They had a giant concierge desk with three guys working the front, and you would think that it would be even tighter security than our building, but NO we just walked right in!

Joseph: And that was New York! You would expect more fear in a big city but, actually, what I feel there is more freedom. In North Vancouver I feel an over need for safety.

Lynn: What happened to most of you in the Sex Seminar was that you got expanded, and for the rest, you got scared; scared because your lives are too tight.

Joseph: Many of you felt good after the seminar because it expanded you; but good is not enough. Therefore, we're looking at it again so we can make a few more adjustments.

Brennan: I felt overwhelmed after the seminar.

Joseph: Overwhelmed? Of course you're going to feel a bit overwhelmed. Did you think we were going to bring you just enough to fill your little tea cups? No, we're going to pour tons of stuff, and you're going to catch what you catch, and it's going to fall where it falls and yet, you're not missing out! You can only take what you can take! We come with extra, just in case! So, of course you're going to feel overwhelmed! That's good. If you don't feel overwhelmed . . . if you feel underwhelmed then we didn't do our jobs, right? And there hasn't been a seminar that anyone has said, "I feel underwhelmed."

(Laughter)

Because that's the point, we make sure that you have enough and the stuff that spills over, which you actually can see, is what makes you come back for more. It's like a large buffet that will take multiple visits and time before you get to taste a lot or a little of what's available. In addition, you'll have to take breaks to digest what you've consumed. Now you're back with empty plates so you can fill and refill. . . . tea cups, buffets . . . how's that for mixed metaphors?

People come to Lynn and I saying, "You know you told me this a year ago and I couldn't get it, but now I do!" Well, that's because you had a tight box back then, not that a tight box is always a bad thing . . . right Lynn?

(Laughter)

. . . now it's larger and it can fit more. And a year from now it will fit even more and the year after that, even more still; but only if you consciously continue to expand your box . . . right Lynn?

(Laughter)

Lynn: You can really be an ass sometimes!

(More laughter)

Joseph: You can only take what you can fit! If I tell you something nine times and you haven't gotten it, it's because nothing's changed; you haven't made the effort to grow! How are you going to get it, if you've provided no space!

Anybody else, what do you need, what do you want to complete, what do you need to make sense of . . . ?

Lynn: What was incomplete for you maybe in the seminar? What did you not say that you wanted to say and left going, "Wish I would have shared that!"

Angie: One thing that I'm kind of trying to make sense of is something about the homework. Mercedes mentioned how, for her, to be fully clothed made her feel, I think the word she used was exposed. For me, I grew up in a home where nudity was practiced; so nudity is very comfortable for me.

While I was away this weekend, all kinds of stuff came up for me from the seminar. I went to the beach and of course there weren't a lot of people there because of the weather, though it really wouldn't matter if there were, and I was butt naked in the water.... It was funny because I bought myself a bikini as a goal, to eventually fit into it. The idea of a bikini is a terrifying thing for me whereas being stark naked and running into the waves is comforting . . . but a bikini, that's terrifying! And there's something that I can't wrap my brain around. It kind of brought me back to the thing with the homework and how Mercedes felt more exposed in clothes than naked. That didn't make sense to me at the time and still doesn't make sense to me.

Joseph: Okay, so this one's an easy one. Thank you for the soft pitch!

(Laughter)

There are cultures in this world, that if you place them indoors, they'll freak out. These are people who have lived outdoors their entire lives. Living indoors is both foreign and frightening to them; it's imprisoning and they want no part of it. They're accustomed to living out in the jungle or in the woods. Living outdoors is what's natural and common for them.

Being outdoors, for them, is comforting. They have a shared series of sensations, sensory perceptions, and experiences with their community, which have been sources of comfort, love, and protection. It's their *common sensory* experience or, in other words, to them its common sense that one should live outdoors; anything else would seem strange. They think we're insane for living indoors, "How do you protect yourself? You're sitting ducks. We get to hear the warnings of animals, of trees, of the wind, of the weather, and you isolate yourself and you isolate all your senses from protecting you and helping you and showing you," that's their way of looking at it.

Most of us grow up with similar sets of shared *indoor* experiences. The smells of food in the home, warmth from a fireplace, and sounds from the television are but a few of the things we associate with the very same feelings of *comfort, love, and protection* these other cultures associate with living outdoors.

The body is a constant receptor--from every pore of our bodies we receive information, even in our sleep! Over time, we become accustomed to these daily bits of information; at least the consistent ones. This experienced consistency creates a sense of comfort. These recurrent experiences become common; they become *our* common sense! Common sense, in its truest definition, is not the misperceived idea of being *street wise,* but the common sensations we share.

So, that's all! You just did it the other way. It became common and safe being naked. Now are you any more free because you choose to be naked rather than clothed? NO, because true freedom comes through exposure, and exposure is never accomplished externally. True exposure is exposing yourself from the inside, out. Exposing and communicating what's really going on, exposing *those* thoughts and feelings that you just can't quite make sense of; those fears, worries, and anxieties that you're afraid to share because maybe "a man doesn't cry" or "a woman shouldn't behave that way" or "I shouldn't be jealous, or scared;" all those shalt's and shalt nots. That's the way to truly expose yourself! You and Mercedes are just two sides of the same coin. You feel exposed with clothes on and Mercedes feels exposed with them off. And maybe, just maybe clothes reveal, to you, too much of the body you don't really like or want to see. It's good to expose; play there, you can expose yourself to yourself, in this way.

Angie: It's so much less weird than I thought it was going to be.

Joseph: Yeah, that's why I said it was an easy one, but that doesn't mean there isn't more for you to look at. I'm glad you asked because this brings you closer to completion. . . . Anybody else?

Simon: I was really pissed off with someone throughout the whole seminar, and I didn't realize until the last day that I was really pissed off at them because their shit is the same shit that I deal with all the time. I think the first time they opened their mouth I just wanted to fuckin' hit em, I was like, "You're such a cunt, shut the fuck up!" . . . I actually met them here first, didn't know them at all prior so when I heard them speak for the first time, when their first sentence came out, I thought, "What a dick!" . . . That's the same thing I always do, and it's that I always talk about myself and I always share how well I'm doing. So since I've seen that, I've been more aware of it and I'm talking less. . . . I'm just stoked how the world is showing me stuff about myself. These days, I'll see stuff when I'm just driving, walking, doing random things. I get all these metaphors out of the blue that give me greater insight. It's making it easier to chuck away all my judgment.

Joseph: Simon can't expose himself through words because he uses words to protect or judge himself and others. How are you going to expose yourself with the very thing you're using to protect yourself with? So, for Simon, silence is the best way for him to expose himself. It's through being quiet, then through listening, that he'll see himself, and others, more clearly. It's allowing for greater exposure. You get that?

Simon: Yeah, even to myself, I was like "Shut the fuck up, shut the fuck up, shut the fuck up" and I can't stop talking!

(Laughter)

I've always waited for my turn to talk instead of just actually listening; now I'm listening. It's changed my relationships. Now that I've started to listen, more and people are calling me up to invite me to do things, instead of me calling them.

Lynn: Well I almost didn't recognize you when you came in!

Simon: Is it my glasses?

(Laughter)

Lynn: No, I had to look twice, because there's an openness about you and it's just what Joseph is saying, there's an accessibility that is there, it's just a little opening.

Simon: Yeah, instead of me walking over to you, you got up to greet me . . .

Joseph: Can you see the similarity, Nathan? Can you see that you both have more space so you're becoming more approachable? There's much less tension about you both.

Nathan: I can feel that. When I saw Jeremy for the first time I totally sized him up, you know what I mean? It's just what I do!

Joseph: This is what we **all** do with Jeremy!

(Laughter)

Jeremy: I put out that vibe right?

(More laughter)

Nathan: I used to walk around with my *chest up* whenever I was around other guys. It's that alpha male thing . . . it makes a lot of sense now, but before I did any work on myself I thought that was the way to be. Now, especially after the seminar, I realize "I have to find a balance but how am I going to find that balance?" . . . and the answer just came to me.

Just knowing there's a problem is a big thing for anybody. Just the awareness has helped me. As soon as it was brought to light, everything changed. Just being aware was a major thing for me. It was just like "Why the hell am I so standoffish to guys when they don't deserve it?" There are a lot of good guys in this world and I just never gave them a chance until I finished testing them; and that would take months! So, just that simple awareness was such a massive thing for me and, on top of that, I can see more is to come because of the openness and expansiveness that I'm feeling. Just accepting those things, and not looking at them as a fault, was such a big deal!

Joseph: What you're illustrating to everyone, thus making our point, is that we hide our shit in Sex. Shit that has nothing to do with Sex. Your issue with men had nothing to do with Sex--not one thing! Yet, when you open your sex closet, guess what's there? Issues that are completely unrelated to Sex; issues with men that were linked to Sex in childhood! This was the same for most of you. You had stuff in your sex closet that had nothing to do with Sex! That's because we hide our junk in that particular trunk.

(Laughter)

So what's happening for you, Nathan, is that you're beginning to see and experience men differently because you've moved them out of the context of Sex. You're dealing with them more directly, more in the present, and, ironically, you're accomplishing this through a Sex Seminar--who would have thunk it!? And the question for Simon is, "What does all your judgment have to do with Sex?" Answer: Absolutely nothing! It's just where you've hidden it, right? We know you hid it in the realm of Sex because it came up so powerfully during a Sex Seminar. Now you can look at it, objectively, without it getting all over your sex life. That's why your relationship is improving. By the way Simon, unlike Nathan, who knows how his issue wound up in the sex trunk, you don't need to know. Not after you've removed it from it.

We hide a lot in Sex because we don't normally go looking there. In addition, even when we invite another to join us in sex they are unable to see our issues because we've buried them too deeply. That is why some of us are unable to experience intimacy because we live superficially on top of our buried issues. Therefore, we're unable to experience any real depth of connection. To change this is to expose it. But again, exposure must be from within. True exposure is performed from the inside out.

Kelly: I learned that everyone has their own issues and it's not all about me. I used to take things very personally and now I see that everyone has their own story, issues, and problems. So now, instead of instantly judging people, I look at their reaction or behaviours and see it as theirs, not mine or because of me . . . and that came out of doing the Sex Seminar.

Follow-up: *The Sex Seminar*

Joseph: Extreme judgement, by the way, is generated from living in a small box. We're not speaking about practical judgement; the kind we need to be able to cross the street, but extreme judgment . . . created by a small tight life.

If you're living in my house and you're constantly leaving dishes in the sink am I going to have more judgement towards you than if you live a mile away from me and you're doing the same in your kitchen? Even if I can see your kitchen through Skype, would it matter to me as much? No, of course not, because there is space between us. If there's space, there's less judgment. When there's less space, you're going to have more judgement of everything and everyone around you. You can see this played out with older people, maybe even with your grandparents. You know the type. They sit at home all day in front of the television, in their tight box, and they just judge away! Right. They put the news on so they can judge away!

(Laughter)

So you've come by this honestly; this is all learned behaviour. The best way to help ourselves with judgment is to create more space; so we can *see*. Seeing is judgment's Kryptonite. As my old, wise professor would say, "The eyes are the only sense that needs distance in order to see." By creating space, thus distance, we can see others more clearly. It becomes easier not to judge because it's no longer so personal. When there's sufficient space, our need to judge diminishes greatly because it doesn't affect our lives as strongly. This is like when there is a snow storm in a distant city. We may feel badly for them, but it's no big deal to us if the temperature, in our city, is 80 degrees Fahrenheit, and it's sunny.

This is why homosexuality is the hot topic today. As a society, we have more space around Sex, so we can finally look at homosexuals and their rights. Supporters can finally ask out loud "Why are you judging them? They don't affect your life!" There's more room to be had for the people who think and are afraid that their morals, their churches, and their views are being attacked. Some of them actually think these homosexuals are going to come in to their house and homo-sexualize their children and their pets and change life as they've known it. All these fears are caused by a tight boxed life. We're not advocating for you to expand your life to the point where you can't even sit through dinner without somebody bothering you because you're so famous. That's not what we're talking about when we speak about a big life. We're suggesting you consider a life that's big enough to accommodate you and the others in your life. A life that has enough room so you don't have to judge so harshly. A life that gives the important people in it space. Enough space so you don't have to be up each other's asses. What do you make of this?

Follow-up: *The Sex Seminar*

Simon: I think society, in general, finds that quite secure: having a small life and trying to control. It's like those magazines at the supermarket where they have all the stupid celebrity gossip. I recently saw, in one of them, a headline that read "Gays on TV" as if it were a bad thing! Crazy. people want to control the TV now because, like you said, they fear that Gay's are trying to get into their homes.

Joseph: Yeah. Joseph completely agrees with you on this one.

(Laughter)

Simon: How do I make that personal?!

Joseph: How do you make it personal? Make it personal . . . don't ask how, just do it. Go ahead.

Simon: I saw something on a magazine.

Joseph: And . . . what did you experience; what was your experience? I don't care about what people do. I want you to tell me about your experience! That's how you make it personal.

Simon: I saw a magazine and I read it . . .

Joseph: . . . and what did it do, what did you believe, and feel, and experience?

Simon: I was just laughing out of disbelief.

Joseph: So it made you laugh.

Simon: Yeah, out of disbelief. I couldn't believe that society would put something that unacceptable out there. That's what it is. It could have said, "Blacks on TV." Unacceptable!

Joseph: So your experience on how others are handling these issues is humorous to you?

Simon: Yeah.

Joseph: Well, then, say that! Why do you tell me about what society thinks! Don't waste your time telling me about what other people think, tell me about your experience. What is your experience of what other people think? You can't tell me with clarity what they're reeeally thinking. There's a lot more value in what you have to say and what you're experiences are than your social commentaries. Leave that to me . . . unless you're looking to take over my position.

Follow-up: *The Sex Seminar*

Simon: I was going to suggest that!

(Laughter)

Joseph: Tell us what you think. We can all feel and understand that! It gives us all something to grab on to because it's alive and vibrant. It's alive because it's personally from you . . . and it's more generous!

Like we said in the seminar, why speak it second person, or third person? This removes you and reduces your contribution. We don't contribute as well when we hide behind the royal "we, people and us." Unless you're doing it from the perspective we do it from, why should you bother? We, intentionally, begin from a generalization so we can then lead you to the specific. We guide you through a personal experience that allows you to access YOU. At which point we ask you "What are your thoughts and reflections," not "What are other people's thoughts and reflections?"

So, the more you take ownership about what you're feeling, thinking, and are experiencing, without judging or blaming, the better off you'll be. Your communication will take on a more impactful and profound quality to it. If you were to tell your partner "I'm feeling angry" for instance, rather than "YOU make me feel angry" you'll create more room for intimate conversation. The only thing the latter can produce is an adversarial position that distances the two of you from one another.

Parisa: It takes two to Tango. There is my reality and another person's reality, and it takes another person to trigger me. But they couldn't if it weren't there to be triggered in the first place!

Joseph: True in part; but it doesn't only "Take two" it can "Take" anything else to trigger you or to trigger me.

Anything could trigger me; a red spot on my white rug could trigger me. "What is that? Who didn't clean that up? What's going on?" I look to see who I can blame, so I don't have to feel, let's say, my anger or disappointment. It doesn't even have to be a person. I can find blame with inanimate objects! "This fuckin' rug sucks, what is it with the color white; why does it have to stain so easily?" It's crazy. It's crazy because instead of looking at myself for the cause to my reaction, I look outside . . . outside to *anything* other than me. So it just takes me!

That's good news, because you can work with you! Now if you have two people who are willing to work on it together, then the potential for growth is exponential.

What you get, with two cooperative individuals who are willing to own their own feelings, is a different kind of dialogue. It will sound more like "Hey, apparently, we trigger each other so let's hang in there together and work through this without kicking each other's asses. So what I'm feeling is . . ." This approach builds trust, loyalty and respect! And with these new commonly shared experiences, a stronger bond is naturally forged.

In contrast, there are many people who don't want to be triggered at all; they think a good relationship is one where they don't ever argue! That's a relationship that uses distance to protect themselves from each other; it uses excessive space. This space, this distance, becomes a protective wall that has the couple be nothing more than *casual acquaintances* to each other. You can live 40 years with a casual acquaintance because this type of relationship is committed to maintaining the status quo. We explain this more thoroughly in *The Communication Seminar.*

What else has come up for you?

Angie: I was talking to a French friend of mine, who also speaks English, and he was saying how it's funny how most of the curse words in French relate to the church and how all of our curse words, in English, pretty much relate to sex. Like every one of them . . . and how the sexual ones are the ones that are considered rude. I, accidentally, let the word fuck slip out in front of my grandmother the other day and she just went off the rails about it! I was just like, "I'm sorry if that offends you, but it's just a word!" It's funny how words relating to sex are swearing words to us. And in other cultures they're things of the church.

Joseph: So what do you make of that?

Angie: How negative Sex is made . . .

Joseph: So, you perceive that others make sex negative?

Angie: Yeah because if I said "Fuck, pussy, cunt" people would get offended by it. Personally, I've learned to, kind of, like those words.

Joseph: That's about space again. Believe it or not, space has everything to do with what you're bringing up. As you know we were recently in New York and we had this experience that I think explains the point.

As we were walking around the city we couldn't help but be aware of all the cell phone conversations people were having. It seemed like everyone who was on the phone was intentionally speaking loud enough for all to hear. On one corner, as we waited for the light to change, we overheard a transsexual yelling, "Fuck him, he owes me $20, tell him to fuck himself!" And next to her was a woman stating matter-of-factly, "I hate that bitch, tell her I'm gonna kick her ass!" and this went on and on. It seemed like we were the only ones who were hearing it, because no one else seemed to have even noticed. Being originally from NYC you'd think I would have been immune to it, but, because I've been in Canada for so long, I guess I was experiencing it more like a Canadian. But what it did do for me was have me remember and appreciate the freedom of expression that I find less forthcoming in Canada. . . . How's that for being diplomatic?

(Laughter)

I noticed the freedom! There was so much more room! Nobody cared! Nobody really cared; it was great!

Lynn: It's strange how eight million people on a small island can create so much room.

Joseph: Now if you're walking on Robson Street, (a busy commercial street in Vancouver) and a transsexual yells out on their cell phone, "Fuck him, tell him to shove the $20 up his ass!" Not only are you going to get most people to turn around, you're also going to feel some of their judgment towards that person. It's much tighter here. There's not a lot of room for the word "fuck" and, maybe even, for transsexuals. Therefore, the real question is what's it going to take to make enough space so you can say the word, "fuck?"

Lynn: There's limited room for expression in Vancouver vs. New York.

Joseph: For those of you who are feeling more free around the subject of Sex, don't forget how resistant you felt when we pushed against your walls. Don't forget how your fear made you want to retreat back into your small boxes. If you do forget then, eventually, you will return to them.

Lynn: Not only were some of you resistant and fearful, you were also sad and angry...

Joseph: And that was, and is, okay! This is just to reveal what's been invisible to us up to now, to reveal where we're at! To give us options on how to continue to expand.

Lisa: I found the "Sex Lab" especially revealing.

Mercedes: Yeah, it was funny how I found it fun and others saw it as offensive to women.

Susan: It was actually some of the men, not the women, who found it offensive to women.

Joseph: Some of you found it offensive while Brennan found it beautiful. That's as different as night and day! It depends on what's there for you. It definitely brought up your individual stuff. There will be times when an individual will see the same thing as *violent to men*.

Lynn: I was actually going to ask all of you if you had reflected on the lab. Because I'd like to know what did you guys think about the man in the film? I heard a lot of you feeling sorry for the woman, but what did you think about the man?

Did any of you see him in pain?

Kelly: Yeah I did, when he was hitting himself in the bathtub.

Joseph: Exactly, it showed right from the beginning that he was in some kind of pain or conflict!

Kelly: It seemed like he was trying not to do what he was doing but he couldn't help himself. He seemed so repressed.

Joseph: You really didn't have to look that deeply to see the enormous amount of repression and confusion he lived under; especially because of his profession. It was through his deviances that he played out his self hatred.

Lynn: We're appropriately concerned about the victimization of women, but not so when it comes to men. We are also properly conscious of the pain and abuse men cause women, but not sufficiently aware when it comes to abuse from women to women, women to themselves, and women to men. As a society, we need to start opening up to the pain and the suffering of men, or else women will never be free . . . Until we can have equal compassion and ability to see men, there will be no freedom for us.

Joseph: No one stopped to ask what the experience was like for the man. Not even the men in the group. Isn't that curious?

A strongly repressed society, as we saw when we looked at the history of Sex, has more prostitution than a less suppressed one, remember? The more suppressed a society, the more prostitution! Why?

Kelly: Because they aren't having their needs fulfilled.

Follow-up: *The Sex Seminar*

Joseph: Right! I'm not passing judgment on prostitution, one way or the other. What I am saying is, when a person is not attending, or cannot attend to, their sexual needs then they will seek it from sources outside of the "normal" realm of human relationships. In addition, since a repressed society doesn't allow women's Sexual power and energy to be expressed, it gets repressed to the point that it's "flushed" to the weaker few.

Now I'm not saying that all prostitutes are weak, some of them outright own their sexual power and choose to monetize it. I'm speaking more of the ones who had fathers, absent or present, who withheld and didn't provide their daughters their emotional needs. So prostitution, in part, is born from the repression of, not only men's, but also women's emotional and sexual needs. This is not to say there aren't male prostitutes; we're speaking of the majority who are women.

Kelly: Are you saying men go to prostitutes for more than just sex?

Joseph: Some men only go to prostitutes for companionship and conversation!

Kelly: What do they talk about?

Lynn: Everything that they can't talk about. Everything they feel they can't talk to their mates about. Sometimes they like to talk to a stranger because nothing they say is going to be held against them. They use them like a therapist, literally like a therapist. That's why so many sex workers feel like therapists.

Joseph: As you can see, going to a prostitute for emotional purposes has very little, if anything, to do with sex. We hide our junk in Sex. So, sometimes, a man will go to a prostitute, not so much for the Sex, even if they have it, but for emotional and mental expression . . . and sometimes healing. These men are usually afraid or unable to speak to their intimates about their fears, hurts, and pain out of fear of being left or judged.

Lynn: To whom can you talk about your darkness? Who? For many of you that's hard to come by.

Simon: Our mates?

Lynn: Yes, but that's difficult, maybe even rare, because it would require that our mates be open and available to such darkness. It would require them to have done some *dark searching* themselves. Who else?

Simon: Joseph!

Follow-up: *The Sex Seminar*

Lynn: True. But what are you looking for?

Simon: For somebody who's objective and non-judgemental; for someone who makes me feel that way.

Lynn: It's difficult for many of us to feel that towards teachers or therapists; especially if we have issues with authority figures.

Joseph: And can you feel that for a therapist when you can't with a mate?

Simon: I guess it depends on the therapist.

Lynn: Yes, but it will depend on where the therapist is. It depends on, not only how well they were trained, but how much self examination they've undertaken.

We've done a lot of work on ourselves, and our own darkness, so that we can be open and available. You can tell me your deviance, and I won't judge it; you can go to the depths of your deviance with me.

Joseph: This kind of work, even today's conversation, creates space. Space creates objectivity and diminishes judgment. I've seen, over the years how we can find space, even in ass-backwards approaches to sexual exploration; especially through porn, porn shops, and strip bars, . . . to mention a few. Because there aren't a lot of healthy ways for us to explore Sex we are often left to our own devices, which often exacerbate our sexual problems. But I still believe something is better than nothing; better than ignorance. But of course, an educated, thoughtful and compassionate approach is always better. We need to understand the consequences of sexual repression and how we've given too much power to institutions like religion and government, who continue to dictate our sex lives through customs, traditions, and laws.

Parisa: And fear.

Joseph: And fear. . . . (Smiling) Good to see we're on the same page, Parisa.

What are some of the things that are hidden in Sex; that show up in Sex?

Kelly: Abuse.

Joseph: Abuse, I get it . . . ab-use, the miss use of something or someone. But what's hidden in the abuse, which is hidden within Sex, is something even more powerful . . . and that is VIOLENCE!

Follow-up: *The Sex Seminar*

Our violence, our anger, our rage is safely tucked away in the Sex closet and we need to expose it. So, how does it manifest . . . violence in sex? Where or how do you see violence being played out in sex? Because it's done all the time. But as you think about it try not to confuse it with *Animal Sex*. Granted, Animal Sex, in its core, is intense and passionate, maybe even violent, but that's a natural violence. No one comes to any real harm when they're having Animal Sex. But when our animal is guided by a twisted or dis-functioning mental or emotional nature, then it becomes harmful; it becomes *unnaturally violent*. So speak about that violence; where do you see it?

Simon: In the gang rapes that are going on in India recently.

Joseph: Gang rapes, absolutely.

Reese: Being East Indian, I have to agree. Sexual repression has a lot to do with this epidemic of gang rapes going on there.

Joseph: Some would argue that these events are unrelated, but not so. We live in not only a physical eco-system but also a delicately balanced and interrelated mental and emotional eco-system.

Where else?

Angie: I see it in the fashion industry, in women's fashion magazines especially. They often have spreads that reinforce and perpetuate rape culture. You have women who are very, very frail and they're made to look even more frail by the poses they're used in. Photographers often ask for models to look broken so they will turn their legs in and hunch their shoulders, and it feels quite violent.

Joseph: Now contrast that to a recent a study done that says rape is one of the top three female sex fantasies.

Parisa: What . . . really!?

Joseph: Yes, one of the top three sexual fantasies for women is being raped. How do you explain that to me? Women fantasize about a stranger taking them. Why would a woman fantasize about a stranger forcibly taking her?

Mercedes: It makes me think that maybe it's a way to act out sexually without responsibility or the possibility of being accused of being a whore or a slut. We . . . I mean, I want sex, but I don't need all the judgment that goes with it, so I can see how a controlled rape fantasy fulfills some of these needs.

Follow-up: *The Sex Seminar*

Joseph: Good. Anything else?

Alexia: So it's a freedom of expression.

Joseph: What do you mean by that?

Alexia: If I'm fantasizing about being raped I might be releasing sexual tension which will leave me feeling relieved or free, somehow.

Joseph: Quite possible. Sexual repression creates deviation and it's through the expression of that deviation that we are often relieved. There are certain freedoms you're missing out on because of sexual repression, so this fantasy could very possibly fulfill some sexual need; even if it's just the need to be taken care of. In addition, if this type of deviance is played out in fantasy, it may not have to play out in your life. So, by all means, imagine it, fantasize about whatever; do it until you can begin to make some sense of all this. There are so many things hidden from us about ourselves and others that it's a great idea to play it out in fantasy. Often, it's through fantasies, that we discover some of our hidden causes and roots to our issues. Sometimes we get to find out who we really are!

Eddie: Is this a way women play out sex and violence without men?

Joseph: What do you think?

Eddie: It sounds like it.

Joseph: Quite possible. . . . What other ways do women perpetuate sexual violence?

Simon: Emotionally, emotional violence . . .

Joseph: Well how?

Simon: Like getting their way if they . . . I don't really know how to explain it.

Joseph: Okay, ladies, tell me a few ways! . . . Ladies, you're with me? Tell me a few ways you castrate a man!

Susan: Say no.

Joseph: Just by saying no? It's how you say no right? . . . "Don't want no short dick man!"

(Laughter)

Follow-up: *The Sex Seminar*

Alexia: We do it in music too, "No one minute man!"

Joseph: Yes, anyone else?

Mercedes: Just by telling him he's not a man or that he doesn't measure up to an ex.

Joseph: Yeah, that's violent. . . . What if there are no victims? What if we're just victimized by stupidity, by how we are enculturated? As long as we assign violence to men, alone, we will perpetuate a deviant expression of violence.

Simon: Are you implying that there is a good violence?

Joseph: Like I said in the seminar, there's natural violence; a healthy and exciting expression of violence. A violence that is enjoyable to men and women alike.

I remember this outtake from a porn movie, where it called for the woman to slap the guy in the face. So she slaps him and apparently he thought it wasn't hard enough so he instructs her to slap him harder. Now this was a big girl, she's was about 5'11, voluptuous and not overweight. So she slaps him harder than he wanted to get slapped.

(Laughter)

He's so shocked that he immediately slaps her back even harder! So she slaps him, even harder! Finally she ducks when he swings at her again and jumps on him and they're rolling in the bed and she yells out, "Are you going to fight me or fuck me?!" That was her response, are you going to fight me, or fuck me. She was awesome! It was none of the, "Oh, a man shouldn't hit a woman!" No! She had full power; she had full sexual power, and she had no trouble expressing her sexual power. "Are you going to fight me, or fuck me? Because I just took your best shot, and so what?" . . . What do you make of that? Because there's power here that women aren't taking sexually. That's their birth right! You've been so trained to play coy that you're losing out on all this energy and power that you're supposed to have, naturally!

Lynn: You think being more aggressive in asking another to bed is enough of this expression; it's not.

Parisa: Men are intimidated when a woman is powerful, so that's why we play low profile.

Joseph: Then you got to fight it! It has to be changed; we have to educate our women, our girls, our boys, all the genders that we're evolving into. You have to change this. I understand there are cultures where it's all about repressing women's power; it's not about art, science and education but about repressing women. You can find them in places like Afghanistan. But just because it's not happening here to the same extent doesn't mean it's not affecting us equally. Each side of the world is affecting the other, powerfully. A change in one affects a change in the other. Just because it's happening in the desert's of Afghanistan doesn't mean it's not affecting us over here. A perfect example of this was illustrated in a science show I recently watched.

Trapped in the sands of the African desert is phosphorous; a key and necessary ingredient for the growth of vegetation. A couple of thousand miles away from there is the rainforest of Latin America, whose soil is lacking greatly from this element. On the surface this appears to be a mistake of nature, because the phosphorous that is needed in the rainforest is stuck in the desert. But recently satellites revealed what was actually going on.

As these satellites were tracking weather patterns, it was noticed that desert windstorms were causing sandstorms. These sandstorms whirled at such a rate that they lifted large amounts of sand into the atmosphere. There the sand mixed with rain clouds causing the phosphorus to be extracted and deposited into the water. Now this is where it gets fascinating. The satellites then further revealed how these clouds then traveled all the way to the rainforest where it dropped the phosphorus filled rain upon the depleted soil that produces the lush forest, which produces the majority of oxygen needed on this planet. How's that for a perfectly regulated ecosystem? The same is going on for us humans. There is a human ecosystem at work that has us all interrelated and interdependent. What we do in one part of the world affects what happens on the other side.

We're in desperate need of balancing our males and females, within and without. Yes, the imbalance shows up in our traditional man to woman relationships, but the real problem is the imbalance within. This goes beyond gender and sexual identity; though it plays out on the surface as such. It's going to take us a long time before we get there but it's been done in part before. The ancient Greeks, for instance, had no discernible distinction around Sexual identification. They didn't even have a name for homosexuals. Today, we have growing distinctions that are causing us more confusion than initially intended.

Initially, the creations of separate sexual identities were intended to exclude one group from the other. For example, individuals were labelled "homosexual" so they could be excluded from power. Recently we've attempted to overthrow that by adding additional titles in the hopes that it would overwhelm and cause a stalemate.

Follow-up: *The Sex Seminar*

Unfortunately, the list of sexual identifiers is growing and we are becoming more obsessed with division rather than oneness.

The Sex Seminar was intended to expose the hidden, expand your consciousness, and widen your box. Our hope was you would walk out on Sunday larger than you arrived on Friday. It didn't matter whether most of the information we provided registered or not; what mattered was that you grew and expanded. That is what lessens the fear and, with less fear, comes more excitement and curiosity.

So, let me ask this question. . . . We have this woman who just told the guy, "Are you going to fuck me or fight me" and he decides, "I can't fuckin' beat this one up" and he has sex with her. What do you think the sex is going to turn into between these two people? Is it going to be violent sex?

Kelly: No

Joseph: No. What is it going to become?

Parisa: Instinct sex?

Joseph: It can, absolutely, but what else can it become?

Nathan: It's going to be, probably, sensual. From the heart, maybe because he's surrendering to her, right? He's going to be like, "Fuck it, I can't beat her!"

Joseph: So what happens if he surrenders to her; to the *female energy*? What happens is he could become *completely* aroused. Because what's actually happening is he is surrendering to Sex! When we surrender to Sex we become alive and awake in its energy; and it doesn't matter what gender we're with at the time. It's easier to surrender to Sex through or with another. What happens to a man when he has to arouse his own energy? Where did we show that in the seminar? Does anyone remember?

Nathan: The porn star dudes.

Joseph: Right, the male porn stars. What happened to them? They had to arouse their own energy.

Kelly: Well they masturbated between shots to keep from going soft.

Joseph: No pun intended, huh?

(Some laughter)

Follow-up: *The Sex Seminar*

. . . And how did that leave them? What did they look like to you?

Kelly: Empty and lonely.

Joseph: Empty, lonely . . . alone, right? Non-intimate. In this situation, it's a woman who arouses a man's energy; yin arouses yang. Unless we're able to access it within us and become self arousing, which is extremely rare, we'll need the other to spark us. Your energy arouses our energy and, when the fire's lit, it can go anywhere! But if I'm blocking you from arousing our energy, if I think I have to control you, if I don't want you to have that kind of power over me, then I might get violent. I might become controlling, I might go in my head and fuck you as an object, and not as a person! On the contrary, if I come to accept that nothing's going to move without the other and I surrender; I'll become *naturally* aroused. I won't have to think about maintaining an erection any longer; Sexual energy will take care of that! When we surrender to Sex, when we commune with Sexual energy itself, we transcend the man-woman representation; we transcend life itself. We are conduits for this energy, which exists independently from you and me. But when we find someone we can surrender together into it with, we'll be able to encounter it firsthand.

Angie: So how does it work for Gay people or Trans individuals?

Joseph: It's the same thing. Gender is on the surface; below that were all the same. It's still yin and yang igniting each other.

Claudia: How about people who practice celibacy? Do they miss out in Sexual energy?

Joseph: The common practice of celibacy is the practice of restraining from Man-made sex. True celibacy is not the avoidance or restraint of Sex, or the Sex act, but the encountering of it for the purpose of expanding into Love. The way we see it, you can have Sex if it leads to Love and still be considered celibate.

Claudia: And nuns and priests?

Joseph: They usually practice repressed celibacy. They don't encounter Sex. It is seen as a block to Love rather than a pathway to it. That's why they have such a hard time with it. Monks tend to practice it properly. They don't avoid Sex; they invite it and travel through it. The only things they avoid are the pitfalls and detours that Sex challenges us humans with. They flow through Sex. Most people don't approach celibacy in that way; like priests and nuns they avoid and repress. This creates tremendous tension and that tension eventually becomes volatile. But if you were to surrender to Sex, all tensions would eventually fall away. Then Sex would be peaceful, whether you partake in the physical act of it or not.

Brennan: So are you saying two people can experience this peace beyond orgasm?

Joseph: Absolutely! Most of our Sexual experiences are far removed, so our orgasms are more about relief than they are about peace. But, when two people approach, encounter and surrender to Sex, then their experience becomes one of peace and bliss. They won't know where they start and the other ends. They'll be connected in a way that a man can literally wonder, "Where's my penis?" When you're truly connected on this deep level, you won't feel your own penises or vaginas. You're just together. Now, that's rare but possible.

Lynn: Then it's not lower case sex any longer, it's upper case Sex.

Joseph: Now that's not to say you can't play around with sex. Like this female comedian once said, "You know, I'd like my lover to be passionate and loving and caressing . . . but that doesn't mean I don't like it up against the fridge once and a while!"

(Laughter)

So, it's all of it! We're not saying one is better than the other, we're saying it's all of it! Explore all of it; we actually tend to be one or two dimensional in this area. This seminar wasn't about *how to*, it was more about the *why's and what's* of Sex. Now you're asking some questions on the how and that's easier to do with all this under your belt. Remember we started with "Where are you at?" Now you can start asking about the *how's* of Sex. You have a better idea of what this thing is and you know it's bigger than you. That's a great start, that's what you all need to hear.

Lynn: The seminar may have revealed a lot to you, including exposing where you're limited. So now you can actually ask yourself, do I want more? And you can provide yourself an honest answer instead of ignoring it.

Joseph: What do you guys make of all this?

Alexia: I feel like after the seminar, I was filled with energy. Without thinking much about it, I was left feeling playfulness and with a new sense of freedom. It has made it easier to see my patterns.

Follow-up: *The Sex Seminar*

One of them is that I push people to their limits, starting with me. So I've worked on that and I've stopped doing it with my boyfriend but I'm finding I still do it with my friends and people at work. I was recently confronted by a co-worker who pointed it out after I was hard on a girl at work. At first I couldn't hear her and I was righteous about not being pushy. But as I meditated and contemplated on it afterwards I realized she was right! Then it came to me that I'm pushy on people around me because it's easier than being pushy with the world. So I made up with the girl. . . . I can now see that I don't have to be so scared of the world anymore and that I can apply this energy outward into life. I've played it too safe up to now. This idea made me feel really excited. That was really profound for me.

Joseph: So what does this have to do with Sex?

Alexia: I've played it too safe with Sex and I've been really judgmental about it. I see that even the glimpse of Sexual energy I had during the seminar changed me. I want to continue to be in the spirit of playfulness that I experienced in one of the Labs. I don't want to continue judging other people, or judging myself; it just blocks me.

Joseph: Okay, so Sexual energy is starting to change you. That's great. But I see that there's violence in your Sex. . . . So, how do women express violence through Sex or Sexual energy?

Parisa: By controlling?

Joseph: Controlling, yes, but be more specific.

Kelly: Withholding.

Joseph: Withholding . . . how else?

Angie: Words, like gossip . . .

Joseph: What do you mean words like gossip?

Angie: Words . . . as in like gossiping and bringing someone down.

Joseph: How so? Be specific, you're heading in the right direction.

Angie: If I wanted to make another woman feel less than me . . .

Follow-up: *The Sex Seminar*

Joseph: And if you wanted to do it sexually . . .

Angie: Yeah. I would speak of her as maybe being loose or not as desirable as me.

Joseph: Women will put other women down so that they are the desired sexual object, that's violent; women on women violence.

Before we ask about how women commit self violence, how else does sexual violence play out between women? What other kind of violence do women commit on each other for sexual attention, energy, power, positioning or advantage?

Claudia: They are just mean to each other.

Joseph: Right. Do you think the concept of "Mean Girls" isn't sexual? One hundred percent it is! The violence that these sexual Prima Dona's commit is extreme and dangerous! They look to achieve compliance, or to destroy the sexual reputation of another female, for sexual power. We only focus on the violence men commit on women, sexually; I want to talk about the violence women commit on themselves and each other sexually. . . . What other ways do women commit violence on themselves sexually?

Kelly: Have sex when they don't really want to.

Joseph: *Have sex when they don't want too* . . . how degrading and violent is that? How else?

Angie: Food.

Joseph: How does that play out? Be specific.

Angie: I was thinking about all the eating disorders.

Joseph: It's easy to argue that eating disorders are sexually based! Many young women don't feel pretty enough, hot enough, or attractive enough so they try to control or rebel through food. They go to extremes from anorexia to obesity and everything in between. That's all forms of sexual abuse, self abuse, and violent self abuse. . . . How else?

Nisha: Similar to that video we saw during the seminar where she cut her labia to have a prettier vagina.

Joseph: Yeah, how violent was that! That still moves me every time I see it, it's so painful.

Kelly: Heavy make-up, maybe piercings?

Joseph: Yeah, it depends if you're doing it to hide or desensitize yourselves. Men do the same by the way, to themselves and to each other. Violence and sex shows up in both genders, it's not a monopoly held by men only. I beg to differ with people who think violence and sex comes mostly from men to women. No. Women do it to each other and to themselves as well!

Angie: Just watch any of the TV housewives!

Joseph: Yes. Those shows are all about sexual violence. Again, it's about sexual attention, power, and control. Now the funny thing is, if Sex could sit here and talk, it would be laughing right now, it would be saying "Are you kidding me? You can't control me; you can't possess me! . . . You can't closet me! . . . You can't contain me! . . . You better just allow me to flow through you, or you'll be left with nothing" . . . But we don't have the privilege to speak to Sex directly so we have to look at it ourselves.

When we hide violence in Sex we distort the Sexual experience. Awareness could change all that. That's what happened to Alexia when she became aware of her violence towards others. It caused her to shift to *playfulness*. Play balances violence in Sex. Now Animal Sex is different because violence is a natural part of it; it's not from an imbalance. Man-made sex, on the other hand, is from our own creation and can easily occur as Animal Sex when it's tinged with violence.

Parisa: So how can you tell the difference?

Joseph: It's very difficult to tell the difference with an untrained mind. An unaware mind sees it the same. It will take practices of self-awareness and objective observation before you'll be able to distinguish the difference. But once you do, it is unmistakeable because the violence in Man-made sex doesn't originate from Sex. That's why, if you add play to Man-made sex, it can shift you to Animal Sex. That's another way out.

Keep looking and, the more you look, the clearer it will get; the deeper you go, the clearer it gets. This is where you have to do your work, and can do your work, if you want to know more about this. We're just here to open the door and set you in the right direction, at least! You are not the source of Sexual energy, it flows through us! I am not the source of Love, it flows through me. Love and Sex are from the realms of the Gods, and they belong to the Gods. I'm blessed and blissed to be able to experience them. I understand they are powerful *influences* that act upon me but, ultimately, with awareness, I can choose whether I want to respond to them or not. But as soon as I start trying to posses them, or be the sole creator of it, I'm going to lose my way.

Lynn: So, Alexia, how do you relate what he's saying to what you shared?

Alexia: Well I think it's talking about abuse on women and I see the abuse that I've done to myself. (Holds back tears)

Joseph: It always starts with the self. The seminar helped you open up to it; now you can complete it.

Alexia, as soon as women turn 11 or 12 on the average, they begin to feel the power of Sex. It provides a new sense of possibility; a possibility of attention, worth, and power. Unfortunately shortly after, you discover you're not the only one feeling this possibility; there are other girls going through this. That's when the competition begins. That's when the power struggle commences and the rage and violence builds. So you start trying to manipulate and control Sex. You don't realize that its initial purpose, for you, was to help you transition from child to adult; to grow you and build you into the unique being that you are meant to be. Today, in your full adulthood and after years of manipulating, controlling and creating sex, you're left with the mess you've made.

Sex is larger than all of us and it's time to come to terms with that. The sooner we do, the easier it will be to balance our Sex lives! We've created our own damages, whether by abusing ourselves and others, abusing children sexually, or abusing Sex itself. It's time for some humility; it's time to turn to Sex with some respect.

The underlining problem is that this has been going on for generations in our families and we can only be as aware as those that have come before us. Therefore, it's important to know whatever strides you make in your life to balance your experience with Sex, will carry over to the next generation. You didn't start this, but you can change it with awareness and education As you lift yourself, you, or your future generation, can begin to see over the wall and see what this is really all about.

Lynn: That's why you want to clear your *storage unit* and make space as you did in the Women's Seminar. . . . Alexia, what is a woman? What is a woman who knows herself?

Alexia: I just see space . . . expansiveness. (Suddenly a crow caws loudly outside the window)

Lynn: So the crow's saying you're on the right path.

Joseph: What do you guys make of this?

Claudia: I've been playing with the concept of sexual power lately. I normally play it out at the gym but recently I decided to practice on the dance floor.

Usually when I go to the gym or a club I'm immediately aware of the attention I'm getting and how I use my body to source attention and power. When I went dancing, I realized that I was diminishing my body and my dancing by being over self conscious of the attention I was getting. I was over sexualizing my dancing and it degraded the whole experience. All of a sudden something that I loved, that I could use to fill me, was being given away freely and leaving me depleted. I was giving away my Sexual power. So, last night, I wore something loose fitting that didn't show my ass and I used dance as mediation; it changed the whole experience. I felt innocent, like Lynn and Joseph were explaining. I let it run through me rather than trying to hold it and possess it every time someone looked at me. I did the same with the music. I relished in it instead of possessing it. I loved it and it didn't matter who was around me! I realized how this plays out the same in my Sex life. It reflects the power struggle that I live with. So it was a huge breakthrough for me!

Kelly: I loved what you said because I love dancing, too, but it also brings unwanted attention; but, at the same time I do like it. So I totally understand what you're saying.

Claudia: It was funny because it was this lie I was playing with myself. I went back and forth, "I don't want this . . . yes I do!! . . . Why are you looking at me that way? But look!"

(Laughter)

Joseph: Can you see how young we are as a civilization in our understanding of Sexuality? Again, we kept saying this world is like elementary school and we're mostly preschoolers and kindergarteners . . . and that's okay! So, once we see the crimes we've committed upon ourselves and others and get past it, we can let ourselves off the hook. By understanding our history, culture, and family systems we can rise to the next grade. That's why we emphasized these variables in the seminar. Now we get a little excited; there's so much to learn and explore. It can become more about possibility than fear. It can be new; Sex can now occur new.

It's unfortunate when somebody older thinks they've experienced everything there is to experience about Sex. That's so silly. There are endless sensations our bodies, minds, and emotions can experience. It's ridiculous to believe otherwise. The human brain is a growing mechanism that is capable of expanding into newer and newer realms. Just think of all the new feelings technology has provided us which didn't even exist 100 years ago; the brain has accommodated them. It will do the same around Sex, as will your body. We are capable of feeling more elaborate and subtle sensations, because of all the recent explorations that other courageous humans have uncovered through Sex.

Therefore knowing these three variables--history, culture, and family amongst others--allows us to be more Sexually spontaneous and exploratory than before we were aware. Without awareness, the most we can be is impulsive and at the worst, reckless. The extensive *research* we undertook last month revealed to us that most of the issues we thought were ours alone actually came from these three variables. We can now see that Sexual repression in a family system can cause one to turn to alcohol as a replacement for Sex, or to facilitate Sex. This can, in turn, cause the younger members of the system to link alcohol with Sex. If continued, generationally, it can become genetic; alcoholism that is.

Kelly: I'm way more free when I'm drunk. . . . I'm even freer when I'm high; I'm way more sexual.

Joseph: We're not more free when we drink. All we've done is temporarily block the issues. True freedom is when these issues are diminished enough that we can connect directly with Sex. When we use drugs or alcohol, we are renting freedom and Sex; we don't own it. That's cheating. You cheat and I cheat when we do drugs and alcohol. When we connect with another through alternative substances we are not coming as ourselves; we're lying. It's a lie because, after we're off the substances, we either can't or have trouble reconnecting with the other the same way. It's Sex that allowed you to feel a connection; not the substances. Therefore, the connection you felt was BULLSHIT! If it weren't for Sex you wouldn't have even gotten a peek of these good feelings. . . . Has there been a time when you drank and it didn't work, Kelly?

Kelly: Yes.

Joseph: Then there's the only proof you need; it should work every time. . . . It was Sex that allowed you to have those experiences and feelings. It's Sex that allows it with or without alternative means. Any blending you achieve with another through artificial means is artificial. The feelings are glimpses of what true blending can bring, but the blending, itself, is an illusion. By the way, the other person can also be a drug for you. If, in your blending with the other, you conclude that he or she sourced it for you, you're in trouble. That's how people lose themselves in sexual relationships. They feel "I'm lost without him, I'm lost without her." Sex is the source and it can be sourced with yourself, with another, or with the entire world!

Angie: There was a part in the seminar where you started talking about how we allow ourselves to be so much more free at night than we do during the day. I consider it okay to be wasted and dancing on a table at 12 o'clock at night. I'm like "Oh yeah fair enough." But if I see them doing it at eleven in the morning, it seems wrong. Can you speak more on that?

Joseph: Recently, as you may remember us saying, we went to New York for one of our daughter's birthdays. The party that was being thrown for her was being held at a lounge that started at two in the afternoon.

 Now, what they do at this lounge is create the illusion of night. They close all the shades, they open the bar, pump up the music and *Voilà* it's night time! Everyone started to behave differently, more Sexual and free. Now the brain responds as if it's night time and the body follows. Therefore, it's more about the dark than it is about the time of day. . . . So I'll throw it back to you, "Why do we give ourselves more permission in the dark?"

Kelly: Because it's like a mask in a way.

Joseph: So one of the ways we use the dark is to mask things. That's true. . . . Any other reasons?

Susan: We're not seen as well.

Joseph: So, there's an aspect of invisibility. Is that why we give ourselves more permission; because we're not seen as much?

Susan: I think so; it's easier to dance in the dark without feeling foolish

Joseph: Good, we can hide, we can mask. But what about those of you who actually come out of hiding in the dark?

Simon: They probably hide during the day and allow themselves to be seen at night because, maybe, there's less judgment at night.

Joseph: According to Angie, she judges less at night. . . . We don't all use the dark the same way. The dark can create a clear canvas just as a white canvas does. So you can *paint* almost any experience you'd like on it.

Reese: Music seems to do the same thing. It gives me more space, especially in the dark.

Joseph: Yes, that's right. You paint on your dark canvas with music, lights, color, sparks, energy, Sexual energy. . . . In the dark your vision is deprived and your other senses are enhanced; smell, touch, taste. . . . What else with the dark?

Lynn: This reminds me of the movie *Nine and a Half Weeks*. There's a scene in the movie where the main character blindfolds his love interest and proceeds to feed her different foods. And because she's *blind,* the food takes on a more sensual quality. She surrenders what she knows, and experiences the foods anew.

Parisa: Where is that movie, I've been looking for it for ages.

Joseph: Um . . . I think it's at the video store . .

Parisa: There are no video stores . . .

Joseph: I'm sure you could find it online.

Parisa: I did see it twice, but I just can't find it again!

(Loud Laughter)

Joseph: That reminds me of an old song called, "The freaks come out at night" . . . Parisa!

(More laughter)

Isn't this why most of you accepted our invitation to this *follow-up;* because you're still somewhat in the dark? So tell us more about the dark . . .

Follow-up: *The Sex Seminar*

Parisa: There's mystery in the dark, it seems very dangerous.

Joseph: Can't you say the same about Sex: that it's mysterious and dangerous?

Parisa: It has been that for me, at times. Yes.

Joseph: Sex and darkness are both unknown to us, at least in part, and larger than us. Is there any wonder, then, why we join the two together? Since there's no doubt that darkness is larger, it's easier to surrender in it than it is to Sex. Darkness has a power, like Sex, that we can tap into. But unlike Sex, it's harder to reach. You have to surrender to it *before* you can access it. It's also easier to surrender in darkness, even semi-darkness because others can't see us fully. As alluded to before, it's harder to judge in the dark. Maybe, Parisa, it's too difficult to hold on to your false self in the dark, and that's what scares you. The dark makes it easy to feel your fears.

Alexia: I just thought of being in your mother's stomach in the dark.

Joseph: My mother's stomach. What the hell were you doing there?!

Alexia: (Laughter)

 . . . I mean *my* mother's stomach!

Joseph: . . . Yeah for some, being in the dark allows us to be in the deepest of comfort, which is mother's womb. So we look to return to that. Darkness is a womb for all of us, regardless of gender. The same goes for Sex. These are powers which hold you, contain you, and envelop you; it doesn't matter how you enter them. It doesn't matter in Sex. Whether you do it through a mouth, anus, or a vagina, it doesn't matter. This is why these two powers are so closely related.

There's a freedom in darkness like in Sex. You can move in any direction and still be held and pleasured. When we have fear of either, it is because of the mind. Through either conditioning or unfortunate events we can easily view them as something to fear. In addition, both can be used destructively or creatively.

Simon: Throughout history the dark is the death day and the day is a rebirth. When the sun comes up the next day, it's a "New day and I can be who I want to be." Aren't you saying the opposite?

Joseph: No. Expansion can come from light and dark. We associate space with darkness and the universe is made up of about 95% of space. Therefore, if the universe is expanding, then darkness is expanding.

We do link death with darkness and darkness with Sex and that makes some sense when speaking about orgasms. As we mentioned in the seminar, an orgasm is considered to be a *little death* because upon having it, you feel temporarily liberated from the body. So in the dark and in Sex we allow ourselves to get closer to death and closer to being okay with it. . . . What else is significant about the dark? There's more?

Parisa: Shadows?
Joseph: No, that's more significant for light; dark is dark.

Jeremy: You can hide in the dark?

Joseph: We mentioned hiding with the masks but there are additional things you can hide. You can hide your feelings, your fears, your bravado, your pain, your worries, and your ugly faces that you think might turn someone off . . . You can hide your body.

Kelly: Yeah, I'm always like, "I like it because it's dark."

Joseph: Yeah we can hide our insecurities, hide our uncertainties, what else about the dark?

Simon: There's an obvious agreement with everyone; it's obvious that it's dark.

Joseph: Yeah it's one of the rare times we all agree. All of us! We 100% agree to the experience of the dark. We might have variations, but we all agree that it's something we're going to surrender to. Okay, let me spoon feed you here. . . . Tell me about *time* in the dark. Because time is very obvious in the light, right? What happens to time as soon as it gets dark?

Kelly: It goes by really fast!

Joseph: No, it disappears . . . don't you see? You don't really conceive of it, you don't, likely, worry about it or concern yourself with it; it gives you the opportunity to go timeless. To feel eternity and what it might feel like to finally feel eternal.

Parisa: In the dark?

Joseph: Yes, in the dark, because how do you measure time in the dark?

Parisa: So if someone is in prison and in the dark and unable to see light, do they surrender to the darkness?

Joseph: Good question! If they surrender to the darkness, they'll do time very well. It will be like that! (Snaps fingers) What do you think? Would YOU eventually surrender?

Parisa: Yes, if I don't go crazy first.

(Laughter)

Joseph: True, the dark will magnify our demons forcing us to surrender or disconnect; or as you put it "Go crazy."

We were watching an old episode of *Fringe,* yesterday, and in it, a guy winds up in a building that is inescapable. No matter what exit he takes he winds up in a different part of the same building, and he's unaware this is happening to him. So when he's asked how long he's been in the building he guesses around five days when, in actuality, it's been 20 years.

Now when you stop to try and conceive how that's possible, you have to realize if you surrender fully, then 20 years is immeasurable. Our earlier form of measuring time was the sundial which operated during the day and only when the sun was out. We needed, and need, light to tell time.

Time can fly or creep by in the dark. Just ask novice mediators. They close their eyes and go into the dark and sit believing they've been sitting for let's say an hour, and when they open their eyes to look at their watches they find it's been only minutes. The same can happen in reverse to a seasoned meditator. Darkness allows you to transcend time! We live in a time-space continuum, and in this continuum we experience space through boundaries and time by observing movement. . . . So what happens in the dark to those two things?

Angie: They kind of dissolve.

Joseph: Yeah, so where are you when you're in darkness, because you're no longer in this time space continuum? . . . I don't want to turn this into *The Darkness Seminar*, but you're asking about the night and Sex.

Angie: This makes me want the Darkness Seminar.

Nathan: Yeah, really!

Joseph: What do you guys make of this? And realize, *everything we just said about darkness applies to Sex; everything!*

Follow-up: *The Sex Seminar*

Riley: I just *never looked at it that way*!?

Joseph: Isn't Sex completely different in the light versus the dark, in the morning versus the night? What's Sex like when you wake up in the middle of the night and you don't know what time it is?

Claudia: A lot of what you've been talking about I feel with music and dance.

Joseph: Dance is another wonderful way we can go into Sex and darkness. When we go into Sex through dance, we allow ourselves to get really close. It becomes harder to see each other clearly so we begin to rely on what we're feeling, rather than what we're seeing. We may even close our eyes and allow our bodies to do the seeing. This, suddenly, enhances things because we're in the dark together. Experiencing the holy trinity of Sex, dance, and darkness is one of the most remarkable transcendent occurrences you can have as a human being.

Lisa: What do you mean by *holy trinity*?

Joseph: Sorry, shouldn't have gone there . . . that's another conversation for another day.

Group: Ahhh, no!

Joseph: Prior to the seminar your *eyes were wide shut*. Today, you have an opportunity to explore Sex with open eyes. There are a lot of things to explore, it's awesome and exciting. There's a lot to try out here, to understand about yourselves and your relationship. Just looking at Sex, through the simple concept of light and dark, can keep you occupied for a long while. Now that you know you're not Sex, you can ask and experience the answer to any question you may want to explore. Sometimes the question turns out to be better than the answer. . . . As long as you thought you were the source of Sex, you weren't going to be asking any questions of significance because that would have exposed you . . . you *Great and Powerful OZ's*.

As we've seen in our Lab experiences, we project our issues on Sex. Sex gets a bad rap. Sex gets blamed for somebody else's violence, somebody else's stupidity, somebody else's sexual abuse towards us, somebody else's anger, or shame, or guilt. It all gets in the way and gives Sex a bad name. What stopped you from exploring Sex before this?

Parisa: My beliefs and culture.

Follow-up: *The Sex Seminar*

Joseph: So beliefs and culture have informed you; this is great to know because you can reform yourself. We can reform our culture, change our beliefs or just plain old find the truth. We can adapt the ancient Greek's view on homosexuality. Remember, it wasn't even a concept--wow! There's so much room to expand and let go. . . . Has this helped or confused you more?

Nisha: It's definitely helped me.

Kelly: It's confused me.

(Laughter)

Lynn: What's confusing, Kelly?

Kelly: I just feel like there's so much to learn, and my values get in the way. Sometimes I have urges, but my values get in the way; they stop me from doing what I want. So I get shy; I want to have more of an open mind.

Joseph: Then you need more space, so you can have less self judgment. With space you can *see* your values objectively. This will allow you to go, "Oh look at me, I'm acting shy right now!" or "Oh look at me, I'm not acting shy right now I'm acting promiscuous!" When we lack space everything occurs like its right on top of us; right in our faces. We're left, then, relying on what we hear, and what you're hearing, Kelly, is not voices from the outside, but a voice from your past. It's your inner moral critic; your *parent voice*. Distance allows us to distinguish this voice from our own; but you need space. You need to expand and stretch and see yourself from where Reese is sitting. *(Reese is sitting on the other side of the room across from Kelly)* Then as you keep looking at yourself, from a distance, rather than from just underneath your own skin, you'll see what you want and what your parent voice wants. Then, and only then, will you be able to choose. As of now, you cannot choose because there is not enough space to distinguish the two. Since you're such an obedient child, your default is to listen to the parent voice. Know that you've taken on one of your parent's shyness. This has left you angry, not shy. You just play shy; it has you feel safe when you're lacking space. The child you once were felt safe in shyness, I know, I was painfully shy as a child and as a young adult I used shyness because it gave me a false sense of safety. But, like with you, it began to work against me. I had to figure out shyness completely and the only way I was able to get out of it was by distancing me from me so I could watch me like a scientist. I became my own guinea pig. This is what you have to do to get out of this. Create space in your life, then observe yourself from the additional available distance. Don't forget, the eyes need distance in order to see.

Lynn: Confusion is often the only thing between you and truth. It's just the ego resisting expansion. You came into the seminar very arrogant believing, as most of you did, you knew Sex because you had Sex. You thought you were mature around Sex because adults have Sex; but neither is true. It's good that you're confused because it means you finally know . . . you don't know.

Joseph: I know fifty and sixty year olds that are not confused, though they should be . . . They think they know Sex because they've been having it for forty years. They don't. All they've been doing is the same thing for forty years. It's old and nothing new is happening for them; there's no growth. What they need to know is that they're stuck in ignorance.

Lynn: I've been with this man for eleven years and I think I know less about Sex today than I did when we first started our relationship. Really, because there are layers and layers and layers of intimacy that I didn't know were possible with not him, but me! Today, I understand Sexual energy can take me there and this insight came to me through this Sex Seminar; we're always, always looking!

Joseph: Your confusion is asking for clarity. It wants more for you. So, we provide the information and experiences to make it a little easier. The main thing to remember is you are not the cause of your Sexual environment: you were born into it. And with education, you can change it.

Kelly: ...This has made me feel bett...no, not better, I feel more aware.

Joseph: It's a good thing you brought this up.

The Sex Seminar was set up to show you the *what*, not the *how* of Sex. So now you're asking the right questions. You're saying, "I see the what, and I'm confused on the how." Good, so that's the next step, that's why we're here today; to tie up loose ends.

Kelly: I think one weekend seminar definitely isn't enough for anyone to get it right. Our life is always going to be evolving and learning. Like you said, I want to grow old, not get old. I love that, because it's true, we need to keep learning and learning and learning; we're always changing.

Joseph: Yes, it's just a beginning. It was meant to get you started. Some people haven't even started yet. Many of you were idling in your sex lives. For some, your entire perception of Sex was based on Man-made sex. You were educated by the sex that was around you not the Sex from inside you. You're over affected by the daily bombardment of sex because you're functioning from the wrong center.

Kelly: Yeah, my energy and body language is affected; everything in my life has been affected!

Joseph: What you see in the mirror, what you see in people around you, how people respond to you, it's all sex, sex, and sex. I'm not saying everything is sex, I'm saying you live stuck on *the sex channel.* You can watch life through hundreds of channels, yet you insist on only staying tuned to the sex channel. And you can switch the channel or watch all of them at the same time. Our consciousness has that capacity! You can watch the friendship channel or the money channel instead, though some of you have bad reception and the sex channel tends to show up no matter what channel you're on. Or even worst, the sex channel will advertise on all your channels confusing you further. By the way, it's important to note that this idea of *channels* was all explained years ago in Ram Dass' *Grist for the Mill*, if you're interested in hearing it from a different perspective.

Simon: The thing you said about men, I was confused about that. Do we get Sexual energy from women alone and does it work the other way around?

Joseph: In the spiritual tradition of sexuality it has been postulated that women are the doorways into Sex. They have been credited as being the luring and necessary force that is needed to bring men to full surrender. That holds true in the world of heterosexual Man-made sex. But in our *brave new world* where gender, and our awareness of gender, is growing and expanding by the day, we have to look at it from the inside out, rather than from the outside in.

We are all male and female; we are made up of 23 chromosomes from our mother's and 23 chromosomes from our fathers; so we are both. Therefore, underneath it all, each individual can be that female force for us and others, regardless of our surface gender. Granted, women's additional nerve endings in their vaginas allow them to access superior feelings of excitement and stimulation; but we are all able to experience the highest of stimulation by transcending the mere physical effects of Sex. Does that help?

Simon: I think so. You're saying that we can cause our own connection to Sexual energy?

Joseph: Yes, we are the causation of our own experiences and we can only affect others to the degree that they are open to us. It's easy to have the illusion that you're *causing* Sexual effects upon another, but you can't cause an affect on anything that's not sensitive to you to begin with. I can't make a wall scream if I hit it with a hammer, if it's not capable of screaming; and that's what we conveniently let ourselves forget. This misconception has caused me some of the greatest pains in my life.

Whenever a relationship of mine ended, whether it was the woman leaving me or me ending it, I would panic about finding out she was with another man. Because I lived with the belief that I was the source of her Sexual arousal. The idea that someone else could do that for her, or do it better, would nearly destroy me! It would mean to me he was a better man than me. It was convoluted and wrong. She never needed him or me! Our mates are attracted to us, as we are to them, usually because of our mutually shared dysfunctions; not because we're so irresistible.

So, Simon, what would it be like to have Sex from your instincts, and not your mind? That would begin to answer your question, because it's through your instincts that you'll be able to access your female self. Both parts of you can be found there. You are overemphasizing your male and you need to connect with your female. Or as the ancient Chinese *Book of Changes* would say, you are in touch with your *Creative* self but not your *Receptive* self. Then you'll be able to unite them creating a oneness in you. This is done Sexually, but not in the classic sense.

Many people try to find spiritual enlightenment by bypassing Sex. This is the problem with Catholic nuns and priests. They're trying to get to God without Sex and they're failing miserably.

Kelly: Sorry, I just have one thing to say.

Joseph: Please . . .

Lynn: Don't be sorry . . .

Kelly: I wanted to ask . . . Lynn, remember when you made us meditate and I felt like I was out of my body? It was when you got us to meditate all together; I saw a

Follow-up: *The Sex Seminar*

white light, and that's never happened to me before, and it freaked me out. I shook out of it, and you told me that it was Sexual energy or something; I didn't really understand it.

Lynn: You think you see only through your two eyes when, in actuality, you have two sources of visions, two types of visions--outer vision and inner vision. Since we over rely on our outer vision, we tend to have foggy inner vision. We often confuse the two, claiming we're having inner visions when in actuality we're projecting our outer visions. But, we literally have inner vision, and if you keep practicing and connecting with it, you'll actually start seeing more with your eyes closed. The light is just the beginning.

Kelly: Well, I loved the feeling.

Joseph: Good, then you have a reason and a motivation to meditate. Meditation is a great way to strengthen your inner vision. I've combined my inner vision and outer vision so now I could see more clearly and give people feedback based on my vision rather than my opinion. But that took a lot of work, inside and outside, for me to get to this point. You don't need a perfect union between the two to find a greater sense of self, but you do need a closer balance between the two. So, all we're saying is strengthen your inner vision with meditation; obviously it resonates for you!

Nisha: The meditation gave me such a weird feeling; but an amazing feeling. I almost felt like a balloon that had no helium or air in it. But about 15 minutes into the meditation it started to feel like I was being pumped by helium. It got larger and taller; it was a crazy feeling!

Joseph: Clearly you got to see that this energy has filled you and will continue to when needed.

Nisha: What energy?

Joseph: Since the meditation directed you through Sexual feelings then it's safe to say it was Sexual energy.

Kelly: You asked the men to be in meditation first; was there a reason for that?

Joseph: Yes . . . the men needed more attention.

Kelly: Was it harder for the men because . . . well, did they get aroused?

(Nervous laugh)

Simon: Not me. I could stand back and actually see what was going on with it rather than being involved with it.

Angie: So, what if you guys had presented it in reverse?

Joseph: Well hold on; let's first see what it was like for the guys. . . . What was it like first doing the meditation, then watching the film clip?

Nathan: It was difficult after meditating. It was like I got hit!

Joseph: No . . . they got slammed! They were put in a highly sensitive position with their senses heightened. When they sat and watched it, it hit them with more intensity than it did you women.

Kelly: So, why did you guys protect the women more than the men?

Joseph: Well, you're assuming we were protecting you.

Kelly: Well, what was it then?

Reese: Why was it done differently? Tell us.

Lynn: Why do you think?

Nisha: The men might not feel it unless they were in that meditative state of mind...

Joseph: You're heading in the right direction, but let's ask the men because they had the experience, so they can speak on it.

Nisha: Would you guys not have felt it if you hadn't meditated beforehand?

Nathan: Well it's like what Joseph has said before; we're more visual, so if we were to just see it first it would just be what it was. It would just be another porno, it would be like, "Holy fuck, that's crazy . . ."

(Laughter)

Instead we actually had to go and sit and be with ourselves inside ourselves. I don't think a lot of men really do that, usually. . . . So, we went and did that and then we went and watched it, and it was like, holy . . . well you heard all our reactions.

Follow-up: *The Sex Seminar*

Simon: The other thing that fucked me up a little is when all the girls looked like they were about to burst out crying, and they were silent. Like Alexia (Simon's girlfriend) didn't even make eye contact, and I was like, "What the fuck are we in for now?"

Alexia: (Looking almost gleeful) I wasn't supposed to!

(Laughter)

Simon: So I felt some weird things when we were meditating and when we walked in, the girls just looked fucked, and I was like "Oh shit, this is going to be hectic." But that was another thing to hide in; I thought that somebody was going to end up dying or something.

(Laughter)

I was thinking something really bad is going to happen. So, I don't know if that helped me feel more . . .

Reese: It was very different because we went in really sensitive.

Women: Awww!

(Laughter)

Lynn: Before we talk about why the difference, or what was the difference; lets share some more . . . women, what was it like for you?

Angie: I just think it's funny. Simon's interpretation of the way we all looked, all shocked and stuff, was so off. Afterwards, when we talked about it, you were saying its funny how the women were more receptive to this than the guys were. I found that a lot of the guys were quite combative about it and when it was done you (Looking at Simon) were like, all up in arms about it. I remember Mercedes and I were like, "It looked like they were having a good time!" A few of the other girls expressed something similar; they weren't really that offended by it.

Joseph: So what do you think caused these diverse reactions?

Nathan: The process in which it was delivered to them, so they got to see it first and were able to calm down . . .

Simon: They were able to reflect.

Nathan: Yeah, they were like, "Oh! That was awesome!"

(Laughter)

Joseph: So, you're saying the women were able to absorb it before they spoke on it reflectively and the men had to speak unreflectively? So, what do you make of that? Isn't this how it's been traditionally, sexually speaking?

Simon: Yeah. I was thinking of the rules of engagement. Say I was single and went into a bar and approached a woman and we went back and had sex. The next day there's always a huge thing about a guy just leaving in the morning and leaving the girl to think about it, and the guy is like, "Okay, next!"

Jeremy: I know when I was young it felt like I was supposed to know what I was doing and it was fine if the girl didn't.

Eddie: Same for me. I lost my virginity to a virgin but she never knew I was a virgin.

Angie: Why didn't you tell her?

Eddie: Because she wouldn't have had sex with me.

Joseph: There are different expectations for boys and young men than there are for their counterparts. It's changing, somewhat, today, but more education is needed.

Lynn: Do men get to *meditate first, and then have Sex* or do they have sex before they could meditate on it?

Joseph: Guys, do you think we handled it any differently than how it is? Don't you just get hit with Sex before you've had a chance to process it? We're not saying it's that different for females; we're saying it's different. It was easier for you men to express your outrage because you're older and more able to communicate it. But believe me, you would have done the same when you were younger, if you were better supported and informed. That's why the guys acted like a bunch of bitches.

(Laughter)

. . . Sorry, I had to say it!

Follow-up: *The Sex Seminar*

Reese: It's so true!

Joseph: Okay. Just halfway joking.

Reese: No, you're not!

(More laughter)

Simon: It's interesting to see that we're expected to be stronger around Sex than women; that women are the weaker sex and have to be protected.

Joseph: Yeah, interesting that some of you thought we did it to protect women.

Lynn: There's an assumption that needs to be broken before we can find compassion for one another and that is that women aren't as strong as men and men have to be stronger and more capable to take care of and protect women. This is an idea that was taught to you and that has been taught since the beginning of time. It has caused our boys to repress their pain and hardships, has forced them to grow up before their time, and become insensitive to other boys who are sensitive. That has really fucked a lot of you men up, thinking you have to take care of mommy. I understand that it was put in place to protect and perpetuate the species but its no longer needed, today. We don't need you to take care of us. We're really strong. We need you to care for us . . . and you need the same. We can take it. Look at the woman in the movie. She could take it.

Joseph: Could? She did!

Kelly: I liked it!

(Laughter)

Lynn: I don't know if Joseph said it in the seminar but he was told he couldn't wear out a hole with a pole by an older man when he was younger; and he really, *really*, tried to prove that man wrong. But that caused him the same pain you witnessed the man having in the video. He needed to get in her! He needed to possess her, and she had already surrendered. Unless you kill us you're not really going to hurt us because you can't even rape me! This is a big one! You can't rape me because I will only let you in, as far as I let you in! You can put your penis in my vagina but you're only in the hallway. I get to say who goes into the ballroom, and men understand that innately.

They've been really angry about that. They want the women's expansiveness, so they try to dominate us to get it. You have to believe we're weak in order to keep doing what you're doing; to keep proving what you think you're proving. You have to so that you feel big and strong! If you let yourself, as men, really feel a woman's power, strength, and expansiveness, you'll start crying! Because you can't match it! You can't give birth, you can't grow life! Unfortunately, most of us women don't even understand that, so we'll compete with each other instead.

We act out violently on each other. We're imploding because we're not expressing our full power. It's sitting in us dormant like TNT that becomes more volatile with time. "I want you to fuck me more than I want you to fuck her! I want you to desire me more and maybe then I'll feel my strength and worth there." But it never happens. We don't understand ourselves as women, but the truth about women is that we're strong. The truth is that we need each other! The truth is we need to understand Sex and Sexual energy more intimately, in order to understand our power. Sex can help us with that, and not by just having it.

Kelly: Wow!

(Laughter)

Simon: What's coming up for me is I can see I had to protect my mom when I was a kid because she had violent partners. So, a lot of it was about letting my parents die, as I was told in the Communication Seminar. That makes even more sense to me now.

Since the seminar, my mom and my relationship has changed. Now, she'll be feeding me things so I can help her and I'm like, "No, I'm not dealing with that." So that's something I'm really thankful for. I see that, and now my relationship with other women has changed. If Alexia comes to me with something, I know she can manage herself, I'll tell her she can do it and she does. I don't feel that overwhelming need to do it for her.

Lynn: In the recent past, I witnessed you resenting her for feeling like you had to take care of her. Good job!

Joseph: We resent when we have to take care of someone who can take care of themselves. Female entitlement and men's need to feel value by taking care a woman, perpetuates this game that ultimately weakens everybody who's involved.

This game is played way too seriously. When we wake up to our full power and the power of others, then the *weakness game* stops working on us. Why not play it out in bed instead? We can play weak, tie each other up, spank each other, dominate and submit . . . let me know when I should stop,

(Laughter)

 . . . we can do whatever! Playing out the weakness game in Sex can be amazingly exciting and fulfilling; then you won't have to play it in the rest of your lives. You can treat each other as equals instead. You need to get what Lynn is saying. It's profound! This misconception of women has formed your perception and approach to Sex. Until we realize that women are stronger than they play or appear, we will continue to participate in this extremely debilitating and harmful power struggle where both sides lose.

Lynn: If you, objectively, watch a woman in her full power walk down the street you'll notice that men, and women alike, look at her like she's a blooming tree or bush, revealing the most beautiful of flowers. Women, at least up to now, have been the peacocks of our species. To assume that the peacock is weak, well that's something that was made up, wasn't it? Fortunately, we're buying into it less and less because of the new female role models and the growing positive depiction of women in movies and television. It's evolving, and women are responding appropriately; but there still is a way to go.

Joseph: When I was a child, it seemed like women didn't know how to run. They ran with their arms and legs flailing.

(Laughter)

You don't see that, at all, anymore. It's been phased out, finally.

Simon: So, it's just throwing they struggle with? (Alexia hits Simon)

(Laughter)

Follow-up: *The Sex Seminar*

Angie: I had a really amazing experience this weekend; I was showing a 38 year old man how to throw a punch. It was interesting because, as a woman, I had a split second of judgment thinking, "You're a man! You're like 6'3, 38 years old and you don't know how to throw a punch, and I'm a girl and I'm teaching you?" But then I realized that it was really beautiful. It was really cool.

Joseph: I thought that when I first met Lynn. If I was ever stuck on a mountain, she could carry my ass down! I like a woman who could carry me off a mountain.

(Laughter)

Susan: But would she?

(Laughter)

Joseph: That's a whole other conversation!

Lynn: Depends on the day!

(More Laughter)

Joseph: We really need to cut each other, and ourselves, some slack. We forget we're only human. Severe judgement is not the answer. Education, awareness, and forgiveness are.

Angie: The seminar made me realize I need to work on forgiveness, not for others but for me.

Joseph: Forgiveness is a big one; especially around sexual abuse. We cannot reduce sexual crimes through ignorance, but by opening our minds and hearts.

For those of us who have been sexually abused, it's harder, but we need to find a way. Healing and education is the place to start.

Kelly: One thing I learned about sexual abuse was to consider what the abuser is feeling and going through. Imagine a person that sexually abuses a child. What must they have been feeling to have done this? Did they feel horrible or guilty or nothing at all? I don't know, it seems like nobody wants to talk about it.

Joseph: There was a movie several years ago called *The Woodsman* with Kevin Bacon that attempted to explore what you're bringing up. It's worth a watch if you want to investigate this further.

I believe genetics plays a role in this but, obviously, there must had been childhood experiences that exacerbated this type of deviation

Kelly: Yeah, exactly.

Angie: Well especially when . . . like for me, I was sexually abused as a kid and I can't imagine it when I'm around children. I think about the people who did it to me, my father and my uncle, and I can't imagine where their brains were at. Sometimes that flashes into my brain, not the act but their actions. It's like "Holy" where were they in their world, that they could do that to me, a child? . . . It's like, I'm hanging out with my little kid right now and I have compassion for them.

Joseph: That's amazing. You need to heal the child in you that experienced that and there's no one better to help her than you.

There's a wonderful Iranian-Canadian Oscar nominated film called *Incendies* that I would highly recommend, which speaks beautifully to forgiveness of sex abuse. The main female character is revealed through the reading of her will to her two estranged adult children. The process brings you through her painful abuse-filled life and concludes with you wondering "How could someone access such depth of compassion?" The character leaves you with the possibility that "Maybe I can give, also."

Nathan: But how do I forgive without forgetting?

Joseph: Forgiveness is not about forgetting. Forgiveness is not condoning. Forgiveness is more about giving yourself additional space and room for other possibilities to show up! Without space, forgiveness is impossible. This is why we believe that time heals all wounds because we experience space through time. But, in actuality, time without space heals nothing! Without space there's no movement, therefore, even if the person could change or grow, it's never going to happen without the room.

Mercedes: So time and space equals forgiveness?

Joseph: No, there's one more stage to include and that's the self work stage. This is the stage where one looks at, sees, and feels the hurt that is begging for forgiveness, even if it involves confronting those who have wronged us.

I've wronged people in my life and forgiving that has been just as difficult as forgiving others. I, first, had to get past my denial of the wrong I had committed.

Then I had to take the time and make the space to see what happened so I could take accountability for my crimes. Next, when possible, I faced those I hurt, I explained myself and then gave them a chance to get their hurt out. Finally, I asked for their forgiveness. Since I've been on both sides of the coin I have become more proactive around giving and receiving forgiveness.

So, Angie, seeing it from their end helps greatly; this is all part of finding compassion. We're all going to leave this Earth one day so isn't it probably better to come to the truth *before* that fateful day?

Can you see that it's in our sex lives and through Sex that we can practice forgiveness the most? That's the one area where we overwhelmingly hurt ourselves and each other; we abuse through Sex more than through any other realm.

Nathan: My father abused me through sex and alcohol.

Joseph: That's the same thing. It's still a form of sex. Alcohol is used as a substitute for sex. When you look deep into a sexually repressed family system you'll always find alcohol to some degree. Your father repressed his homosexuality so, in his case, he used alcohol to alleviate his pain and maybe find permission, when intoxicated, to express it. We do the same with drugs. Also, mentally and emotionally immature people overindulge in alcohol in order to have or at least pursue sex. They'll drink, have sex, maybe feel some shame, and shut down. They learn nothing because they fail to reflect on their experiences and repeat the cycle all over again . . . over and over again.

When this type of behavior is perpetuated over several generations you wind up with a sexually immature family. Their humor is always crude and rude and their sexual conversations are never serious. They know no boundaries and sex abuse is rampant.

Lynn: What you did that weekend was very healthy. You took time out from your lives so you could come and explore. And explore you did! You endured challenging conversations, difficult Labs, and you were honest with your thoughts and pain. That was more than we could have asked for. In return, you grew. I can see it today! And there's still more work to be done because a few of you did try to hide.

Parisa: I *definitely* was protecting myself.

Lynn: Yeah, so that's beautiful that you got to see it, because we couldn't tell you that. You had to come to it on your own. You had to experience it.

Follow-up: *The Sex Seminar*

Parisa: So many of my beliefs have gone *poof* since then!

Joseph: We figured since you all did it the healthy way, we should give you an opportunity to complete. So we have another 45 minutes. We could stop here or continue. Is there anything else that you guys want to discuss?

Parisa: I have to thank you both, because of this seminar, I found the strength to return to Dubai.

Joseph: Wow! Good for you. I hope.

Parisa: Yeah I don't know what to expect. I'm just going to try my luck again, over there.

Joseph: Well you're going back a different person.

Parisa: Yes, and I'm going back to a culture where women know nothing about Sex and men watch porn all the time.

(Laughter)

Parisa: So, I hope I can do some good there.

Joseph: That's sadly funny because I read that when they found Bin Laden he had a sizeable porn collection. It makes sense what you're saying.

Lynn: Well, just don't end up in jail!

(Laughter)

Parisa: Yeah I need to be careful because I've learned all of these curse words like "fuck" that I have to get out of the habit of saying. I don't know how; it's difficult because it's so expressive!

(Laughter)

Reese: What would happen if you said "fuck" there?

Parisa: I might lose my job because if they want me to do something and I don't want to do it I say, "Fuck no." I'm a different person . . .

(Laughter)

Angie: Yeah, I swear a lot because of you guys!

Follow-up: *The Sex Seminar*

Parisa: When I was there last I worked like a prostitute, accepting all the shit just to keep my job and keep my salary. I'm no longer that person so I don't know what's going to happen. I just pray that I am safe because I'm not good at keeping this mouth shut; but I plan to be careful on how I use my words. So, I'm coming to you for one-on-one because I think that I need it before I go.

Joseph: It's just about refining us and our communication. You can refine and still express yourself fully. I understand that more will be required of you, but you can do it. You were stretched here so that you'd have more space to see yourself. That's why you appear so different to all of us than you did in the seminar.

Group: Yes . . . yeah . . . absolutely, you really do!

Joseph: That's because you expanded and then adapted to the new you. You'll do it again. This is how we grow. Don't worry, any of you; you'll grow into the new you easily enough. Growing gives us the opportunity to see more, so you'll see things differently in Dubai; you'll see things you couldn't see before. So try to resist predicting what will happen and trust that your instincts and new insights will guide you.

I speak as I speak, and I'll speak like this in front of ten thousand people, if it's called for. But if the situation changes I will shift my language, accordingly, because what's most important is communication. I control my communication, it doesn't control me. That's the result of my commitment to being heard and understood. It's a skill and power you can build. Think of it that way. This experience may be a great opportunity. Don't waste time narrowing it down.

Lynn: You can see what's appropriate for each situation.

Joseph: Great stories, great humour, comes from a person learning how to say something without saying it. It's the little clip we showed you about Lenny Bruce with the "Blah Blah" . . . right!?

(Laughter)

He refined it, and was still fully expressed. He got his point across brilliantly! And that's the opportunity you now have.

Follow-up: *The Sex Seminar*

Eddie: It would be no different than what I would do with my children. I can repress certain things, when appropriate, and then choose to be more defined and precise when needed. There are right times and a wrong times to say certain words, I feel.

Joseph: Absolutely, especially with children. You have to gauge what age you can say these things to them. And if you were to communicate too softly or too harshly they'd either not hear you or they'd shut down.

Lynn: The same can be said about adults.

Joseph: That's true.

We can adapt. I can say "fudge" with the same impact as I can say "fuck" so I still get relieved, if you're going to restrict me to just saying "fudge."

Simon: It feels so much better just saying, "fuck."

Joseph: When our oldest daughter was little she was quite reserved. So, whenever she got angry at me she'd just repress it. So, one day I said to her "I know you want to give me the finger right now" and she just looked at me like I had read her mind. So I suggested to her "Just do this (holds up index finger) instead" . . . and that gave her so much joy!

(Laughter)

Lynn: He gave her an out that didn't leave her feeling like she had crossed an inappropriate boundary.

Joseph: Curse words are part of sexual expression. Therefore, how do we keep it within the boundaries, while at the same time, giving children some freedom of Sexual expression? We need to start considering how we're going to speak to our children about Sex. How do we show them what healthy Sexual expression is before they have Sex? We're inundated with sex today at every turn so how do you prepare them for that? You want to begin to consider this and think about it, because you clearly know now what limited communication and repression creates.

Lynn: What else . . . anything?

Angie: The way you related Sexual energy to the ocean in one of the Labs, was quite profound for me. I've been spending a lot of time around the ocean and I'm just like "Jesus Christ, it's amazing how little I know about the ocean!" Just the little bit I've experienced has taken up a chunk of my lifetime. I could not fully fathom or explore it all, and Sex is just like that. I've only experienced a small tiny little slice of Sex, I now realize . . . Sex covers the entire world, and I've competed with other females over a small slice of it!

Joseph: How insane is that scene!

Angie: Well, what I thought of was being at the beach, and I'm standing in the water with a bunch of other girls, and I'm taunting them with a cup of water from it going "Ha-ha, I have it and you don't!"

(Laughter)

And, we're all waist deep in the ocean water!

Joseph: How would it feel if you perceived it that clearly all the time? How would you live? Would it change how you live; how you behave towards other people? By the way, Sexual energy dwarfs the ocean in its size.

Angie: I can't handle that!

(Laughter)

Parisa: What is jealousy?

Joseph: Jealousy comes from the belief that love is limited and another has more than you. Like an apple pie, where there are only so many pieces to go around and someone has a larger piece than you. No one can take love away from you, it's unlimited. What you fight over is Man-made love. So, it's the belief that love is limited.

Parisa: So, I want to understand. When two people are in a relationship and the partner . . . the man, is free to have sex with someone else, and I know that person loves me, but he's also with someone else, that definitely makes me jealous.

Joseph: Are you in a committed relationship?

Parisa: No.

Joseph: Then what is it you want?

Parisa: I want him to want me, only. But, I understand we don't have a commitment and I still get jealous.

Joseph: It's funny how we're okay with our pleasure and fulfillment but not that of our partners. You want something from the relationship that the other person doesn't want. So, really, it has nothing to do with the third person at all. It has to do with the man not wanting the commitment you want. Jealousy is your reaction to not getting what you want. Somewhere you think he's giving it to someone else instead of you.

You think love is limited, and that he's the only one you can get it from. There are other people who are willing to give you that commitment but, the truth is, you're not interested. As long as you have walls up around your heart and unresolved pain in it; you'll push intimacy away. That's why you're choosing unavailable men. In your case, jealousy is a symptom of a larger problem.

Lynn: As you shared, your father was a cheat, so you learned "apple-pie love" from your family system. Somebody took two pieces and you only received one; that's what you're always afraid of. You project your system on the rest of the world, convincing yourself that is how the world is. You do the same with your mates. . . . Love is as abundant as is Sexual energy. It's so abundant, but we're not raised to know that.

Joseph: This generation of parents, who were raised with apple pie love, have tried to change it by having fewer children. Their thinking is "Okay, we're not going to have seven kids, we're going to have two or three and we're going to give them lots of attention so that they never feel the way we felt." So, you take this little girl and give her all your attention and when she grows up and goes out into the world, she expects the same treatment; she feels entitled. But the real world doesn't comply, and when she sees other women getting attention she gets jealous! We're right back where we started. You're not going to change a coin just because you've flipped it. There's still a belief of lack underneath it all; belief of limitations. You over-love your kid because you feel that there's limited love in the world for her. In turn, you set her up for jealousy, either way.

Angie: So how do I get past that belief?

Lynn: By experiencing love in its largeness. You'll have to allow yourself to go into what *is love,* and that can easily be done like you did in the Lab.

Joseph: Right. Go into love's ocean. Feel it, know that you are inside love. Notice what it's like when others are playing in the water, also. How do you feel when you watch others playing in it? How do you feel when you find your loved ones playing in it? It takes a lot to be able to be there with your partner and allow them to make love to someone else in front of you. But, if you truly love them and want them to have full pleasure, it may turn out easier than you think. It may not be your preference. I'm not saying it's the best way to show love, I'm saying it's one way. The way to be okay with it is to really want their happiness. This *disappears* jealousy. Anything that allows you to experience love as unlimited will do the trick. Of course, it doesn't have to be as extreme as having your lover be with another. What we're getting at is we have the ability to be okay with the happiness of others. That's what an adult can do. When a person can't; well aren't we then describing a child? *"You can't have any fun without me, no!"*

(Laughter)

That's the child in us; so when that's playing out and you're feeling jealous, know your child is present. Then take this opportunity to ask her "What do you want; what do you want right now?" What are you needing?" And give her the love and attention, and leave your partner out of it. Your child needs to feel special in your case. Therefore, make her feel special by loving her!

Most of you only know *special love*, you don't know love. You know possessive special love. "You're special," or "I'm special." We use it as an excuse to possess the other. That's a limited type of love. We say we want to feel special, we say we want our lover or friend to see us as the most special person in the world. Why? Are you willing to do that for another, for the rest of your life? Are you willing to exclude the rest of the world? That's not likely, especially if they stop seeing you as special! The people I love are special to me, because I love them. Love makes it special, not people.

Simon: Can I ask you about the Sexual energy in terms of creativity? With my making film and taking photos, I've got absolutely no drive, now, to do that.

Joseph: You're trying to rebalance your whole Sex center. You're in an adjustment period. Previously you used Sexual energy for your man-made purposes and it worked within those confines. Now you're looking to expand beyond it and you need to be willing to wait for it to take charge. Sex needs to know you've surrendered before it takes over the steering wheel. If you're truly committed to an even larger creative life then you'll have to wait.

Simon: So, just don't force it . . .

Joseph: Right, no forcing for now. As I said to Nisha, just breathe. Just breathe through it. And if you're feeling apathetic, just breathe. It will pass. It's just a feeling. Anyone else?

Nisha: So that's how you expand? I know there's not only one thing to do, but if I watch myself then . . .

Joseph: This is the first place you begin expanding . . . (Takes deep breath)

Nisha: Breathe, right.

Joseph: Yes, but there's more. Notice, I expanded my diaphragm, I expanded my chest, I expanded oxygen intake. I started expanding, which immediately brings more of the world in. Short breath, less world; larger breath, more world. We, initially, get dizzy when we suddenly take in more air than we are accustomed to taking. That's because it's too big, too much world. But if we persist, we expand and it gets easier. So we have to get used to it. We have to breathe it in for a while until it becomes normal and we enlarge. When we breathe slower and more deeply we start feeling broadened, so that's the first place to begin. Next, Angie and Parisa, close your eyes and see the object of your jealousy from a distance. Set him far off enough until you feel neutral towards him. Lastly, visualize yourselves on this Earth and see how long you've lived and how much longer you're likely to remain, and see that from a distance. This will give you even further perspective. By creating additional time and space you'll, not only be able to see the limited time you have remaining here and value it more, but you'll also have the space to see that the person you're focusing on is just one in a sea of people. This will diminish your possessiveness and jealousy. Additional time and space creates expansiveness, and this expansiveness slows up your breathing. Ultimately, this generates an easier, larger life which will appear to be so full that even the idea of possessing another will seem absurd.

Observe your breath and you'll notice when you feel tight, it will shorten and when you feel expansive, it will deepen. Use this knowledge and work with your breath. Create your expansion with it. You don't have to wait around for it to come through external things and people. That's the key; this is how to do it. It starts with the breath.

Lynn: That's why we do our seminars and these open forums in a circle. It generates the space to see! The circle creates an opening that ironically, brings us closer. The combination of distance and enclosure, caused by the circle, makes the work easier. In a circle, you don't have to be anyone else but you. In a circle there is no possibility of jealousy because everyone in it has their own distinct place. The opposite happens when you sit rank and file where there's less space and the number of people you can be intimate with decreases.

Eddie: You spoke a lot about meditation during the seminar and I was wondering if you can speak more on why you think it's such a big part of Sex?

Joseph: Would anyone like to tackle that?

Parisa: When I did Vipassana the first time, I was with focusing on breathing, concentration, and just trying to sharpen the brain. As my chattering lessened, which wasn't until seven or eight days later, I started to feel love and Sex. You feel it, which I didn't understand until Joseph and Lynn explained it to me. You don't feel you need another person, I can see, now, that I was connected to Sexual energy. I had an orgasm. As I shared in the seminar I was like "Oh, I shouldn't have this" because I misunderstood their instruction on Sex. I was getting aroused; I was happy. I was happy that I didn't need anyone to feel pleasure. I was self content and just loving me. Meditation gave me this, along with surrendering to Sexual energy. The ten days led me to the point where I slowly started to reflect and the reflection wasn't only thinking, *no*! Pictures started popping up in front of my face, and I saw my life from an observer's point of view rather than seeing it from my usual minds view. I started to see the shit that was my fault and it took a lot of courage to accept it; to not talk or argue it!

There's no *because* when you cannot talk, when you cannot share it with someone else. When there's no one to listen and support you, and say, "Yeah you're right; I can see your point of view." You're just there and the brain gets tired of justifying you, and that's when I saw the truth and after I saw the truth, I started to feel aroused by breathing, and I had an orgasm, and I was like, "Why do I need men, again?"

(Laughter)

. . . Thanks for reminding me of that; that answers my earlier question.

Joseph: It's unrealistic to stop Sexual thoughts, they (Vipassana) only insist you avoid *fixating* on Sexual thoughts and refrain from Sex. This makes it easier to find objectivity in your meditation. These boundaries allow you to strengthen your breathing and mental concentration leaving you better equipped to manage your mind rather than it managing you. So when they say no praying, Sex or Sexual indulgences, they only mean it for the duration of your meditation; it makes it easier to develop meditative skills that way.

Meditation is an offshoot of Sex; it's evolved from Sex. Therefore, it makes sense to follow this evolutionary path, just as you would follow the paths of your children. One expands the other and their basic components are the same. They require breathing, rhythm, movement--the equivalent in meditation would be the movement of thoughts and emotions--focus, and surrender to be fully experienced. Lastly, meditation is an efficient tool and vehicle for Sex; you can use it to travel and explore this massive terrain. We can always explore it, whether it's through gathering information and doing a study, writing a book, researching, talking about it, having it, or all the above. Meditation makes it easier to create space and expansiveness so that you can get a deeper and clearer connection to Sex. Teach children meditation and you're teaching them about Sex.

The *Dhamma Brother's* showed you that meditation can be done anywhere, even in prison. Vipassana provides it under the safest environment possible. So, that's why we recommend it to beginners; it's a great place to train in mediation.

Eddie: How is it that the prisoners didn't feel worse after meditating, especially the ones doing life?

Joseph: Meditation can often be painful and excruciating, depending on what you're working on. It's not about feeling good but, rather, about clearing yourself. So, know that it doesn't matter whether you're in a prison or not; it all depends on your attachments. Every day, I see people walking around in deeper prisons than the ones behind bars; so it's relative.

Nonetheless, we are impressed by these men, these killers, who came to terms and have come to an understanding of *their role* in their lives. As you heard, many of them have fully accepted accountability for their actions. They're not saying, Eddie, "I now see the error of my ways so let me out!" No. They're saying instead, "I accept I'm going to be here for the rest of my life." That's pretty profound! So you see the results of this practice and what it can do for you. Imagine what it can do for you in your Sexual research. You are all Sexual researchers now, you are searching again.

Jeremy: I can't believe how much it's helped to look at it historically. When I think of Sex now it's no longer about sex only.... It just seems enormous.

Joseph: It was our research on the ancient civilizations that started it all. We have a context to work with. We know where we are--Main & Vine. This makes it easier to travel forth. There is no need to return to a repetitive and predictable sex life.

Lynn: If I may get back to you Parisa . . . that was a beautiful share, thank you!

Parisa: I'm not sure if I gave . . .

Lynn: No you did. Thank you!

Joseph: Anybody else want to share, or any more questions on this? Do you feel satisfied? Is there something still confusing?

Angie: I don't think I'm ever going to feel completely satisfied with this work. I feel like I could do the Sex Seminar ten or fifteen times and still get something out of it. Part of me is wishing I'd recorded it so I could listen to it over and over and over again! . . . Over the next like couple of years

Nathan: Well isn't that the point of it though, it's the exciting part of it! It's so huge, it's bigger than the ocean, so just accept it and enjoy the fact that we can play forever!

Joseph: Yeah it's very exciting and you can do the same thing over again from different angles, getting a hundred different experiences, at a hundred different times. That could be a metaphor for your Sex life.

Angie: Yeah.

Lynn: Let me ask; . . . those of you who had done the previous Sex Seminar, was this one anything like the first one?

Alexia: No.

Nathan: Way different.

Angie: It's was a little bit more stressful, because I just wanted to know more! Yet, it was exciting!

Joseph: Well, be in that excitement. That's the naturally enthusiastic child in us being excited. What do you need though? Do you need to do ten Sex Seminars?

Angie: No but I'd like too.

Joseph: So your adult has to determine that; it has to determine what you need.

Parisa: I'm actually grateful for the group dynamic, because it's everybody's contribution that made the picture full. Sessions are important and specialized but I prefer group work; seminar work. I like that I get to share and hear all your shares. It opens a lot of things up for me. Nathan, I'm grateful to have you. Seriously, you're the one that I remember the most. When I was so scared to look at my past, just looking in your direction calmed me. You were so courageous that weekend. You lead by example and it made me reflect. I'm sure I wouldn't have reflected as much if you weren't part of the group.

Nathan: Yes. You had me.

(Laughter)

Parisa: Because of the support I felt from the group I was able to look deep and take ownership of it.

Joseph: No one has really spoken on that, so let's take a moment and ask: what do you guys think about your group?

Kelly: Everyone's very sexual.

(Laughter)

. . . No, I liked everyone and I enjoyed it.

Joseph: What else do you think?

Jeremy: This has been a very unique experience. I think that *you* (Looking at Parisa) came so far from the Communication Seminar to the end of this one. I thought that you were very, I don't want to say outspoken, but you were very angry. . . It seemed that way to me, in the beginning. Now you seem way more chill.

Parisa: Thanks, I am an angry person and I'm working on my anger.

(Laughter)

Follow-up: *The Sex Seminar*

Jeremy: No, but I think that you um . . . well what I feel from you is that you are a very strong woman. No question. I don't find you weak at all; I didn't think that you were being rude. Today I can just see that you're much more content with yourself.

Nathan: Yeah I would say the same.

Jeremy: But you two were great! You and Joseph!

Parisa: He pushes my buttons!

Jeremy: Yeah, but at the time I thought, "Wow this is going to blow up!" I really did! A couple of times I thought for sure it was going to go sideways. But that just goes to show--you, or I, need to give this work some time. . . and good luck in Dubai!

Parisa: Thank you. I mean that, thank you so much.

Joseph: Anybody else? What do you think of your group?

Simon: I found that I was actually, for once, happy to have people in the world that pissed me off more than I did myself. It showed me how pissed off with myself I am. The people that really fucked me up are the ones I learned the most from, so it was really good. . . . I lose my shit all the time about stupid stuff, and those are the things I need to work on and you (Looking at Joseph) just kept drilling that. In the thing that you said about Kelly, you gave the same lesson repeatedly. You kept saying the same thing over and over again until it clicked . . . so that was good to find out: "Oh, it's me that I'm pissed off at."

Joseph: So you appreciate the group being able to help you with that?

Simon: Hmmm, yes, but not just the ones who I feel are giving useful things, even people who say useless things, I think are actually helpful to me.

Joseph: Absolutely, got it!

Angie: (Looking at Simon) . . . That was my experience of you in the Communication Seminar. I told you that! I was like "Ugggh" . . . you drove me nuts!

(Laughter)

So it was really good for me in a similar way.

Follow-up: *The Sex Seminar*

Lynn: So what would you say is the most profound thing you've learned through working in a group?

Simon: That we're all in it together, and everyone's the same.

Joseph: That's huge, especially for you self pitying and loner types.

(Laughter)

Simon: Before the seminar I saw, everyone separately, like, "Oh that's her, that's her, that's him, that's him." I can now see something about everyone that I can relate to and that relates to everyone else, as well.

Alexia: I see that we're all having our own internal battles. I have mine and I can see everyone else's just highlights mine. This makes me feel compassion because I know I'm in my own hell sometimes, and others are too.

Joseph: From childhood we're run by the belief that there is always someone else who has their shit together and we just happen not to. But the truth is, *we all have our shit, and when you put shit together it becomes nothing more than a bigger pile of stinky ass shit!*

(Laughter)

If we understood this earlier in our lives there'd be a lot less kids killing themselves. This is an unfortunate illusion we sell ourselves. Kids actually buy that others are better off.

Angie: I learned that in school. . . . I didn't do well in school so I would sit in the back of the class. I found it terribly dull and boring there, and, of course, there would be the girl with the straight A's, and skinny little body sitting up front. I thought I was worthless next to her because she was, you know, killing it in class. That sort of thing and the comparing caused me a lot of pain. It was further emphasized with grades; the comparing, it's brutal!

Joseph: If we come to terms and realize that we're pre-schoolers being taught by kindergarteners, then this burden will be lifted. You're not going to learn a lot from a kindergartener. You have to get that. There's plenty of room for us to learn from everything and everyone. No one's cornered the market, though they'd like you to think they have. This is what has stopped you from surrendering to something larger than yourselves. There really isn't anybody who's that much further ahead. There really isn't... Anything else? Or anything about anyone else?

Nathan: I don't know the girls name, she was the one with the man issues. She's not here...

Lynn: Tami.

Nathan: Yes, Tami... I wish she was here because she shared stuff with me that was just amazing to hear. I didn't realize that I am being looked at by other people and she saw something that I've never seen in myself. It was surprising what she said, especially coming from somebody like her. She said she was sharing with her friend about me and that she saw me as a *full, complete male*. It was just amazing to find out after the fact. She said she had issues with men and that I helped her see them differently. So I wish she was here because she was really impactful for me. So I'm just going to put it out into the universe right here.

Joseph: Yeah there's a lot to give thanks for. We feel thankful when we are thinking fully. When we are able to think--fully, more deeply--it brings up a natural thankfulness. Hence, why the German thinker, Martin Heidegger, said, "To think is to thank." To truly think, not just to spin, but to think, automatically brings up appreciation. We become naturally grateful. To think about what somebody's done for us brings up a gratitude that is contagious. It makes us more grateful to life itself. Therefore, when you bring yourself to a seminar where you allow yourselves to think, you give yourselves the gift of gratitude! Real thinking, as my old, wise professor would suggest, is what ultimately leads us to love. So for all of you who hung in there during the stormy periods, for those of you who shared and exposed yourselves during your pain... congratulations, because the thankfulness you feel now, was earned! For those who couldn't fully reach that point, its okay, you did well. It's a step in the right direction. You returned each day and you shifted and now you're more curious than ever. We couldn't have asked for more.

This is why we do what we do. We're here to show you the door and maybe help you through it. The rest is up to you; this is when the real thinking starts. Without it, this world becomes nothing more than a robot state. It doesn't change on its own; we need to make the effort to think. Otherwise, we leave the *burden of awakening* to the next generation; and that's not necessary.

Lynn: It's very rare that a group of people get together and fight for truth. That's why we consider you all to be brave and courageous. No matter how hard, no matter how angry, no matter how scared, no matter how sad you became . . . you stayed in your seats and you didn't run. No matter how much fighting there was with Joseph, who provoked so much pain, you stayed in your seat. That's what makes you courageous.

Joseph: There are always moments when we think, "I can't. I can't do this anymore." This is when we have to lean on another--and you did. You brought yourself to a place where you can lean on another because you can't do it alone in a room. When you're alone and you say "I can't," there's no one there to counter you; so you don't.

This has been good, you've practiced expressing yourselves, telling on yourselves, and asking for help. You've said out loud "I can't today!" and we said in return, "Yeah, you can!" We were there for each other.

Lisa: Yeah, even during the breaks, I received so much help!

Joseph: You put yourselves in a position to receive help, rather than waiting at home for an imaginary someone to come and save you. Also know, you came because you needed help. We need to accept that we're not meant to do this life thing alone! We have to ask for help, assistance, and insight! It's not going to just come. You know that because you've already tried it.

Sex is one of the biggest subjects you could have tackled with us. You could have chosen family or friendship, which are important, yet smaller, subjects. No, you chose Sex! And as large as the Ego Seminar might have been for you; The Sex Seminar is even bigger!

We've swum the *ocean* together and now you know you're not alone in it. You can be with something larger than you without feeling "less than." As I read yesterday, "If you're the biggest thing in your life, how big can you get?"

. . . Thank you for all for your questions, comments, and shares. We appreciate what you brought today. . . . I would also like to thank you on behalf of each and every one of us for being there and for being as strong as you've been. I hope this gives you some sense of completion so you can continue once again on this search!

Group: THANK YOU!! I'm so grateful for you two!

Joseph & Lynn: You're welcome.

Angie: I feel we are so fortunate. Those of us that have met you and have gotten to work with you guys . . . it's something that billions of people in the world don't have access to.

Joseph: Well, thank you.

Lynn: We'd like billions of people to have access!

Angie: I'd also like to see billions have access to this!

Follow-up: *The Sex Seminar*

One year later...

"I had a real breakthrough in the sex seminar that had been about 8 years in the making. I finally surrendered to all of the pressure and expectation I had been placing on myself for my whole life, it was painful but extremely satisfying to finally let go of some of that backed up baggage I didn't know myself without.

I learned how much I didn't actually know about sex and just how expansive 'sex' truly is. I left the seminar with a much more curious way of being around what we call sex and how much I've let myself be 'run' by it on a daily basis!

I want to thank Joseph and Lynn for proving the space for me and the other group members to have such an amazingly unique experience!"

-Reese

"As a young girl I was taught to repress my sexuality, that it was shameful to be sexy. As a result, I had a breast reduction at the age of 20. My reason at the time was that my breasts didn't suit my body but after doing the Sex Seminar I discovered the real reason... that I was so uncomfortable with the attention I got from men that I physically changed my body to try to erase the shame. Had I known this back then I don't know if I would have done it.

The seminar changed the way I see myself, I am a sexual being and that is a beautiful thing. I recommend this book to anyone who wants to create more freedom in their life, sexually or otherwise.

Thank you so much for helping me become the woman I am today and the woman I am still becoming. I love you both."

-Lisa

*"You know, we're told how to do it- kind of. But along with that, young women- most people, really- are given a whole slew of other things to stew on before, during, and after the act itself. Guilt, shame, fear, pride... The list goes on and on. What I took away from The Sex Seminar more than anything, is that I was taking sex way too fucking seriously. As Joseph said "You guys need to stop taking this so fucking seriously. You're **fucking**, seriously. How about fucking PLAYFULLY?" It's amazing how simple it is, really. I didn't realize how much I was complicating something that could be so easy, beautiful, FUN, and something that I could really learn about myself from. My whole sex life- or I should really just say my whole life- has had a huge shift in perspective since the seminar.*

I can honestly say that I give, and receive love more freely now. I'm experiencing and exploring real intimacy for the first time in my life. There's always more work to do, and I'm really excited to keep doing it. Pun intended." -Angie

Follow-up: *The Sex Seminar*

"There is something very powerful that happens when 18 or so people voluntarily sit in a room for two and a half days to talk about SEX. You find out it goes way deeper than that. I walked into that room on Friday just having left a courtroom for assault charges, from a night I don't remember. My life one year before that was falling apart. I was a drug addict for ten years but have always wanted more for myself and better.

This seminar woke me up to myself and how I walked in the world with a hate for men and want to help women. My hate for men always got in the way of experiencing the kindness that can come from a man. Not even two days after the seminar and back in everyday real life my interactions with men changed. Instead of the old stare down on the street that I needed to win, it was friendly smiles and even a hello that I was open to receiving.

The whole helping women and protecting them thing is still in the works but the seminar shone the light for me to be able to see what I wasn't willing to see prior. Every single person in that room for that weekend helped each other just by being in that room. When I run into them in the street, there is a level of intimacy that is shared that you will be hard pressed to find anywhere else. It has been one year since the seminar and the person I was then compared to who I am now is unrecognizable.

That seminar couldn't have come at a better time for me, it truly did change the direction of my journey in this crazy beautiful thing
we call life. I may not know every bodies names who shared that weekend with me but I will never forget them. They showed me that I do have something to offer and that I am not alone. I no longer turn to drugs or alcohol, everything I could ever need I can now find from within.
 Thank you, Lynn and Joseph for providing such an amazing platform for personal growth. Love you all!"

-*Nathan*

"The seminar showed me that life is sex energy. Creation and destruction, including the creation of me and all that I do is connected to this energy, my choices, actions, reactions, interactions, are all a mirror reflection of how I perceive and be in the world.

The sex seminar made me aware of the shame I accumulated in my past.

Unconsciously I can be insecure, awkward, needy and vulnerable. From the ages 8-17 I was raised in 9 different foster homes, some caring positive experiences and some uncaring negative experiences all which made me the warrior I am today. I felt unloved and abandoned by both of my parents, feeling unwanted and unaccepted in all areas growing up, having to care for myself with help from siblings most of my childhood. I see how conditioned I had become; I truly believed that I was a burden to the world.

All of my actions reflected this, it wasn't until I worked with Lynn and Joseph enough, that I realised I had been lying to myself. I had to see it on my own. Children cannot take care of children. It wasn't personal, my parents never intended to abandon me, but my belief was so strong. It came out in all areas of my life such as being insecure in social situations, around other families, not fitting in with peers, having problems with authority. My main reflection was not having a strong father figure in my life from birth; it had me act most of my unlovable, needy, burden issues out with men.

I finally understood why I had been out in the world searching for unconditional love through a man, while all along it was at home in my eyes.

I became clear on how my shameful feelings get in the way of my relationships and everyday life experiences, tying to the lack I was so familiar to feeling which always had me feel less than and not worthy of love or happiness.

I didn't wanna be dirty or accept that I was imperfect, but now realise that my imperfections are what make me beautiful, to be real, silly and un inhibited like I am meant to be, to embrace my true essence... spontaneously as it comes.

Having the courage to look within and see what's really there, I feel a let go, trust within that has me be less self conscious and more self aware. In a sense where I am sensitive to and aware of all that's around me but my focus is within me, not looking out worrying about how I "should be" behaving.

Meditating, observing and accepting hard truthful realisations I've found a freedom within myself to be myself.

Thanks to the sex seminar and all of the tools I have learnt and the support I have felt.

I am so grateful for Lynn, Joseph and the seminar they worked so hard to create.

The gifts I have received are little miracles and I cherish every one.

Love you, no ifs ands or buts, and I celebrate you."

-Alexis

"It was liberating and eye opening to realize that my sexual parts are much more than breasts and private areas of the body. Freeing myself from limiting beliefs, shame and guilt increased my intimacy in relationships and reduced anger and sexual frustration. I finally understand that there is no right or wrong way to enjoy sex; what is important is the mutual respect of individuals and their boundaries."   -Parisa

"The sex seminar was a life altering experience that has led me on a new journey in my personal sexual life.

It was truly an eye opening, jaw dropping "light bulb" moment that I will carry with me in my years to come.

Follow-up: *The Sex Seminar*

I walked into that seminar sexually insecure/shy, embarrassed of myself and my lack of "sexiness". Consistently comparing myself to others and to society's ideal of what sexy means. Not knowing what to expect, thinking "well it can't do any harm" I sat in a chair blushing and waiting... (much like my sex life prior to this experience). Little did I know, my life and personal perspective on the word sexy would change forever.

I left that seminar feeling empowered and confident. Now having the knowledge to understand this sexual energy, we as humans posses. I now am starting to understand myself, my body and my personal love life. Lynn and Joseph handed me the tools I needed to create my new sexual awaking. Who would of thoughts sex could be this much fun? Seriously!!

I learned what intimacy meant to me, the true sensation of human touch. I learned how to connect with myself and I'm learning how to connect with my partner. I've since been taken to new highs I didn't think were possible; to be able to have these amazing tools to explore and have fun with sex. To let go of all of I thought I knew and open my heart, mind and body... by letting go of what I thought I knew. By simplifying and feeling; to not place judgement on others regarding their sexual fantasies, preferences or kinks. To have the power to know and understand how the mind works and connects with the human body. This sexual energy we as humans posses is undeniable, we are sexual beings. So embrace it. To know undoubtedly, that I am not alone in my worries, fears or insecurities. The idea of healthy mind blowing sex was never an option for me...until I took this seminar. I am free of the walls I created. I feel alive!

The seminar helped me find out what was holding me back from myself. All too often, I was having sex but not fully enjoying it due to my "head sex" mentality. To learn my body, what I like, how to sexually explore and pleasure myself, my needs, my deep dark fantasies and how to share that with someone.

I highly recommend this book to everyone and anyone! Forget what you thought you knew and open your mind to the unknown, you won't regret it.
-Tami

About the Authors

Joseph Angel Maldonado, M.A., and Lynn Traub-Maldonado CHT are experts in the field of self development. They have a combined 50 years experience in seminar development and , as well as individual and couples therapy. They dig into areas of the subconscious that most don't dare to explore and expose the reality of what is blocking ultimate freedom and fulfillment.

References

Berman, B. (Producer) & Wachowski, A. and Wachowski, L. (Directors). (1999). The Matrix [Motion Picture]. Warner Bros. Pictures.

"Comprehensive Sex Education: Research and Results." Advocates for Youth (Website). Retrieved from http://www.advocatesforyouth.org/publications/1487.

Foucault, M. & Hurley R. (1990). The History of Sexuality, Vol. 1: An Introduction (p. 69). U.S.A: Vintage Books Edition.

Kirsta, A. (2003, May 16). Genetic Sexual Attraction. The Guardian (p. 13).

Linder, D. (2003). "Selected Bits from Bruce's Monologues Cited in the Cafe Au Go Go Obscenity Prosecution of Comedian Lenny Bruce." Famous Trials: The Lenny Bruce Trial 1964. Retrieved from http://law2.umkc.edu/faculty/projects/ftrials/bruce/brucemonologues.html.

Marquis de Sade. (1965). Justine, Philosophy in the Bedroom, and Other Writings (p. 188). (Compilation by R. Seaver & A. Wainhouse, Trans.). New York, NY: Grove Press.

Osho. (1998). *The Supreme Doctrine (p.168)*. Eastbourne, UK: Sussex Academic Press.

Robinson, L. (2010, August 2). Lady Gaga On Sex, Fame, Drugs, and Her Fans. Vanity Fair. Retrieved from http://www.vanityfair.com/online/daily/2010/08/lady-gaga-september-issue.

TabulaRasaFilm. (2011, February 20). Lenny Bruce - Blah blah blah [Video file]. Retrieved from https://www.youtube.com/watch?v=rMkN8bMWTdw.

Michelle, A. (Writer) & John, M. (Director) (September 29, 2013). Pilot. Michelle, M. (Producer) *Masters of Sex*. St. Louis, Missouri: Showtime

www.ingramcontent.com/pod-product-compliance
Lightning Source LLC
Chambersburg PA
CBHW070336240426
43665CB00045B/2049